CW01617588

Eduqas GCSE Religious Studies (9-1)

Catholic Christianity

Route B

Laura Skinner-Howe
Rebecca Jinks
Ann-Marie Bridle

OXFORD
UNIVERSITY PRESS

OXFORD
UNIVERSITY PRESS

Great Clarendon Street, Oxford, OX2 6DP, United Kingdom

Oxford University Press is a department of the University of Oxford.

It furthers the University's objective of excellence in research, scholarship, and education by publishing worldwide. Oxford is a registered trade mark of Oxford University Press in the UK and in certain other countries

First published in 2021

British Library Cataloguing in Publication Data
Data available

978-1-38-200954-6

10 9 8 7 6 5

The manufacturing process conforms to the environmental regulations of the country of origin.

Printed in Great Britain by Bell and Bain ltd, Glasgow

MIX
Paper | Supporting responsible forestry
FSC® C007785
FSC www.fsc.org

Thank you

The publishers would like to thank Rabbi Benjy Rickman, Ann Angel, Philip Robinson and Julie Haigh for their help in reviewing this book The publishers would also like to thank James Helling for compiling the index for this book.

The teaching content of this resource is endorsed by WJEC Eduqas to support WJEC Eduqas GCSE in Religious Studies Route B. This resource has been reviewed against WJEC Eduqas' endorsement criteria. As this resource belongs to a third party, there may be occasions where a specification may be updated and that update will not be reflected in the third party resource. Users should always refer to WJEC Eduqas' specification and Sample Assessment Materials to ensure that learners are studying the most up to date course. It is recommended that teachers use a range of resources to fully prepare their learners for the exam and not rely solely on one textbook or digital resource. WJEC, nor anyone employed by WJEC has been paid for the endorsement of this resource, nor does WJEC receive any royalties from its sale.

Nihil obstat: Philip Robinson, Censor Deputatus

Imprimatur + Bernard Longley, Archbishop of Birmingham

12th February 2021

The Nihil obstat and Imprimatur are a declaration from within the Catholic Church that the parts of this publication concerned with doctrine and morals are free from error. The Nihil obstat and Imprimatur apply to Chapters 1-4. It is not implied that those who have granted the Nihil obstat and Imprimatur agree with the contents, opinions or statements expressed.

Contents

Contents

Eduqas GCSE in Religious Studies

This book covers all you will need to study for a GCSE examination in Religious Studies with Eduqas Route B. It includes the knowledge that you need for all your examinations, plus help in developing those crucial examination skills.

How is the specification covered?

The content that you will need is divided into three examination papers or 'components'. This book covers all three of those papers.

Component 1 – Foundational Catholic Theology

This paper is worth 37.5% of your overall marks. It is a compulsory paper and you are expected to answer every question.

The examination paper for this component is split into two sections:

- Origins and meaning
- Good and evil

Component 2 – Applied Catholic Theology

This paper is worth 37.5% of your overall marks. It is also a compulsory paper and you are expected to answer every question.

The examination for this component is split into two sections:

- Life and death
- Sin and forgiveness

Component 3 – Study of Judaism

This paper is worth 25% of your overall marks. You are expected to answer every question on this paper.

The examination for this component is split into two sections:

- Beliefs and teachings
- Practices

It is vital that you study the whole course and do not miss any bits out because there will be questions on all three of these components. This book contains everything you will need to be able to do this.

How do I use this book?

As you work through this book, you will find features to help you develop your knowledge and your examination skills so that you can feel confident on the day of your examination. Bible quotations in this book have been taken from the New Revised Standard Version: Catholic Edition, except for chapters 5–6 on Judaism, where quotes have been taken from the Jewish Publication Society's edition of the Tanach.

There is an Introduction to every new chapter.

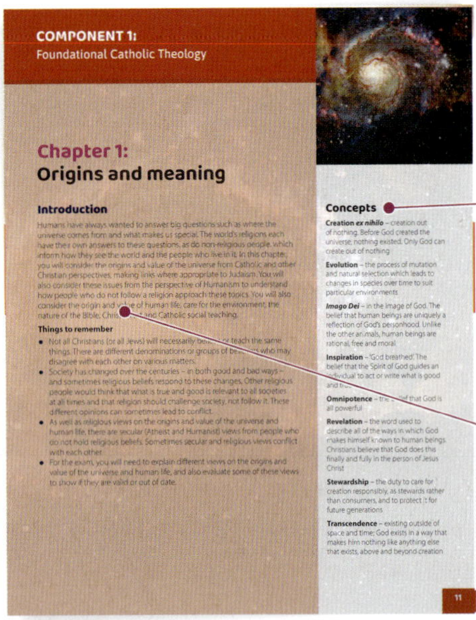

Concepts – At the start of every chapter is a list of the concepts you are expected to know and the definitions that Eduqas have provided. These terms are then highlighted in the main text, so you can see how and when they are used.

Things to remember – These are points that are important to bear in mind as you study the religions or themes. They will help you to understand the material in each chapter.

The content that you will need to study is covered in a number of double page spreads.

The Jewish perspective – In Chapters 1 and 2 only, Jewish perspectives are offered.

Specification focus – This shows you which detail from the specification is being covered on these pages, so you can be confident you are covering all the required content.

Quotes – Quotes from religious texts are shown in yellow boxes. We have included all the essential quotations named in the specification – these appear with a blue outline.

Useful terms – These boxes give definitions of some specialist language used on the pages that has not been included in the list of concepts but is still helpful to know. These terms are in bold and blue on the main page.

Knowledge recall – There are three questions at the end of each double page that ask you to recall knowledge and understanding from the pages you have just covered. These help you to repeat key information so that it sticks in your mind.

Evaluation practice – There are two questions at the end of each double page that ask you to provide arguments and weigh up how effective they are. These questions help you to practise thinking of ideas and reasoning, just as you will in an exam.

There are skills practice pages at the end of each chapter that will help you to become familiar with the different question types that you will encounter in the exam.

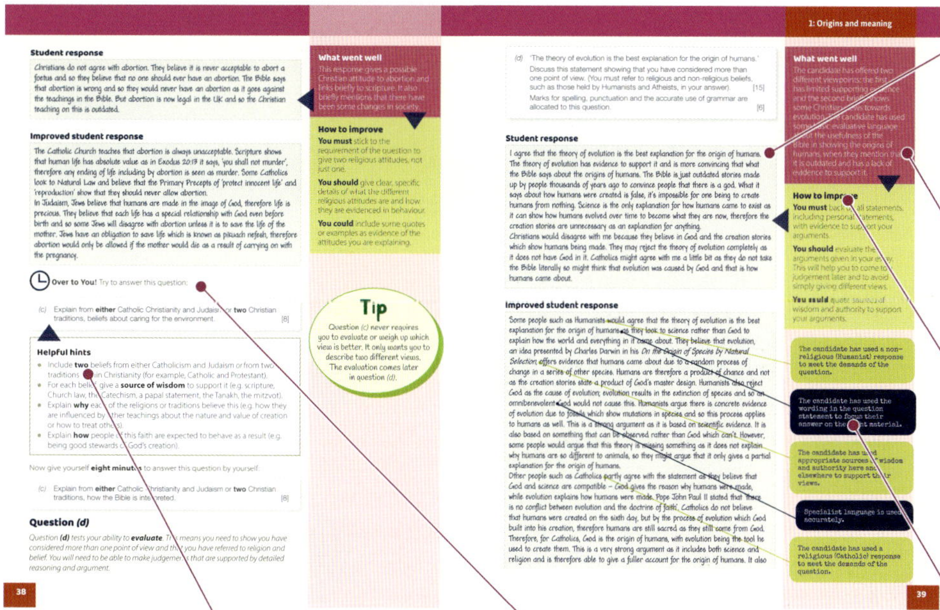

Exemplar questions – Each skills section contains examples of questions from real examination papers, and some exemplar answers. In each case, there is an answer with some problems and an improved response.

What went well – An explanation of the successful features of a student's answer.

How to improve – These boxes suggest things you must, should and could do to improve an examination response.

Helpful hints and Tips – Support and guidance in writing your own answers.

Over to You – Opportunities to try your hand at real examination questions.

Commentaries – These show how and why an improved answer is successful.

What will the exams be like?

To match the three components that you will study, there are three examination papers that you will have to answer.

Examination 1:
Component 1 –
1 hour 30 minutes

In this examination paper, there are two questions with four parts each. Question 1 will always be about Origins and meanings and question 2 will be about Good and evil.

Examination 2:
Component 2 –
1 hour 30 minutes

In this examination paper, there are two questions with four parts each. Question 1 will always be about Life and death and question 2 will always be about Sin and forgiveness.

Examination 3:
Component 3 – 1 hour

In this examination paper, there are two questions with four parts each. Question 1 will always be about Beliefs and teachings and question 2 will always be about Practices.

Tip

You need to answer every question on each examination paper. If you have enough time, always try to write something, even if you are not sure of the answer. You won't lose marks for writing the wrong thing!

What kinds of questions will be asked?

Each question is always divided into four parts: *(a)*, *(b)*, *(c)* and *(d)*.

(a) question

(a) will always begin with the words:

What is meant by…

Or *What do Catholics mean by…*

Or *What do Jews mean by…*

Question *(a)* is worth two marks and it always requires you to define one of the concepts listed on the specification. These are listed for you at the start of each chapter. You should aim to spend no longer than two minutes on an *(a)* question before you move on.

A partially correct answer will get 1 mark. You will need an accurate and appropriate definition for the full 2 marks.

Tip

Learn the definitions for the concepts provided by Eduqas and listed at the start of each chapter. These definitions will get you two marks with no need for extra information to be added.

(b) question

(b) will always begin with the word:

Describe…

Question *(b)* is worth five marks and always requires you to show your knowledge and understanding of a specific area of religion. You will find the content needed for these questions in the main body of each chapter. The skills pages will help you learn to answer these kinds of questions. You should aim to spend no longer than five minutes on a *(b)* question before you move on.

Here is what Eduqas want to see in your answer for a *(b)* question:

- Knowledge – of a religious idea, belief, practice, teaching or concept.
- Understanding – of how belief influences individuals, communities and societies.
- Specialist language – used correctly and in context.
- Sources of authority – quoted or referred to accurately and in context.

Tip

Avoid writing a list of bullet points in answer to a *(b)* question, but remember you are not expected to include large amounts of detail. It is more important to answer the question clearly and accurately than to give lots of detailed information.

(c) question

(c) will always begin with the word:

Explain…

In Component 1 only, you will be asked to show an understanding of diversity. This means that the question will always go on to say:

… from **either** *Catholic Christianity and Judaism* ***or two*** *Christian traditions…*

Responses to a *(c)* question in Paper 1 only should always clearly show two different religious responses. These can be from Catholic Christianity and Judaism, or you can give two different responses from within Christianity (e.g. Catholic and Church of England). This book shows you both options. This is not required in either of the other papers.

Question *(c)* on all the papers is worth 8 marks and requires more detail than a *(b)* question. You still need to show knowledge and understanding, but you also need to include supporting evidence or reasoning. You can find help with this on the skills pages. You should aim to spend roughly 8 minutes on a *(c)* question.

As with the *(b)* question, Eduqas will credit you for showing knowledge and understanding, for using specialist language and sources of authority, but the *(c)* question is worth 8 marks and requires more detail.

In a *(c)* question, Eduqas want you to show ***how*** or ***why*** a belief or practice is ***important*** OR to give details on the ***main features*** of beliefs, teachings or attitudes about a topic.

- Include supporting evidence or reasoning to 'explain' your answer.
- Give a detailed response – spend up to 8 minutes answering this question.
- For Paper 1 only, show an understanding of ideas, beliefs, practices, teachings and concepts from Catholic Christianity and Judaism, or two Christian traditions.

Tip

Question *(c)* requires you to write about *religious* beliefs and attitudes. You will not gain any marks for writing about Atheists or Humanists in your response.

(d) question

(d) will always begin with a controversial statement and then tell you to:

Discuss this statement showing that you have considered more than one point of view (you must refer to religion and belief in your answer).

Question *(d)* is worth 15 marks and you should aim to spend 15 minutes on it. This question is different from the others because instead of testing your knowledge and understanding, it tests your evaluation skills. You will need to look at the statement and show how some religious people might argue one response, but other religious people may argue differently. In some questions you will also need to refer to non-religious viewpoints. You then need to weigh up which response is better and give reasons why. You can see lots of hints and ideas for how to do this on the skills pages of this book.

Tip

The *(d)* question asks you to demonstrate your evaluative skills. The examiner wants to see you analyse and evaluate the issues so that you can make a reasoned judgement.

Here is what Eduqas want to see in your answer for a *(d)* question.

- Analysis and evaluation – of the issue raised in the question statement.
- Judgement – backed up by knowledge of religion, teaching or moral reasoning.
- Understanding – of how belief influences individuals, communities and societies.
- Specialist language – used correctly and in context.
- Sources of authority – quoted or referred to accurately and in context.

On Question 1 in Paper 1 (Origins and meaning) and Paper 2 (Life and death) you will be marked on **SPaG** (spelling, punctuation and grammar). So always try to use your best written English as it is a chance to pick up extra marks. There are 6 SPaG marks for each question and 12 in total for the course.

Tip

On Question 1 in Component 1 only (Origins and meaning), you will be asked to include beliefs of non-religious people such as Humanists or Atheists in your answer.

COMPONENT 1:
Foundational Catholic Theology

Chapter 1: Origins and meaning

Introduction

Humans have always wanted to answer big questions such as where the universe comes from and what makes us special. The world's religions each have their own answers to these questions, as do non-religious people, which inform how they see the world and the people who live in it. In this chapter, you will consider the origins and value of the universe from Catholic and other Christian perspectives, making links where appropriate to Judaism. You will also consider these issues from the perspective of Humanism to understand how people who do not follow a religion approach these topics. You will also consider the origin and value of human life, care for the environment, the nature of the Bible, Christian art and Catholic social teaching.

Things to remember

- Not all Christians (or all Jews) will necessarily believe or teach the same things. There are different denominations or groups of believers who may disagree with each other on various matters.
- Society has changed over the centuries – in both good and bad ways – and sometimes religious beliefs respond to these changes. Other religious people would think that what is true and good is relevant to all societies at all times and that religion should challenge society, not follow it. These different opinions can sometimes lead to conflict.
- As well as religious views on the origins and value of the universe and human life, there are secular (Atheist and Humanist) views from people who do not hold religious beliefs. Sometimes secular and religious views conflict with each other.
- For the exam, you will need to explain different views on the origins and value of the universe and human life, and also evaluate some of these views to show if they are valid or out of date.

Concepts

Creation *ex nihilo* – creation out of nothing. Before God created the universe, nothing existed. Only God can create out of nothing

Evolution – the process of mutation and natural selection which leads to changes in species over time to suit particular environments

Imago Dei – in the image of God. The belief that human beings are uniquely a reflection of God's personhood. Unlike the other animals, human beings are rational, free and moral

Inspiration – 'God breathed'. The belief that the Spirit of God guides an individual to act or write what is good and true

Omnipotence – the belief that God is all powerful

Revelation – the word used to describe all of the ways in which God makes himself known to human beings. Christians believe that God does this finally and fully in the person of Jesus Christ

Stewardship – the duty to care for creation responsibly, as stewards rather than consumers, and to protect it for future generations

Transcendence – existing outside of space and time; God exists in a way that makes him nothing like anything else that exists, above and beyond creation

The origins of the universe

Creation in Genesis

The Catholic Church teaches that there is one **omnipotent**, **omniscient** and **omnibenevolent** God who is responsible for creating the universe and everything in it.

The opening words of the Bible clearly show God's creative power, stating 'In the beginning God created the heavens and the earth' (Genesis 1:1). God's creative role continues in Genesis 1 as he creates the world in six days and rests on the seventh day. This is followed by a second creation story in Genesis 2, in which God creates the world and where the humans he creates are named Adam and Eve.

Certain themes are unmistakable in both stories: God creates, God is **eternal** and God is **transcendent**. For Catholics, creation reflects God's power and benevolence. He made the universe to fit the needs of humans and due to his own goodness, creation is intrinsically good.

Most Catholics read the Genesis accounts of creation as symbolic stories. They do not interpret them literally, but instead believe they give insights into the nature of God and why creation came into existence. This means that Catholics accept scientific theories of creation, which they believe give the specifics of how the universe originated without undermining God as creator of the universe.

Creation *ex nihilo*

Creation *ex nihilo* means to create from nothing. The Bible teaches that this ability to create is unique to God due to his **omnipotence**. In Genesis 1, God creates everything in the universe without the need for other materials. Other passages in both the Old and New Testaments reinforce the belief that God alone is the architect of the universe. Catholics believe the universe had no other beginning before God. God is the only eternal being, and the only thing to have existed before the creation of the universe.

St Aquinas was a Catholic priest in the thirteenth century who supported the concept of creation *ex nihilo*. He developed his **causation** argument to show God as the 'uncaused first cause'. St Aquinas observed the process of cause and effect in the world and concluded that every effect has a cause, so logically the universe must have had a cause too. God is the first cause of the universe as he exists before anything else.

St Augustine and creation *ex nihilo*

St Augustine was an early Christian theologian who wrote a series of short books called *Confessions*. In his twelfth book he wrote about God creating the universe *ex nihilo*. He said that nothing existed before the universe was created except God, and that the universe was created good. God is shown as superior to and different from the universe he created.

Specification focus

Catholic beliefs and teachings about the origin of the universe and the concept of creation *ex nihilo* as expressed in the writing of St Augustine (specifically *Confessions XII, 7*); the relationship between Catholic views and other Christian views on the origin of the universe and the extent to which these conflict.

‘All things came into being through him, and without him not one thing came into being.’
John 1:3 (NRSV)

The Bible teaches that the world was created by God from nothing in seven days

‘I am the first and I am the last; besides me there is no God.’
Isaiah 44:6 (NRSV)

Useful terms

omnipotent – all powerful
omniscient – all knowing
omnibenevolent – all loving
eternal – without beginning or end
transcendent – existing outside of space and time
causation – the idea that everything has a cause and God is the cause of the universe

*But besides yourself, O God, who are Trinity in Unity, Unity in Trinity, **there was nothing from which you could make heaven and earth**. Therefore **you must have created them from nothing**, the one great, the other small. For there is **nothing that you cannot do. You are good and all that you make must be good**, both the great Heaven of Heavens and this little earth. **You were, and besides you nothing was. From nothing, then, you created heaven and earth**, distinct from one another; the one close to yourself, the other close to being nothing; the one surpassed only by yourself, the other little more than nothing.'

Confessions XII, 7

- Augustine shows God as an eternal being who existed before the universe.
- God created the universe *ex nihilo* as he is omnipotent.
- God is omnibenevolent and good, so the universe is good.

St Augustine said that the universe was created from nothing by an omnipotent and omnibenevolent God

Catholic and Fundamentalist Christian views on the creation of the universe

Most Catholics understand the Genesis creation accounts to be symbolic stories because there are two accounts written at different times and in different styles. For Catholics, these stories have underlying truths which help to show the nature of God and creation. Other Christians, such as Liberal Christians, also interpret the Genesis accounts in this way.

In contrast, some Fundamentalist Christians interpret the creation stories literally. They view the Bible as the word of God and believe everything in it is true. Most believe the universe was created in six days as described in Genesis. Most reject scientific attempts to explain creation, which they believe are flawed and undermine the creative power of God.

Catholics and Fundamentalists may conflict in how they interpret the creation stories but they both agree Genesis shows:

- God is omnipotent and the ultimate creator
- God created the universe and everything in it
- God's creation was good.

The Jewish perspective

The Hebrew Bible talks about one God who created the universe from nothing, who is the source and sustainer of all life. Genesis is the first book of the Hebrew Bible, so Jews and Christians share similar beliefs about the creation of the universe and the nature of God as the ultimate creator.

Most Orthodox Jews believe that God created the universe in six days with order and purpose and rested on the seventh day. Like Fundamentalist Christians, most Orthodox Jews see Genesis as a factual account of creation. However, most Reform Jews, like Catholics, see Genesis as a metaphorical explanation for creation.

'Blessed be He who spoke and the world came into being.'

Barukh She'amar prayer

Many Jews observe Shabbat each week as a reminder of creation. They do not engage in creative activities and give thanks to God. Jews also celebrate Rosh Hashanah each year as the birthday of the world and the anniversary of the sixth day of creation. It is a time when they confirm that there is one God who is King.

Knowledge recall

1. Define the following concepts: creation *ex nihilo*, omnipotence, revelation. (You can find these definitions on page 11.)
2. Give three reasons why Catholics believe God created the world *ex nihilo*.
3. State one reason why most Fundamentalists reject scientific explanations of the universe.

Evaluation practice

4. 'Genesis literally shows how the world was made.' Give one Catholic response to this statement.
5. Do you think Fundamentalists are right to reject the Catholic interpretation of the Genesis creation stories? Give two reasons for your view.

The Big Bang theory and the theory of evolution

The Big Bang theory

One of the most important discoveries within cosmology (the branch of science that studies the origins of the universe) is the expansion of the universe. The Catholic priest George Lemaître first proposed that the entire universe began from a 'big bang'. This theory was developed by Stephen Hawking and has become the leading scientific explanation for the origin of the universe.

Hawking proposed that all matter in the universe was originally focused in a small, single point. Around 13.7 billion years ago there was a 'big bang' and this matter rapidly expanded and then cooled, forming stars and galaxies over time. This process occurred over billions of years, meaning the earth is a lot older than some religious explanations would suggest.

Scientific evidence supports the Big Bang theory. Scientists have been able to observe galaxies moving away from each other through the Hubble telescope. The speed of expansion suggests the age of the universe is around 14 billion years. Scientists have also discovered cosmic microwave background radiation that is present throughout the universe, which supports the theory that a huge explosion occurred.

Catholic views on the Big Bang theory

Pope Francis said that:

> 'The Big Bang theory, which is proposed today as the origin of the world, does not contradict the intervention of a divine creator but depends on it.'
> *Pope Francis*

Here the Pope is saying that the Big Bang required God – for Catholics, the Big Bang could simply be how God chose to create the universe. God must have created the matter and caused the conditions to enable the explosion, therefore the universe was still created *ex nihilo* by God. This means that for Catholics, science and religion are compatible, with God remaining the ultimate omnipotent and omniscient creator.

Darwin's theory of evolution

In his book *On the Origin of Species by Natural Selection*, the naturalist Charles Darwin proposed a theory for how animals and humans developed: the theory of **evolution**. He based this theory on variations he saw between animals across the Galapagos Islands. He focused on finches and noticed that their beaks varied depending on what food sources were available to them. These variations enabled survival by allowing the finches to extract food from their environment in the most efficient way.

Specification focus

The relationship between Catholic and non-religious views about the origins of the universe and of human beings (Stephen Hawking's theory of the Big Bang) and the extent to which these conflict; comparison of the scientific theory of evolution (Charles Darwin, Richard Dawkins), with Catholic beliefs about the purposeful creation of human beings; the extent to which creation and evolution are compatible, with reference to Pope John Paul II's *Message To The Pontifical Academy Of Sciences: On Evolution*.

The Big Bang theory proposes that the universe expanded over billions of years from a single point

Useful terms

natural selection – a process in which animals that are better adapted to their environment are more likely to survive

Atheist – a person who does not believe in God

Humanist – a non-religious person who follows the principles of Humanism

Darwin determined that a process of **natural selection** occurs within species. Over millions of years, gradual changes take place and a new species will develop (or evolve) with the traits needed to help it survive. Darwin traced the evolution of humans back through ape-like species and reptiles all the way to a single bacterium.

From his observations, Darwin concluded that God had no part in creation, stating:

> ‘I cannot persuade myself that a beneficent and omnipotent God would have designedly created the Ichneumonidae [a parasitic wasp] with the express intention of their feeding within the living bodies of caterpillars.’
> *Charles Darwin*

Darwin's observations on the Galapagos Islands found variations between finches. He concluded that species evolve over time to better suit their environments

Scientific evidence supports the theory of evolution. Fossils show many species have become extinct or evolved into new species. DNA technology is also able to show genetic connections between species, suggesting they have evolved from the same point.

Dawkins' views on the theory of evolution

The **Atheist** and **Humanist** Richard Dawkins agrees with Darwin's theory of evolution. He believes it is more logical than a god creating all life on earth. He has stated that natural selection 'has no purpose in mind'; there is no creator God guiding the process.

Building on Darwin's work, Dawkins argues that whole organisms do not evolve – rather, the genes within organisms evolve. Genes that are beneficial to the organism survive while flawed genes become extinct, meaning that over time the organism becomes better suited to survival. Dawkins believes that this process of natural selection has driven the development of all life (including humans), without the involvement of a creator God.

Are Christianity and evolution compatible?

In his *Message to the Pontifical Academy of Sciences: on Evolution*, Pope St John Paul II stated:

> ‘There is no conflict between evolution and the doctrine of faith regarding man and his vocation.’
> *Pope St John Paul II*

The Catholic Church accepts the theory of evolution but argues that it does not mean that humans are not sacred. Evolution is how God chose to create humans and he did so out of love and according to his plan. It is the idea of God having a loving plan for humans that is important, rather than the process of evolution itself. The Catholic Church believes that science can help theologians to better understand scripture and so scientific research should be encouraged. Many Liberal Christians agree with this viewpoint.

Many Fundamentalist Christians reject evolution and see it as undermining God's role as creator of the universe. They believe that God created the universe and placed all life on earth with the characteristics that it has now, so evolution is fundamentally contrary to their beliefs.

Knowledge recall

1 Define the following concepts: evolution, transcendence, stewardship. (You can find these definitions on page 11.)
2 List three reasons why the Big Bang theory is compatible with Catholic beliefs about creation.
3 State two reasons why some Fundamentalists reject the theory of evolution.

Evaluation practice

4 'Science and religion are incompatible.' Give one Fundamentalist Christian response to this statement.
5 Do you think scientific theories are the best way to understand how the universe was created? Give two reasons for your view.

The sanctity and value of human life

Catholic views on the sanctity of life and *imago Dei*

The Catholic Church takes an **absolute** approach to the value of human life: all human life is sacred, without exception. This belief is known as the **sanctity of life**. Catholics believe in the sanctity of life because they believe God created humans differently from other animals, giving them a soul and the ability to make rational decisions. Humans are unique, and human life should be treated with respect and dignity.

> 'Human life is sacred because from its beginning it involves the creative action of God.'
> *CCC 2258*

Catholics believe that life is a gift from God that should be cherished from **conception** to a natural death. Any deliberate killing of innocent people is always wrong, no matter how small, old or sick they are. Catholics believe the Holy Spirit is present within each human body and that each person is created ***imago Dei***; humans are God's most special creation.

> 'So God created humankind in his image.'
> *Genesis 1:27 (NRSV)*

St Catherine of Siena and *imago Dei*

St Catherine of Siena is known for her spiritual writings, and for helping the poor and those in need during the fourteenth century. She believed that all people are created *imago Dei* and deserve to be treated with dignity as they are all loved by God.

In her work 'of Discretion', she gives the following messages on *imago Dei*:

> '**Her dignity is that of her creation, seeing that she is the image of God**, and this has been given her by grace, and not as her due. **In that same mirror of the goodness of God, the soul knows her own indignity, which is the consequence of her own fault.**
> What made you establish man in so great a dignity? Certainly the incalculable love by which you have looked on your creature in yourself! You are taken with love for her; for **by love indeed you created her, by love you have given her a being capable of tasting your eternal Good.**'
> *St Catherine of Siena*

Specification focus

Catholic beliefs and teachings about the origin and sanctity of human life and the concept of *imago Dei* as expressed in the writings of St Catherine of Siena; the relationship between Catholic views, other fundamentalist Christian views and non-religious views about the value of human life, including attitudes towards abortion.

'CCC' stands for 'Catechism of the Catholic Church'. This is a book that was published to summarise the teachings of the Catholic Church.

St Catherine of Siena taught that God loves humans and created them in his image, gifting them a special dignity and value

- Humans come from and are like mirrors of God; this helps them to see their own dignity and worth.
- Humans understand their faults. They are able to see the ways they do not reflect God.
- God creates out of love. Humans have dignity and worth because God loves them.

Catholic views on abortion

Since 1967, **abortion** has been legal in England, Scotland and Wales. However it must meet the following criteria:

- In most circumstances abortion is only allowed up to 24 weeks.
- Two doctors must agree.
- There must be a risk to the physical or mental health of the mother or existing children, or a significant risk that the baby will be born with a physical or mental disability.

The Catholic Church opposes abortion in all circumstances as it believes life starts from the moment of conception, so ending a pregnancy violates the sanctity of life and is always wrong. God gives life and creates humans *imago Dei*, so to abort a foetus is to destroy a life that already has value, dignity and a relationship with God.

The Catholic Church teaches that a foetus is unique in God's eyes. The parents should consider adoption rather than abortion, as this does not violate the foetus' rights (including its right to life). In situations where an abortion is being considered, emotional and spiritual guidance as well as practical support should be offered from the wider community to help the parents.

Even in situations where there is a risk to the mother's life, abortion is still not permitted. However, the Catholic Church does allow life-saving treatment if the intention is saving the mother. This could have the effect of ending the life of the foetus, but as this is not the intention but an unintended side effect, it is permissible. This is known as the doctrine of double effect.

‘From the first moment of his existence, a human being must be recognised as having the rights of a person.’
CCC 2270

Other approaches to the value of life and abortion

The Church of England, like the Catholic Church, disagrees with abortion due to the sanctity of life. Instead, the Church encourages better sex education and for parents to consider adoption. However, in rare situations the Church of England sees abortion as the 'lesser of two evils', such as ending a pregnancy to save the life of the mother.

Fundamentalist Christians completely disagree with abortion as they believe the foetus is a human being with the same rights as the mother. They take a pro-life stance to abortion, believing the foetus has the right to grow and be born.

There are a wide variety of non-religious views on abortion. Some non-religious people argue that the mother's life is more valuable than the foetus', and it is up to the individual to choose what they want to do with their own body. Others believe that abortion is wrong as life begins at conception, therefore it is equivalent to murder.

Useful terms

absolute – the idea that truth and principles are final and universal
sanctity of life – the belief that human life is sacred because it is a gift from God
conception – when sperm meets an egg and fertilisation occurs
abortion – the removal of a foetus from the womb to terminate a pregnancy

‘Before I formed you in the womb I knew you.’
Jeremiah 1:5 (NRSV)

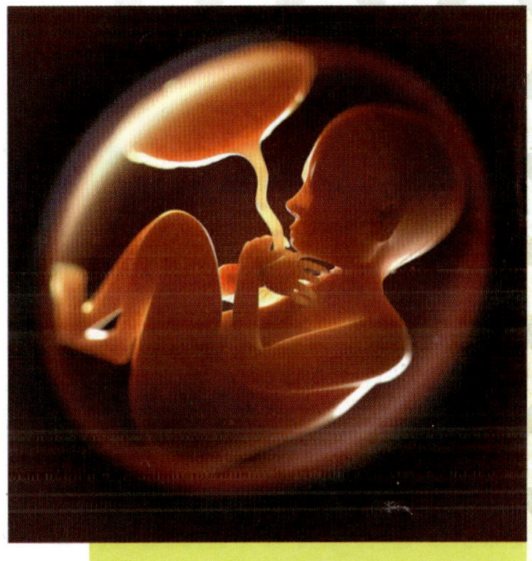

Catholics believe that from the moment of conception the foetus is sacred and should be protected as life is planned and given by God

Read about Humanist attitudes to abortion on page 18.

Knowledge recall

1. Define the following concepts: *imago Dei*, omnipotence, inspiration. (You can find these definitions on page 11.)
2. List three reasons why Catholics reject abortion.
3. State one source of wisdom to support the concept of *imago Dei*.

Evaluation practice

4. Give a reason why Catholics reject abortion.
5. Do you think abortion is acceptable? Give two reasons for your view.

Humanist views on the value of life

Specification focus

Humanist critiques of Catholic beliefs about sanctity of life issues (for example, Peter Singer's views on 'speciesism') and Catholic responses to these challenges.

Humanist views on the value of life and abortion

Humanism is a system of belief focused on the importance of human beings. It rejects any notions of God and looks to science and reason for answers to moral and ethical issues. It believes that the only thing which is real is physical matter or material, and discards belief in anything spiritual such as the soul, the afterlife and God. When making moral decisions, Humanists would tend to promote those decisions that increase the freedom of individuals the most and reduce harm to others.

Most Humanists have a **relative** attitude to the value of life. They may argue that life is special but not because it has been gifted by God. Most agree that everyone should have the right to choose how they want to live based on their **quality of life**. Many Humanists also reject the Catholic Church's **pro-life** stance on abortion because they believe it removes choice, and tend to take a **pro-choice** approach instead.

One pro-choice argument is that a foetus is not a person at conception and so does not have a right to life. Therefore the mother's established life takes precedence over the unborn life.

Humanism advocates for:

- Better sex education and contraception to reduce unwanted pregnancies.
- Maintaining legislation for abortion to reduce unwanted pregnancies and unsafe abortions.
- Understanding the effects that abortion can have on a person's quality of life (both positive and negative), and where appropriate considering adoption.

Peter Singer believes that human life does not have absolute value (in some cases, animal life has more value than human life)

Peter Singer's views on the value of life and abortion

Peter Singer is a controversial figure when it comes to the value of life. He is an Australian moral philosopher and supporter of Humanism who rejects the sanctity of life in favour of the quality of life. Singer believes it is important to increase pleasure and decrease suffering in life, and this is how the quality of life should be measured. He argues that it is acceptable to abort a foetus which will have a poor quality of life when born, as this will cause less suffering.

Singer disagrees with **speciesism** as he does not believe that human life has a special, intrinsic value. He argues that anthropocentrism (where humans are central and more important than other animals) is wrong and sees this as a form of discrimination. He argues that animals, like humans, have the ability to feel and think so should be of equal value. In fact, animals can sometimes have *more* value than humans: an animal that can feel and think is more valuable than a human who is not considered a 'person', such as a newborn baby.

> 'What we must do is bring nonhuman animals within our sphere of moral concern and cease to treat their lives as expendable for whatever trivial purposes we may have.'
> *Peter Singer, Animal Liberation: A New Ethics for our Treatment of Animals*

Useful terms

relative – the idea that truth and moral values are not fixed but depend on the situation

quality of life – the idea that life must have benefits for it to be worth living

pro-life – the belief that abortion is wrong in every circumstance and all humans have the right to life

pro-choice – the belief that the mother has the right to choose what happens to her body and so can have an abortion if she wants one

speciesism – the idea that human life is more important than any other life

For Singer, personhood (the qualities that someone has that makes them a person) is not absolute. He argues that human life begins at conception, but these humans are not persons. Embryos lack the ability to think, feel, reason, communicate and choose. In fact, any human who lacks the qualities of a person (such as a newborn baby or someone in a coma) is classed as a non-person. It is acceptable to end the life of a non-person to reduce their suffering. As a foetus is a non-person, abortion is morally acceptable.

The Catholic response

The Catholic Church strongly disagrees with Peter Singer due to the Christian belief that all humans have dignity and value because all humans are sacred. The idea that a disabled human has lesser value is completely wrong for most Catholics. The Catholic Church teaches that personhood is absolute and so it does not matter what condition a human is in: they remain a person as they were created by God in his image.

The Catholic Church believes that suffering is a part of God's plan. It allows people to share in the suffering of Jesus, and can make them stronger and more resilient. Suffering does not reduce a person's value as each person is sacred regardless of their quality of life.

The Catholic Church teaches that humans have more value than animals as they are made in God's image, but it also teaches that Catholics should be good stewards of the earth. This includes caring for animals as they are also part of God's creation. Catholics might agree they are speciesist in that they value human life more than animal life, but this does not mean they approve of animals being unnecessarily harmed.

Catholics believe they have a God-given responsibility to care for animals, but animals do not have the same value as humans as God did not create them in his image

The Jewish perspective

Jews and Christians share similar beliefs about God as the creator of life. Most Jews believe that God created life and made humans in his own image. They believe in pikuach nefesh (the obligation to save a life), which demonstrates that human life has special value and should be preserved. Pikuach nefesh is so important that it is permissible to break all but three mitzvot (Jewish rules) to save a life.

Many Orthodox Jews believe pikuach nefesh applies to unborn babies too and so abortion is unacceptable. The mitzvah 'do not kill' is a general universal command to not take life, and for some Jews this includes the unborn.

Most Reform Jews believe that abortion is allowed in extreme cases, such as where the mother would not survive the pregnancy, or the baby would be severely disabled.

Knowledge recall

1. Define the following concepts: stewardship, evolution, transcendence. (You can find these definitions on page 11.)
2. List three reasons why Humanists might reject the Catholic view that abortion is always wrong.
3. Suggest one biblical teaching that could be used in a debate about abortion.

Evaluation practice

4. 'All life has equal value.' Give one Catholic response to this statement.
5. Do you believe that the quality of life is more important than the sanctity of life? Give two reasons for your view.

Creation in Genesis 1 and 2

Specification focus

Creation: Comparison of the first and second creation accounts, and their respective representations of God and human beings.

The book of Genesis

The first book of the Old Testament is Genesis. It is the first word of the Bible in Greek and is usually translated 'in the beginning', which tells us that Genesis deals with the creation of the universe. In its opening chapters, it gives two separate accounts of creation which detail how the universe came about.

These two accounts have some differences. Genesis 1:1–2:3 explains how God created the earth and all things in six days, then rested on the seventh day. In contrast, Genesis 2:4–2:24 gives no timeframe for creation and instead shows God as more closely linked to his creation. In order to avoid confusion and contradiction, most Catholics do not read these accounts literally but view them as myths or symbolic stories which reveal truths about the nature of God and the nature of human beings.

Useful terms

transcendent – existing outside of space and time
immanent – God is close to his creation and involved with the world so that he can make himself known

What Genesis 1 and 2 show about the nature of God

The two Genesis accounts show that God has the following qualities:

Genesis 1	Genesis 2
Creator	
God creates in a 6-day period, calling forth creation with just his word, showing his **omnipotence** and purposeful plan. 'Then God said, "Let there be light;" and there was light.' (Genesis 1:3)	The opening sentence states that God created the universe. 'the LORD God made the earth and the heavens.' (Genesis 2:4)
Omnipotent	
God alone creates the universe and everything in it *ex nihilo*. 'The earth was a formless void.' (Genesis 1:2)	God is so powerful he was able to create the vast universe. 'the heavens and earth were completed in all their vast array.' (Genesis 2:1)
Transcendent	
God is outside of creation, making him unique, not subject to space and time. 'In the beginning God created the heavens and the earth.' (Genesis 1:1)	God was not created; he created everything. 'the LORD God made the earth and the heavens.' (Genesis 2:4)
Eternal	
God existed before he created the universe; he has no beginning or end. 'In the beginning God created the heavens and the earth.' (Genesis 1:1)	God existed before creation, showing he has no beginning or end. 'the LORD God made the earth and the heavens.' (Genesis 2:4)
Omnibenevolent	
God created everything good for the benefit of humans. 'And God saw that it was good.' (Genesis 1:10)	God created the universe and provided humans with everything they need (including a companion) out of love. 'The LORD God made to grow every tree that is pleasant to the sight and good for food.' (Genesis 2:9)
Immanent	
God creates humans in his image and then blesses them, showing the closeness between God and humans. 'God blessed them, and God said to them, "Be fruitful and multiply, and fill the earth and subdue it".' (Genesis 1:28)	God is involved with all aspects of creation and the lives of those he creates. This shows his omnipresence. 'Then the LORD God formed a man from the dust of the ground, and breathed into his nostrils the breath of life, and the man became a living being.' (Genesis 2:7)

What Genesis 1 and 2 show about the nature of humans

In Genesis 1 and 2, humans are shown as being special with a unique place in God's creation. In Genesis 1, God loves humans so much that he created the earth in such a way that humans have everything they need to eat and thrive, while in Genesis 2 God's love is shown when he makes Eve for Adam so that he has a companion. Both accounts have the same themes about humans that teach us about their nature and their place within creation.

The two accounts show that humans are made:

- ***Imago Dei*** – God created man and woman to be his likeness in the world, and this makes them different to all the other creations of God as they are more like him. 'So God created humankind in his image, in the image of God he created them' (Genesis 1:27).
- Sacred and with a special dignity – as humans are made in the image of God, God has set them apart to be the most unique and important part of his creation. Humans have sanctity of life and as a result have a special value which cannot be measured. They were also gifted a soul unlike any other creature. 'Then the LORD God formed man from the dust of the ground, and breathed into his nostrils the breath of life, and the man became a living being' (Genesis 2:7).
- To have freedom and free will – God gives Adam and Eve the ability to make their own free choices. This means that all humans have the ability to make rational, free choices and to obey or disobey God. 'You may freely eat of every tree of the garden; but of the tree of the knowledge of good and evil you shall not eat, for in the day that you eat of it you shall die' (Genesis 2:16–17).
- To be stewards – God gives humans a special responsibility to care for his creation. In Genesis 1 humans are given dominion to rule over the earth, but not in a way that damages or abuses it. This is more clearly seen in Genesis 2 when Adam is given the responsibility to 'till and keep the garden' as a caretaker would. He has authority over nature and is entrusted with naming all the animals.

Humans have special dignity and worth as they are the pinnacle of God's creation

The Genesis accounts teach that humans have been given a special relationship with God, but at the same time they have responsibilities towards creation to ensure that it stays as God planned and created it. Despite being told in different ways, both creation accounts agree on the nature of God and the nature of humans.

Knowledge recall

1. Define the following concepts: omnipotence, transcendence, creation *ex nihilo*. (You can find these definitions on page 11.)
2. List three things that the Genesis accounts show about the nature of humans.
3. State one source of wisdom to support the belief that God is omnipotent.

Evaluation practice

4. 'Creation shows God's transcendence.' Give one way in which Genesis 2 might challenge this.
5. Do you think that having two stories of creation undermines the belief that God created the world *ex nihilo*? Give two reasons for your point of view.

Catholic and Humanist views on caring for the environment

Specification focus

Creation: The significance of the Creation narratives with regards to Catholic beliefs about the nature of human beings and their relationship with creation; a comparison of Catholic and Humanist beliefs on the importance of preserving the planet and the environment.

Catholic beliefs about humanity's relationship with creation

The Catholic Church teaches that humans have a special relationship with creation because in both Genesis accounts, God gives humans responsibility over his creation. In Genesis 1 man is given **dominion** over creation, to rule and care for it, while in Genesis 2 man is given the job of tending to creation. Both stories show that humans have **stewardship** over God's creation.

Most Catholics believe it is humanity's duty to care for the environment as humans are not the owners of creation. God has simply gifted creation to humans for us to be caretakers of the earth who have been trusted to ensure its wealth is shared with all those currently alive and all future generations.

In addition, environmental issues such as pollution, overpopulation and climate change not only damage the environment but threaten human life. God created humans ***imago Dei*** and with dignity, and so every care should be taken to preserve life. The Church teaches that protecting the environment will help ensure social justice for future generations by making sure they have access to the same natural resources available today.

God created the universe to be 'good' for the benefit of humans and their survival

> 'God blessed them and said to them, "Be fruitful and multiply, and fill the earth and subdue it; and have dominion over the fish of the sea and over the birds of the air and over every living thing that moves upon the earth."'
> *Genesis 1:28 (NRSV)*

Catholic views on caring for the environment

Both creation accounts in Genesis teach that humans have stewardship over the earth and everything in it. Humans are God's caretakers and should work to stop people taking advantage of the world's resources and environment. The Catholic Church promotes **sustainable** living to preserve the earth, for example by recycling, reducing consumption and using clean, renewable resources.

> 'The destruction of the human environment is extremely serious, not only because God has entrusted the world to us men and women, but because human life is itself a gift which must be defended.'
> *Laudato Si, 6*

The Catholic Church teaches that every human has a responsibility to work for the common good and share the world's resources to ensure that future generations can live in a world fit for their needs. This is a practical way of showing love of one's neighbour and means that all people in society will profit from living in a just society. The world is humanity's common home and so working for the common good means that each person will have an equal stake in it.

Useful terms

dominion – having power or control over nature and the environment

sustainable – using natural resources responsibly to ensure they do not run out

Those who live in poverty are often the most dependent on the environment for survival. The Catholic Church works to put the poor first; this is known as 'the preferential option for the poor'. It believes that reducing the impact of climate change and environmental issues on the poor is a way to recognise that every human has the sanctity of life.

> 'Today, however, we have to realize that a true ecological approach *always* becomes a social approach; it must integrate questions of justice in debates on the environment, so as to hear both the cry of the earth and the cry of the poor.'
> *Laudato Si, 49*

The Catholic Church teaches that humans must look after the earth and all that is in it as stewards of God's creation

Humanist views on caring for the environment

Like Catholics, Humanists believe it is humanity's responsibility to care for the environment.

Similarities	Differences
Most Humanists and Catholics believe: • Humans need to be stewards of the earth to protect the environment, which is humanity's common home. • Sustainable living protects the environment. • Working for social justice will help the world's resources to be shared more equally. • Upholding human rights and equality is the responsibility of all people.	**Most Humanists, but not Catholics, believe:** • God is not a reason why humans should protect the environment. It should be cared for as the natural world is beautiful and without it humans will not survive. • Humans only get one life. If we damage the environment, we are damaging lives now and in the future. • It is important to control the population to stop overcrowding, to ensure all people have enough. • Some Humanists also believe humans are equal to other animals and so have an equal share in the earth's goods. They reject speciesism.

Read about speciesism on page 18.

The Jewish perspective

Jews believe that God created the world and all life. This is reflected in Orthodox prayers which thank God for creation. Most Jews believe it is very important to respect and care for the environment as it is a gift from God.

> 'Blessed be He who spoke and the world came into being.'
> *Barukh She'amar prayer*

The Torah demands that nature be respected. The weekly Shabbat reminds Jews of the limits of their engagement with the world. The festival of Sukkot was celebrated as a harvest festival, reminding Jews to be grateful for what they have been given and the gift of nature.

Most Jews believe that they have a responsibility to 'heal the world': this is known as tikkun olam. It is a way of making the world a better place to live and includes using the world's resources responsibly and showing respect for life.

Knowledge recall

1 Define the following concepts: *imago Dei*, stewardship, inspiration. (You can find these definitions on page 11.)
2 List three reasons why Catholics believe they need to care for creation.
3 State one source of wisdom to support the idea of stewardship.

Evaluation practice

4 'Everyone needs to care for environment.' Give one Humanist response to this statement.
5 Do you think that the world is ours to do what we like with? Give two reasons for your point of view.

Revelation and inspiration in the Bible

Specification focus

The Bible: The Catholic understanding of the nature of revelation and inspiration, with reference to the structure and origins of scripture and its literary forms; different Christian views on the literary form of Genesis and the significance of this for the interpretation of the accounts.

The structure and literary forms of the Bible

The word **Bible** is derived from the Greek word *biblia*, which means 'book'. The Bible is made up of many small 'books', written over a period of about 1500 years by around 40 different authors. It has a clear two-part structure: the Old Testament followed by the New Testament.

The Old Testament is part of the Christian Bible because it reveals God's love for his people which, for Christians, culminates with the coming of Jesus which the New Testament describes. Jesus was Jewish and so were his followers so they all would have venerated what we now call the Old Testament as the scriptures that revealed God to them.

The second part of the Bible is the New Testament, which details the life of Jesus and the work and writings of his early followers, and was written in Greek. The books in the Bible today were agreed by the Church around the fourth or fifth century.

As the Bible was written by numerous authors at different times, there are many literary forms within it. To understand each form properly it is important to understand who wrote it, why and when they wrote it, and how this influences the text.

Old Testament	Law	The five books of Moses, known as the Pentateuch. They give guidance on how to live and follow God.
	History	These books explain the history of the Jewish people and their relationship with God.
	Prophets	These books give messages from God about the future including warnings, instructions and reminders to keep God's laws. A prophet is an inspired messenger of God.
	Wisdom	These books give information about the nature of God, how to stay close to God and how to be a good person. They contain a variety of styles such as poetry and songs.
New Testament	Gospels	These books describe the life and teachings of Jesus. There were four gospel writers: Matthew, Mark, Luke and John. The word gospel means 'good news'.
	Letters	Also known as Epistles, these were largely written by the apostles and witnesses of Jesus, to help give guidance and support to the early Church.
	The Book of Revelation	This is different to the other writings in the New Testament and was written by John. It is an apocalyptic book that deals with the end of the world.

The Bible is divided into two parts: the Old Testament and the New Testament

Revelation and inspiration in the Bible

For Christians, the Bible is the way that God makes himself known and so they see it as the Word of God. The Bible is **revelation**, meaning that God reveals messages about himself through his actions and the prophets. It also shows Christians that God is omnibenevolent and loves his people, particularly through the Incarnation of Jesus. The Bible also teaches Christians how to live a life of goodness and holiness through its moral teachings.

Useful terms

Bible – the Christian scriptures, which contain the Old Testament and the New Testament

metaphorical – to read the words of the Bible as stories or myths that contain truths

literal – to read the words of the Bible as factually true

God shared his Holy Spirit with humans when he created Adam, which allowed humans to be guided along the right path and to live correctly. The Bible continues this guidance as God sent the Holy Spirit to the Bible writers, to guide them to write down God's messages so people could know his truth and the right way of living. This is **inspiration**; the Bible writers were inspired by the Holy Spirit to write the Word of God.

Revelation and inspiration mean that the Bible has authority for Catholics as it is God's Word.

> 'All scripture is inspired by God and is useful for teaching, for reproof, for correction, and for training in righteousness.'
> *2 Timothy 3:16 (NRSV)*

Different Christian interpretations of Genesis

The Catholic Church teaches that the Bible is a text inspired by God's Holy Spirit, the authors of the Bible wrote down the things God wanted to be recorded. The Church also teaches that as the Bible's authors were human, they were limited in their understanding due to the time and place they were living in. For example, they would not have known about scientific explanations of the universe and this would have shown in their writing.

For Catholics, the truths revealed in the Bible need to be authoritatively interpreted by the Church, which teaches that the creation stories in Genesis should be read in a **metaphorical** way. This means Catholics can accept scientific theories about creation such as the Big Bang theory and the theory of **evolution**.

Some Christians (such as Fundamentalist Christians) believe God gave humans the ability to write down exactly what he wanted and so they take a **literal** view of the Bible. They believe that every word in the Bible is true and does not need interpreting. They reject scientific theories of creation, believing instead that the world was made exactly as it says in Genesis.

✡ The Jewish perspective

Jews believe that the Torah (the first five books of the Tenakh) is the most authoritative scripture as Moses received this directly from God on Mount Sinai. Due to this, Orthodox Jews believe the Torah must not be altered and should be understood literally.

> 'The Torah will never be abrogated, nothing will be added to it or subtracted from it; God will never give another Law.'
> *Maimonides*

Most Reform Jews believe that taking the Torah literally is impossible as it was written in a very different time and place and cannot apply to modern life without some modifications. Therefore, the text needs to be understood in a modern context and interpreted to fit in with modern life.

Catholics interpret the creation stories in Genesis metaphorically while some other Christians interpret these literally

Knowledge recall

1. Define the following concepts: revelation, inspiration. (You can find these definitions on page 11.)
2. List three reasons why Catholics believe the Bible has authority.
3. State one source of wisdom which shows that the Bible is inspired by God.

Evaluation practice

4. Give a reason why some Christians interpret the Bible literally.
5. Do you think that the Bible should be read literally? Give two reasons for your point of view.

Michelangelo's *Creation of Adam*

Specification focus

Painting: The meaning of Michelangelo's *Creation of Adam* in the Sistine chapel; the extent to which Michelangelo's *Creation of Adam* expresses Catholic beliefs about creation, God and human beings.

Art in Christianity

Since its beginnings Christianity has used art to help people understand its messages and teachings. This was particularly needed in the medieval period when Christianity had spread to the wider world which did not have the same educational habits or access as the Greeks, Romans or Jews did at the time of the early Church. The medieval period was a time when most people in Europe could not read and would not have access to the Bible. Art became a way of sharing the Bible and its messages, a way of showing the power and radiance of God, and a way for a person to deepen their own faith.

The Catholic Church has expressed its faith through various forms of art, such as sculptures, statues, stained glass windows and paintings. One important point to remember is Christians do not worship the artwork – they use it to help them to focus on and worship God.

Michelangelo's *Creation of Adam*

Michelangelo Buonarroti (1475–1564) is one of the most famous Renaissance artists. He made a name for himself in Italy as a sculptor with his famous work *Pieta*. He was noticed by the Pope at the time and was commissioned to sculpt his tomb, a job he never finished. Michelangelo was then commissioned to paint the ceiling of the Sistine Chapel in the Vatican in Rome. It took him four years to complete, lying on his back on a scaffold. It was immediately seen as a great work of art.

Michelangelo decorated the ceiling with nine different scenes, but the *Creation of Adam* is probably the most famous. It shows God giving life to Adam. It portrays various ideas about the nature of God and the nature of humans (in the image Adam represents all of humanity). It shows humans are dependent on God and have a special relationship with God.

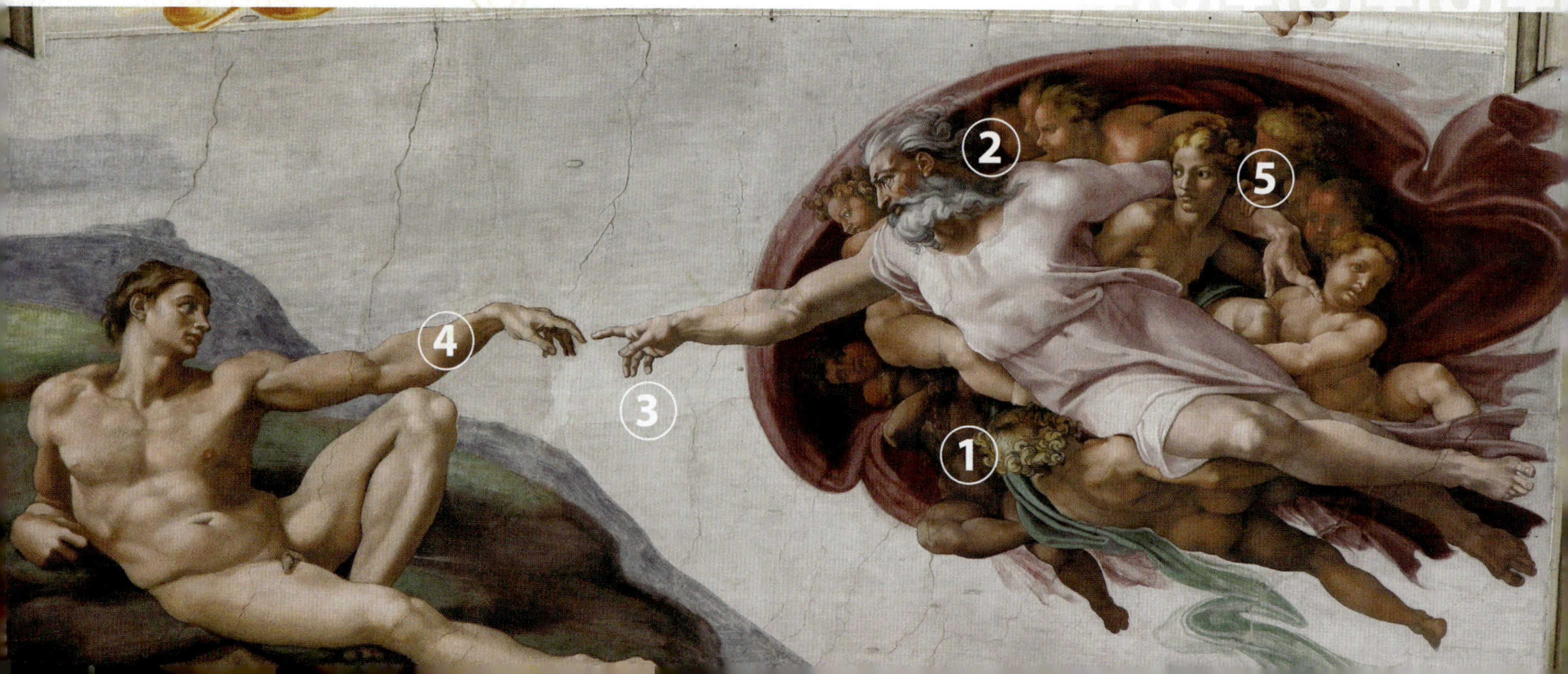

How Michelangelo's *Creation of Adam* expresses Catholic beliefs

① God is sat within a cloud surrounded by floating angels, showing his **transcendence**. This suggests that God is not confined to the limits of this world. Some believe the cloud is in fact a brain, showing that God is omniscient.

② God appears very different to Adam. He is elderly, with grey hair, but he is also muscular and healthy. This indicates that God is the father of Adam, and also suggests wisdom: God is omniscient.

③ God is shown almost touching Adam. In doing so he is about to give life to Adam. God is therefore an omnipotent creator. He makes Adam healthy and strong, demonstrating his love for him as his father, showing that God is omnibenevolent.

④ God is shown next to a woman who some believe is Eve, suggesting that he has planned for Adam to have a companion. This shows God's omnibenevolence and omniscience. Others believe the woman to be the Virgin Mary, with the Christ Child to her left. This indicates that God knows Adam will sin and fall from grace, so he has planned for a 'last Adam' – Jesus – to come and save humans and bring them back to grace. ('The first man, Adam, became a living being; the last Adam became a life-giving spirit.' – 1 Corinthians 15:45).

⑤ Adam is portrayed in a relaxed position opposite God, lazily reaching his hand towards God. He appears to not be fully animated and requires God's touch to bring him to life. As Adam represents all humanity, this means that humans are dependent on God to give them life. By giving humans the spark of life, God gave humanity the sanctity of life. ('Then the Lord God formed man from the dust of the ground, and breathed into his nostrils the breath of life; and the man became a living being' – Genesis 2:7).

⑥ Adam represents the belief that humans are the children of God as life comes from God. This is seen in the age of Adam compared to God. He is much younger than God, with God looking down on him like a father. This suggests humans have a special dignity as they come from God.

⑦ Adam mirrors God: he has similar features and build, and echoes God's position. St Catherine of Siena taught that the soul is the mirror of God, and this can be seen clearly here in Adam. Humans are made ***imago Dei*** and so have a special likeness and resemblance to God. This means that God loves humans as he makes them like him. ('So God created humankind in his image, in the image of God he created them; male and female he created them.' – Genesis 1:27).

⑧ God's creation is shown as beautiful. Adam is a healthy and handsome man; this illustrates that God's creation is good. God is good and so he shows this in humans and the rest of creation. Adam's outward beauty reflects the inner beauty of the soul that God gifted to him. Humans are the pinnacle of God's creation, and God is the Father of all creation. ('Yet for us there is one God, the Father, from whom are all things and for whom we exist, and one Lord, Jesus Christ, through whom are all things and through whom we live.' – 1 Corinthians 8:6).

Knowledge recall

1 Define the following concepts: *imago Dei*, transcendence, revelation. (You can find these definitions on page 11.)

2 List three ways in which *Creation of Adam* reflects Catholic beliefs about creation.

3 State one source of wisdom to support the Catholic belief in *imago Dei*.

Evaluation practice

4 '*Creation of Adam* accurately portrays Christian beliefs about the creation of humans.' Give one Christian response to this statement.

5 Do you think the nature of God is shown accurately in the *Creation of Adam*? Give two reasons for your view.

1.9

Symbolism in the Tree of Life mosaic

Specification focus

Symbolism: The use of symbolism and imagery in Christian art, with particular reference to the Tree of Life apse mosaic in San Clemente in Rome and the meanings of the symbols contained within it, for example, the Alpha and Omega, the Chi-Rho, lamb, dove and the four evangelists; the symbol of the cross as the Tree of Life with reference to the theology of Christ as the New Adam and how this is expressed in the San Clemente mosaic.

Symbolism and the Tree of Life mosaic

Symbolism is used extensively in Christianity as a way of giving messages and showing religious beliefs. The Tree of Life mosaic is an example of Christian art which is filled with symbolism. It is a highly detailed mosaic located in the **apse** in San Clemente (a minor basilica in Rome), and is believed to have been created around the twelfth century.

The Alpha and Omega

Alpha (A) and Omega (ω) are the first and last letters of the Greek alphabet. Together they suggest eternity and are used to refer to Jesus. In the book of Revelation, it states '"I am the Alpha and Omega", says the Lord God, who is and who was and who is to come, the Almighty' (Revelations 1:8). God is referred to first as Alpha and Omega, then in Revelations 1:18, Jesus is also referred to as Alpha and Omega. This shows not just Jesus' connection with God, but also his identity with God. They represent Jesus' connection to God, showing that Jesus is also eternal. He is God Incarnate (God made flesh) and thus was there at the beginning of creation and will be there at the end.

α Ω

The Chi-Rho

This is another symbol to represent Jesus. It is made from the first two letters of the Greek word for Christ (Chi is represented by X and rho is represented by ρ). This symbol was used frequently in the early Church and is still used today, for example on the baptismal candle. The Chi-Rho is shown with the Alpha and Omega in this mosaic to reinforce the central importance of Jesus.

The lamb

In the story of Passover in the Old Testament, lambs were sacrificed and their blood was put on the lintels and doorposts of every Israelite home to save the first-borns. Jesus has become known as the sacrificial 'Lamb of God' in Christianity as he saved humanity with his death and resurrection.

At the bottom of the mosaic there are thirteen lambs, representing the twelve apostles and Jesus. The central lamb pictured with a halo is Jesus. Jesus' sacrifice on the cross paid the debt of humanity and saved them from sin and death, in the same way that lambs saved the Israelites.

The apostles are also portrayed as lambs as they lived lives of sacrifice. Jesus is also portrayed as the good shepherd, and the apostles as his flock.

Useful terms

symbolism – images used to show or represent religious beliefs
apse – a large, usually domed roof at the eastern end of a church
evangelist – one of the four Gospel writers: Matthew, Mark, Luke and John

The dove

The twelve doves in the mosaic represent both the twelve apostles and the Holy Spirit, as doves are a traditional symbol of the Holy Spirit. Portraying the apostles as doves shows they are guided by the Holy Spirit. During Pentecost the Holy Spirit came down upon the apostles, giving them the courage to evangelise, leading to the expansion of the Church.

The four evangelists

The four **evangelists** are of central importance to the early spread of Christianity and so are shown in their symbolic forms at the top of the apse next to the risen Christ.

- Mark is shown as a lion.
- Luke is shown as an ox.
- Matthew is shown as a human.
- John is shown as an eagle.

The symbolism attached to the four evangelists originates from Revelations 4:6–7: 'Around the throne, and on each side of the throne, are four living creatures, full of eyes in front and behind: the first living creature like a lion, the second living creature like an ox, the third living creature with a face like a human face, and the fourth living creature like a flying eagle.'

The Tree of Life and Christ as the New Adam

The central image in the mosaic is Jesus on the cross, surrounded by 12 doves, with the hand of God above. The Trinity is therefore at the centre of the apse, with a transcendent God becoming immanent in the person of Jesus.

Jesus' crucifixion and death are portrayed as a symbol of hope, as he radiates light. Mary and St John stand on either side of the cross, with God the Father above handing Jesus a victory wreath, showing that his sacrifice has been a victory over sin and death.

The cross is growing from the Tree of Life, showing that the cross is the Tree of Life. This shows that through the death of Jesus on the cross, salvation is given to everyone and all people are given eternal life.

The mosaic reflects the idea that Christ is the New Adam, who removes the stain of sin from humanity, restoring the relationship between humankind and God that was damaged in the Fall. The serpent coiled at the base of the tree echoes Genesis 2, when Adam and Eve ate the forbidden fruit.

The vibrant and swirling vines that sprout from the Tree of Life cover the whole mosaic and reach all of humanity. The vines unite humanity and are fed by Christ on the cross, showing that life comes from Christ's sacrifice. Jesus said in John's Gospel that 'I am the vine, you are the branches' (John 15:5). The mosaic shows that just as branches rely on the vine for life, so too does humankind rely on Jesus for life.

Knowledge recall

1. Define the following concepts: revelation, omnipotence, creation *ex nihilo*. (You can find these definitions on page 11.)
2. List three symbols shown in the Tree of Life mosaic and briefly explain their meaning.
3. State one source of wisdom to support the idea that Jesus is the Tree of Life.

Evaluation practice

4. 'Religious symbols in Christian art give us a better understanding of God.' Give one way in which a Christian would respond to this statement.
5. Do you think the Tree of Life mosaic accurately portrays Christ as the New Adam? Give two reasons for your view.

Catholic social teaching

The nature of Catholic social teaching

Catholic social teaching is the group of principles the Catholic Church has formed which deal with issues of **social justice**, poverty, distribution of wealth and the dignity of people. Pope Leo XIII is considered to have first made Catholic social teaching an important part of the Church's agenda when he called for improvements for the working class and those in poverty at the end of the nineteenth century, but its roots can be traced back to the work and teachings of Jesus in the Bible.

Jesus taught that people should 'love your neighbour as yourself' (Mark 12:31) and help those in need regardless of who they are. Catholics therefore believe that all humans are their neighbour and they have a duty to help those in need. Social justice is of utmost importance to the Catholic Church; making sure that every person has equal opportunities and freedoms follows the example and teaching of Jesus.

There are seven key themes in Catholic social teaching which aim to promote equality for all:

- The sanctity of life and the dignity of the person – every person is made in God's image, so every person is equally valuable.
- The common good – thinking about the needs of the wider community.
- Social justice – fair distribution of wealth, opportunities, resources and privileges in society.
- The preferential option for the poor – the needs of the poor should be put first.
- Dignity of work – all types of jobs should be respected equally, workers should receive fair pay for their work and should not be subjected to work that is demeaning or dehumanising.
- Solidarity – showing support for each other and working for the common good.
- **Stewardship** – the duty to care for creation responsibly and protect it for future generations.

> 'Some opportune remedy must be found quickly for the misery and wretchedness pressing so unjustly on the majority of the working class.'
> *Pope Leo XIII, Rerum Novarum 3*

Catholic social teaching and *imago Dei*

The core of Catholic social teaching is the belief that every human is created ***imago Dei*** and so has dignity. Humans are created in the image of God, so from the moment of conception until natural death they possess the sanctity of life. Anything that threatens to destroy human life – such as war, abortion or euthanasia – is completely wrong.

Poverty, inequality and injustice are also seen as attacks on human life and therefore the Catholic Church teaches that 'with respect to the fundamental rights of the person, every type of discrimination, whether social or cultural,

Specification focus

Loving and Serving in Catholic communities: The influence of the concept of *imago Dei* on Catholic Social Teaching about justice, peace and reconciliation, with reference to *Gaudium et Spes* 29 and 78.

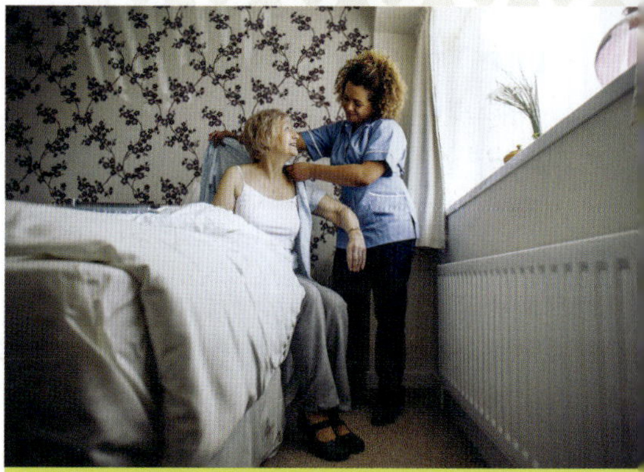

Catholic social teachings form the basis for how all people should be treated: with dignity and respect as they are made imago Dei

Useful terms

Catholic social teaching – the official teachings of the Catholic Church on matters of social justice
social justice – the aim to have a society that is fair, where all people have access to and an equal share in wealth, opportunities and basic necessities
reconciliation – the act of bringing individuals or groups together in peace after conflict

whether based on sex, race, colour, social condition, language or religion, is to be overcome and eradicated as contrary to God's intent' (*Gaudium et Spes* 29). The Catholic Church calls for people to work for the common good and to put the poor first so that inequality is eradicated.

> 'Since all men possess a rational soul and are created in God's likeness, since they have the same nature and origin, have been redeemed by Christ and enjoy the same divine calling and destiny, the basic equality of all must receive increasingly greater recognition.'
> *Gaudium et Spes 29*

The Catholic Church teaches that justice, peace and reconciliation in society mean that all people can live their lives without injustice or suffering, and can enjoy their common home

Justice, peace and reconciliation

Justice is the basis of Catholic social teaching, which aims to ensure that all people can live in a world where they are treated fairly and have equal opportunities. To create social justice, it is important to recognise that everyone has dignity and should be respected equally.

Injustice leads to suffering and pain. The Catholic Church advocates for its followers to right the wrongs that injustice causes and work towards creating the common good for all in humanity's common home. The Church asks for Catholics to make 'an enterprise of justice' (*Gaudium et Spes* 78) to uphold human dignity and combat injustice.

The Catholic Church has always promoted peace as it reflects one of the main themes of the gospels; Jesus taught 'Blessed are the peacemakers, for they will be called children of God' (Matthew 5:9). The Church believes that peace allows people to live without fear, pain and suffering. It allows them to live a secure life with access to work, education and necessities. Conflict is not just confined to war: it can be smaller and more personal and can lead to injustice and a breakdown of community. The Church teaches that individuals have a duty to work for peace and should try to overcome personal conflicts, while Catholic groups like Pax Christi work to resolve conflict on a larger scale.

> 'A firm determination to respect other men and peoples and their dignity, as well as the studied practice of brotherhood are absolutely necessary for the establishment of peace. Hence peace is likewise the fruit of love.'
> *Gaudium et Spes 78*

Catholic social teaching argues that the only way to achieve genuine peace is to ensure that those who have been in conflict go through a process of **reconciliation**. This removes lasting issues on both sides to leave harmony. It is only when harmony is achieved that there is no more injustice, pain or suffering. Reconciliation encourages social justice and allows people to move on with their lives. The gospels promote reconciliation as a way of building good relationships with others and with God, as shown in the parable of the forgiving father.

Working for justice, peace and reconciliation is essential to the Catholic Church. Catholic social teaching calls for individuals to act when needed and to show love for their neighbour in a practical sense. This means recognising that all people are created *imago Dei*, caring for the poor and oppressed, and working to create a just society for the common good of all those who live in humanity's common home. It is also essential to work to bring about the end of injustice, as injustice can cause conflict.

Knowledge recall

1 Define the following concepts: *imago Dei*, stewardship, inspiration. (You can find these definitions on page 11.)
2 List three reasons why Catholics believe that social justice is important.
3 State one source of wisdom that supports the preferential option for the poor.

Evaluation practice

4 'Not all people are equal.' Give one way in which a Catholic would respond to this statement.
5 Do you think Catholic social teaching supports the idea that all people are made *imago Dei*? Give two reasons for your view.

The role of the Catholic Church in interfaith dialogue

Specification focus

Loving and Serving in Catholic communities: The importance of the role of the Catholic Church in interfaith dialogue to promote understanding, respect, tolerance and harmony between the different religious and non-religious traditions in Great Britain, including: Christianity, Buddhism, Hinduism, Islam, Judaism, Sikhism, Humanism and Atheism.

What is interfaith dialogue?

Interfaith dialogue describes communication, discussion and collaboration between people of different faiths and no faiths, including Humanists and Atheists. It allows these different groups to find shared aims and common ground, so they can move forward in cooperation. It tries to overcome barriers between people of different faiths and reduce conflict in society for the mutual benefit of all people. It attempts to build **social cohesion** by promoting commonality and inclusivity.

The law in the UK protects an individual's right to religious freedom. Effective interfaith dialogue respects this by trying to ensure that people can practise their faith safely in society, where their beliefs and traditions are respected and tolerated. The work of groups like the Interfaith Network promotes understanding, cooperation and good relationships between faiths so that social cohesion is possible.

> ‘Every type of discrimination, whether social or cultural discrimination, whether based on sex, race, colour, social condition, language or religion is to be overcome and eradicated as contrary to God's intent.’
> *Gaudium et Spes 29*

The UK is home to people of many different religions and ethnicities who all add to its culture

Britain as a multi-faith society

The UK is very diverse in its religious makeup. Christianity is the main religion; other religious and non-religious traditions include Islam, Buddhism, Hinduism, Judaism, Sikhism, Humanism and Atheism. This means the UK is a **multi-faith society**, as well as a multi-ethnic society. This is not a recent change to British society: Britain has always had people of many faiths and ethnicities as part of its population.

In its early history Britain was invaded by numerous groups, such as the Romans, Saxons and Vikings, and each has had an influence on the religious and ethnic composition of the UK. Many people from the British Empire and later the Commonwealth countries also moved to Britain. Britain has also become home to refugees from many different countries due to wars that have occurred over the centuries. All of this has led to Britain today being very religiously and ethnically diverse.

There are many positives to living in a multi-faith society:

- As people experience different religions they can become more tolerant and understanding.
- Misconceptions about different religions can be corrected.
- Interfaith events can unite people of different faiths in one community.

However, living in a multi-faith society can also bring challenges:

- Minority religions or ethnicities can experience racism and discrimination.

Useful terms

interfaith dialogue – engagement between those of different faiths and no faith to bring about positive outcomes such as respect, tolerance and social harmony

social cohesion – when members of society are bound together through respect and tolerance, and share common values

multi-faith society – a society in which there are people of many different religions and people of no religion

- Fear of a religious group based on misunderstanding can lead to violence and terrorism.
- Religious extremism can lead some people to be more intolerant of mainstream religions.
- Religious or ethnic groups may be blamed for problems in society.

The Catholic Church and its role in interfaith dialogue

One of the roles of the Catholic Church is to promote interfaith dialogue. The Church believes this is a way of showing love for one's neighbour as it builds respect for people of other faiths. The Church teaches that all people are created ***imago Dei*** regardless of their religion and as a result they have the right to be treated with dignity. Likewise, every person has the sanctity of life, therefore their human rights, including their right to freely practise the religion of their choice, must be upheld. Interfaith dialogue for Catholics is a way of showing love for all and respect for different religions.

The Second Vatican Council argued the need for better relationships with Jews and Muslims, and as a result, the Church has stressed interfaith dialogue as essential to finding universal truths which are shared by all religions. Understanding the similarities between faiths brings them closer together and reduces the possibility of conflict. Although the Catholic Church teaches that it alone holds the whole truth, it believes other religions do have some truths and acknowledging these is important for building good relationships and ending religious intolerance and discrimination.

> 'The Church gladly acknowledges whatever is true and holy in the religious traditions of Buddhism, Hinduism and Islam.'
> *Redemptoris Missio 55*

Today in the UK, the Catholic Bishops' Conference of England and Wales (CBCEW) works to promote interfaith dialogue and social harmony by encouraging Christian unity and good relations with other religions. A few examples of its work include:

- Encouraging remembrance of the Holocaust.
- Organising visits where Catholic bishops are welcomed into other places of worship to promote tolerance and pray for peace across religions.
- Hosting the Benedict VXI lectures, where key figures from different faiths are invited to speak.
- Providing resources such as the podcast series 'In Their Own Words', where people from nine different religions talk about their faith.

Pope Francis actively encourages interfaith dialogue as he believes this is a way to recognise each person's special value and dignity. He visits many countries and speaks about the need for tolerance and respect for all people. In 2019 he travelled to Abu Dhabi and addressed over 700 people representing Islam, Judaism, Christianity and other faiths, stating that 'religions, in particular, cannot renounce the urgent task of building bridges between peoples and cultures.' This shows his desire for all religions to cooperate.

> 'The Church therefore, urges her sons to enter with prudence and charity into discussion and collaboration with members of other religions.'
> *Nostra Aetate 2*

Interfaith dialogue helps people to come together and find similarities to create a tolerant and harmonious society

Knowledge recall

1 Define the following concepts: *imago Dei*, revelation, evolution. (You can find these definitions on page 11.)
2 List three reasons why Catholics believe interfaith dialogue is important.
3 State one source of wisdom to support the Catholic belief that tolerance and harmony are important within society.

Evaluation practice

4 'The Catholic Church alone is responsible for social cohesion.' Give one way in which a Catholic would respond to this statement.
5 Do you agree that interfaith dialogue is important for society? Give two reasons for your view.

The work of CAFOD and SVP

Specification focus

Loving and Serving in Catholic communities: The extent to which the work of one Catholic charity, such as CAFOD and one local charity, such as SVP, reflect Catholic beliefs about the dignity of human beings, the importance of loving one's neighbour, and respecting creation.

Catholic charities and Catholic social teaching

The Catholic Church believes in the dignity of humans as they are made ***imago Dei***. Catholics are called to eradicate poverty as it goes against loving one's neighbour and respecting their dignity. Supporting Catholic **charities** is one way of doing this.

Globally, over a billion people live in severe poverty, with thousands dying daily due to lack of food, clean water or access to medical care. The Catholic Church teaches that the poorest in society should come first; this is known as the 'preferential option for the poor'. In May 2020 Pope Francis stated that the 'Church's preferential option for the poor is non-negotiable'. The Church believes the poorest should be put first because their needs are greatest; working towards equality by helping the poor shows love of neighbour and respects everyone's sanctity of life.

The work of CAFOD

'CAFOD' stands for the Catholic Agency for Overseas Development. It is the official aid and development charity of the Catholic Church in England and Wales. CAFOD's charity work is mainly carried out in areas of extreme poverty in Africa, Latin America and the Middle East.

CAFOD is a Catholic charity that works to alleviate poverty in developing countries by giving aid and support to those most in need

Human dignity

CAFOD recognises the dignity in each person and tries to help everyone in need as they are *imago Dei*. CAFOD does not discriminate about who it helps: the charity supports people of any race, religion, gender and background, showing the value of every human in their work.

CAFOD's work is inspired by the teachings of Jesus, such as the parable of the sheep and the goats. The charity gives to those in need and teaches valuable skills to enable people to become self-sufficient. For example, CAFOD has worked in Zimbabwe for over 30 years, providing tools, seeds and training so that families are able to farm independently and earn their own living. By doing this, CAFOD enables people to see their own value and recover their dignity.

> ‘As St Ambrose put it: "You are not making a gift of what is yours to the poor man, but you are giving him back what is his."’
> *Populorum Progressio 23*

Loving one's neighbour

CAFOD provides short-term aid and disaster relief for those who have experienced a natural disaster, disease or war. For example, the charity helped developing countries respond to the coronavirus pandemic by distributing hygiene kits and masks to communities living in poverty. CAFOD shows love of neighbour by ensuring that people have the resources they need to survive.

Useful terms

charity – an organisation set up to help those who are less fortunate

CAFOD – the Catholic Agency for Overseas Development, a Catholic charity which works to bring about social justice

SVP – the St Vincent de Paul Society, a Catholic charity which aims to alleviate poverty by helping those who are in need in local communities

The charity also provides long-term aid to allow individuals and communities to become more independent. CAFOD's website allows people to buy 'world gifts' that can help those in need in the long term, such as a sewing kit that will help a woman to learn to be a seamstress and earn her own income.

In the UK, CAFOD works to educate people on the causes of poverty. It campaigns for just policies and holds fundraising events to fund projects overseas.

Respect for creation

CAFOD also believes that care for creation is an important part of its work, as the common good is connected to the state of humanity's common home. CAFOD campaigns for people to tackle the climate crisis as the poorest will be the most badly affected by it. The charity sees sustainable development as a means of protecting the environment and looks for new ways of carrying this out.

SVP is a Catholic charity that works to end poverty in local communities by offering practical support and help to those in need

The work of SVP

'SVP' stands for the St Vincent de Paul Society. It is a charity founded in Paris in 1833 by Frederic Ozanam, based on the charitable work of St Vincent de Paul. SVP gives hands-on support and helps those in need. The work of SVP has spread to many countries around the world, with groups in many parishes offering local support.

Human dignity

The work of SVP reflects its belief that each person has dignity and is created *imago Dei*. Like CAFOD, SVP works with all people, including the most marginalised and isolated, such as the elderly, the sick and those in prison. The charity believes that all people have the right to a good life and its practical work in communities reflects this.

Loving one's neighbour

SVP's work is a practical expression of 'love your neighbour'. It is inspired by the parable of the sheep and the goats to work to fulfil the needs of others. For example, SVP members make home visits to the sick and housebound, and visit care facilities, prisons and hospitals. SVP runs centres where those in need can access food, clean clothing and washing facilities. The charity also helps people to access training and education to improve their job opportunities. SVP treats all people with compassion and does not judge people on their situation.

> 'I was hungry and you gave me food, I was thirsty and you gave me something to drink, I was a stranger and you welcomed me, I was naked and you gave me clothing, I was sick and you took care of me, I was in prison and you visited me.'
> *Matthew 25:35–36 (NRSV)*

Respect for creation

One way in which SVP shows care for creation is through its community shops and furniture stores, where people can donate clothing, household items and furniture. This means that people have access to affordable second-hand items, which helps individuals in need but also helps to protect the environment, as it reduces the amount of waste going to landfill.

Knowledge recall

1. Define the following concepts: stewardship, omnipotence, creation *ex nihilo*. (You can find these definitions on page 11.)
2. List three ways that Catholics try to help alleviate poverty.
3. State one source of wisdom that explains why Catholics work to alleviate poverty.

Evaluation practice

4. 'It is everyone's responsibility to help the poor.' Give one way in which a Catholic would respond to this statement.
5. Do you agree that supporting charities is a way of showing love of one's neighbour? Give two reasons for your view.

Skills practice

On these exam practice pages, you will see example answers for each of the exam question types: **a**, **b**, **c** and **d**. You can find out more about these on pages 8–9.

Question *(a)*

*Question **(a)** tests your knowledge and understanding. You will always be asked to **define a key concept** in this question. You can find a list of the concepts at the beginning of the chapter.*

(a) What do Catholics mean by 'inspiration'? [2]

Student response

When the Holy Spirit gives you inspiration to do something.

Improved student response

Inspiration means 'God breathed'. It is the belief that the Spirit of God guides an individual to act or write what is good and true.

What went well

The candidate has given a general definition of what inspiration means and linked to the Holy Spirit.

How to improve

You must use a synonym (another word that has the same or similar meaning) for 'inspiration' to show that you understand what it means.

You should learn the exam board's definition of the word at the start of this chapter.

You could learn more than one synonym to improve your definition.

Over to You! Try to answer this question:

(a) What do Catholics mean by 'stewardship'? [2]

Helpful hints

To help you answer this question effectively, you could use the check list below to make sure you include the most important things:

- Include a **synonym** for the word 'steward/stewardship'.
- Give an **example** of how someone could be a good steward.

Tip

The easiest way to make sure you get full marks for this question is to learn the definitions found on page 11.

Now give yourself **two minutes** to answer this question by yourself:

(a) What do Catholics mean by 'omnipotence'? [2]

Question *(b)*

*Question **(b)** tests your knowledge and understanding. It will always ask you to **describe** a belief, a teaching, a practice or an event that is included on the specification.*

(b) Describe what **two** of the symbols in the 'Tree of Life' apse mosaic in San Clemente in Rome represent. [5]

Student response

There are many symbols on the 'Tree of Life' apse which represent many things. One symbol is the Alpha and Omega which are the first and last letters of the Greek alphabet and symbolise beginning and end. Another symbol is the thirteen lambs. One has a halo showing that it is different to the others.

What went well

The candidate mentions two separate symbols shown on the 'Tree of Life' apse.

How to improve

You must make sure you have fully described what each symbol is.

You should include what the symbols represent in relation to Christian beliefs.

You could make reference to or even quote sources of wisdom or authority to support your answer.

Improved student response

The 'Tree of Life' apse contains many different symbols which reflect core Christian beliefs. For example, one symbol shown on the apse is the Alpha and Omega. These are the first and last letters of the Greek alphabet and they are a symbol of Jesus. They represent that Jesus is God and is eternal, he was there at the beginning and will be there at the end.
Another symbol shown on the apse is the thirteen lambs. The central lamb is shown with a halo which represents Jesus as the Lamb of God, whose sacrifice 'takes away the sins of the world' and brings salvation. The other twelve lambs are looking at the Lamb of God showing they are followers or apostles of Christ. They are shown as lambs as they lived a life of hardship and sacrifice for their faith.

Tip

The best answers reference all aspects of the question. Here, the candidate talks about:
- two separate symbols on the 'Tree of Life' apse
- what each symbol represents
- scripture which supports one of the points made.

Over to You! Try to answer this question:

(b) Describe St Catherine of Siena's teaching about being made in the image of God. [5]

Helpful hints

Use the check list below to make sure you include the most important things:

- **Describe** one of St Catherine of Siena's teachings about *imago Dei.*
- Give an **example** of a statement from St Catherine of Siena's 'Of Discretion' to support your point.
- Then **repeat** the above process to give two more teachings from St Catherine of Siena about *imago Dei.*

Now give yourself **five minutes** to answer this question by yourself:

(b) Describe **two** ways in which the work of CAFOD reflects Catholic teaching about human dignity. [5]

Question *(c)*

*Question **(c)** tests your knowledge and understanding. You need to give detailed evidence and reasoning to support your explanation of the topic. For the Origins and Meaning paper, you will always be asked to **explain two different viewpoints**, but you don't need to evaluate which is the better view.*

(c) Explain from **either** Catholic Christianity and Judaism **or two** Christian traditions, beliefs about abortion. [8]

Student response

Christians do not agree with abortion. They believe it is never acceptable to abort a foetus and so they believe that no one should ever have an abortion. The Bible says that abortion is wrong and so they would never have an abortion as it goes against the teachings in the Bible. But abortion is now legal in the UK and so the Christian teaching on this is outdated.

What went well

This response gives a possible Christian attitude to abortion and links briefly to scripture. It also briefly mentions that there have been some changes in society.

How to improve

You must stick to the requirement of the question to give two religious attitudes, not just one.

You should give clear, specific details of what the different religious attitudes are and how they are evidenced in behaviour.

You could include some quotes or examples as evidence of the attitudes you are explaining.

Improved student response

The Catholic Church teaches that abortion is always unacceptable. Scripture shows that human life has absolute value as in Exodus 20:13 it says, 'you shall not murder', therefore any ending of life including by abortion is seen as murder. Some Catholics look to Natural Law and believe that the Primary Precepts of 'protect innocent life' and 'reproduction' show that they should never allow abortion.

In Judaism, Jews believe that humans are made in the image of God, therefore life is precious. They believe that each life has a special relationship with God even before birth and so some Jews will disagree with abortion unless it is to save the life of the mother. Jews have an obligation to save life which is known as pikuach nefesh, therefore abortion would only be allowed if the mother would die as a result of carrying on with the pregnancy.

Over to You! Try to answer this question:

(c) Explain from **either** Catholic Christianity and Judaism or **two** Christian traditions, beliefs about caring for the environment. [8]

Helpful hints

- Include **two** beliefs from either Catholicism and Judaism *or* from two traditions within Christianity (for example, Catholic and Protestant).
- For each belief, give a **source of wisdom** to support it (e.g. scripture, Church law, the Catechism, a papal statement, the Tanakh, the mitzvot).
- Explain **why** each of the religions or traditions believe this (e.g. how they are influenced by other teachings about the nature and value of creation or how to treat others).
- Explain **how** people of this faith are expected to behave as a result (e.g. being good stewards of God's creation).

Tip

Question *(c)* never requires you to evaluate or weigh up which view is better. It only wants you to describe two different views. The evaluation comes later in question *(d)*.

Now give yourself **eight minutes** to answer this question by yourself:

(c) Explain from **either** Catholic Christianity and Judaism or **two** Christian traditions, how the Bible is interpreted. [8]

Question *(d)*

*Question **(d)** tests your ability to **evaluate**. This means you need to show you have considered more than one point of view and that you have referred to religion and belief. You will need to be able to make judgements that are supported by detailed reasoning and argument.*

(d) 'The theory of evolution is the best explanation for the origin of humans.'

Discuss this statement showing that you have considered more than one point of view. (You must refer to religious and non-religious beliefs, such as those held by Humanists and Atheists, in your answer). [15]

Marks for spelling, punctuation and the accurate use of grammar are allocated to this question. [6]

Student response

I agree that the theory of evolution is the best explanation for the origin of humans. The theory of evolution has evidence to support it and is more convincing that what the Bible says about the origins of humans. The Bible is just outdated stories made up by people thousands of years ago to convince people that there is a god. What it says about how humans were created is false, it's impossible for one being to create humans from nothing. Science is the only explanation for how humans came to exist as it can show how humans evolved over time to become what they are now, therefore the creation stories are unnecessary as an explanation for anything.

Christians would disagree with me because they believe in God and the creation stories which show humans being made. They may reject the theory of evolution completely as it does not have God in it. Catholics might agree with me a little bit as they do not take the Bible literally so might think that evolution was caused by God and that is how humans came about.

What went well

The candidate has offered two different viewpoints; the first has limited supporting evidence and the second briefly shows some Christian views towards evolution. The candidate has used some basic evaluative language about the usefulness of the Bible in showing the origins of humans, when they mention that it is outdated and has a lack of evidence to support it.

How to improve

You must back up all statements, including personal statements, with evidence to support your arguments.

You should evaluate the arguments given in your essay. This will help you to come to a judgement later and to avoid simply giving different views.

You could quote sources of wisdom and authority to support your arguments.

Improved student response

Some people such as Humanists would agree that the theory of evolution is the best explanation for the origin of humans as they look to science rather than God to explain how the world and everything in it came about. They believe that evolution, an idea presented by Charles Darwin in his *On the Origin of Species by Natural Selection*, offers evidence that humans came about due to a random process of change in a series of other species. Humans are therefore a product of chance and not as the creation stories state a product of God's master design. Humanists also reject God as the cause of evolution; evolution results in the extinction of species and so an omnibenevolent God would not cause this. Humanists argue there is concrete evidence of evolution due to fossils which show mutations in species and so this process applies to humans as well. This is a strong argument as it is based on scientific evidence. It is also based on something that can be observed rather than God which can't. However, some people would argue that this theory is missing something as it does not explain why humans are so different to animals, so they might argue that it only gives a partial explanation for the origin of humans.

Other people such as Catholics partly agree with the statement as they believe that God and science are compatible – God gives the reason why humans were made, while evolution explains how humans were made. Pope John Paul II stated that 'there is no conflict between evolution and the doctrine of faith'. Catholics do not believe that humans were created on the sixth day, but by the process of evolution which God built into his creation, therefore humans are still sacred as they still come from God. Therefore, for Catholics, God is the origin of humans, with evolution being the tool he used to create them. This is a very strong argument as it includes both science and religion and is therefore able to give a fuller account for the origin of humans. It also

The candidate has used a non-religious (Humanist) response to meet the demands of the question.

The candidate has used the wording in the question statement to focus their answer on the right material.

The candidate has used appropriate sources of wisdom and authority here and elsewhere to support their views.

Specialist language is used accurately.

The candidate has used a religious (Catholic) response to meet the demands of the question.

supports religious belief as it maintains God as an omnipotent creator, rather than reducing or removing his part in the creation of humans.
In contrast, Fundamentalist Christians completely disagree with the statement. They believe that evolution undermines God as an omnipotent and omniscient creator as shown in the Bible. As they believe the Bible is the literal Word of God, anything that contradicts it is incorrect, therefore God is the only explanation for the origin of humans as he created them in his likeness on the sixth day (Genesis 1:27). This is a weak argument as the Bible was written thousands of years ago when there was no real scientific understanding. Therefore, this belief is outdated and conflicts with modern society as there is physical evidence to support the idea that humans evolved, rather than God simply creating them on the sixth day as they are now.
I ultimately believe that the Catholic approach is the best as it gives the fullest explanation for the origin of humans. It also accepts scientific explanations for the origin of humans and therefore is not in conflict with modern society. Also, the Catholic view upholds the sanctity of life while still supporting evolution, meaning that the concept of God as the giver of life is not undermined, rather it is just understood in a different way. Science and religion give the whole picture of the origin of humans, with science giving the how and religion giving the why.

At the end of each paragraph the candidate has evaluated the arguments made.

There is evidence of diverse views within Christianity.

Over to You! Try to answer this question:

(d) 'Only Humanists have a duty to care for the environment.'
Discuss this statement showing that you have considered more than one point of view. (You must refer to religious and non-religious beliefs, such as those held by Humanists and Atheists, in your answer.) [15]
Marks for spelling, punctuation and the accurate use of grammar are allocated to this question. [6]

Helpful hints

If you find it difficult to answer this question effectively, you could try using the structure below to help you set out your paragraphs:

- **Argument** – Clearly state a religious view about the question.
- **Back it up** – Give some evidence or an example of teaching or behaviour that shows this view.
- **Challenge** – Offer a counterargument that directly opposes the view you have previously stated.
- **Back it up** – Support this response with evidence or examples.
- **Decide** – Weigh up which views are the best and why.

This could be one paragraph. Repeat the formula again for a second paragraph and at the end conclude with a final decision. Make sure one of these paragraphs is a non-religious/Humanist perspective!

Tip

You can gain 6 marks for spelling, punctuation and grammar in this question. Make sure you learn how to spell key words and check your answer when finished.

Now give yourself **fifteen minutes** to answer this question by yourself:

(d) 'The world is ours to do what we like with.'
Discuss this statement showing that you have considered more than one point of view. (You must refer to religious and non-religious beliefs, such as those held by Humanists and Atheists, in your answer.) [15]
Marks for spelling, punctuation and the accurate use of grammar are allocated to this question. [6]

Chapter 2:
Good and evil

Introduction

In this chapter, you will explore some of the biggest philosophical questions generated by belief in God, such as why God allows evil and suffering. This is a question that has occupied generations of thinkers and believers; for Atheists it is one of the main arguments against the existence of God. We will also look at teachings that form the foundation of Christianity, such as the Trinity and the Incarnation. At times we will look at topics from a Jewish perspective, but most of the chapter is focused on discussions surrounding Christian belief.

Things to remember

- There are diverse views towards some of the topics in this chapter, even among Christians. It is important to acknowledge and understand these different perspectives.
- In this topic you will learn why some people find it too challenging to believe in an omnibenevolent and omnipotent God. You will need to know why some Atheists use the problem of evil to dispute belief in God – and how Christians respond to this. You may have strong opinions on this but you will need to provide evidence to back them up, and you should be able to put forward the opposing view even if you do not agree with it.
- Quotes and extracts from the key texts in the specification are included in this chapter. Try to learn some of these quotes so you can use them in your responses (but remember it is important to understand and be able to explain the quote – not just repeat it!).

Concepts

Conscience – human reason making moral decisions. The knowledge we have of what is right and wrong and the God-given compulsion within all human beings to do what is right and to avoid what is evil

Evil – the absence of good and the impulse to seek our own desires at the expense of the good of others which often results in suffering

Free will – the decision making part of a person's mind is called the will. A will is free if a person is able to choose right from wrong without being controlled by other forces

Goodness – the quality of being like God: seeking the well-being of others selflessly

Incarnation – 'made flesh'. The Christian belief that God became man in the person of Jesus, fully human and fully divine

Natural Law – the moral laws of right and wrong which are universal and not dependent on human laws. The belief in natural law is the belief that the moral law is discoverable by every human being and is the same for all human beings in all places at all times

Privation – the loss or absence of a quality or something that is normally present. Evil is a privation of good

Suffering – pain or loss which harms human beings. Some suffering is caused by other human beings (often called moral evil); some is not (often called natural evil)

The Trinity

Specification focus

Trinity: The nature of the Trinity as expressed in the Nicene Creed; the biblical support for the doctrine and its historical development, with reference to the metaphorical explanation of the doctrine as a trinity of love, lover and beloved in St Augustine's *De Trinitate* 8.10.

What is the Trinity?

Belief in the Trinity is central to all **denominations** of Christianity. It is the belief that the one God comprises three persons: the Father, the Son and the Holy Spirit. The three persons of the Trinity are distinct from each other and yet each person is fully God (and there are not three Gods). In Christianity this is described as a 'mystery' because it is impossible for humans to fully understand it.

The Trinity in the Nicene Creed

The **doctrine** of the Trinity was fully defined in the fourth century after some debate among theologians about who Jesus Christ was in relation to the Father and the Holy Spirit. Before this, questions had arisen about the implications of Christ being God. For example, if Christ is God then is Christianity still **monotheistic**?

The **Council of Nicaea** took place in 325 AD to answer these questions and establish a creed that would outline the fundamental beliefs of Christianity, including belief in the Trinity. The resulting Nicene Creed is a statement of faith that is still said regularly in Mass today. It outlines the Church's official teaching on the Trinity.

The Nicene Creed takes each person of the Trinity in turn:

I believe in one God,
The Father almighty,
maker of heaven and earth,
of all things visible and invisible.

- This makes it clear there is only one God, even though God is also three persons.
- The first person is God the Father, who created the universe and is the source of all life.

I believe in one Lord Jesus Christ,
the Only Begotten Son of God,
born of the Father before all ages.
God from God, Light from Light,
true God from true God,
begotten, not made, consubstantial with the Father...

- The second person is the Son of God.
- 'Begotten, not made' means the Son came from the Father, but the Father did not create him.
- 'Born of the Father before all ages' means the Son has always existed along with the Father.
- 'Consubstantial' means the Son is of the same substance as the Father. They have the same nature and are of equal importance.
- The Son became human in Jesus Christ to save humanity from sin.

I believe in the Holy Spirit, the Lord, the giver of life,
who proceeds from the Father and the Son,
who with the Father and the Son
is adored and glorified,
who has spoken through the prophets...

- The third person is the Holy Spirit.
- The Spirit comes from the loving relationship between the Father and the Son.
- The Spirit has equal power and majesty to the Father and the Son.
- The Spirit inspires people and can be seen at work through the prophets.

The Trinity in the Bible

The doctrine of the Trinity is not specifically mentioned in either the Old Testament or the New Testament, but there are many individual references to each of the three persons in the Bible. There are also a few places when the whole of the Trinity is referred to at once.

- In Matthew 28:19, Jesus tells the apostles to 'Go therefore and make disciples of all nations, baptising them in the name of the Father and of the Son and of the Holy Spirit'. This is the only place in the Bible where Jesus refers directly to all three persons of the Trinity.
- St Paul also refers to all three persons of the Trinity in his final blessing and farewell at the end of his letter to the Corinthians (2 Corinthians 13:13): 'The grace of the Lord Jesus Christ, the love of God, and the communion of the Holy Spirit be with all of you.'
- At Jesus' Baptism (Mark 1:11), Jesus himself is of course present; a dove which is a symbol for the Holy Spirit appears; and God the Father's voice can be heard from heaven saying 'You are my Son, the Beloved; with you I am well pleased.'

St Augustine's teaching on the Trinity

St Augustine was a bishop and theologian in the early Christian Church. In his book *De Trinitate* ('On the Trinity'), he offered an analogy based on love to help explain the mystery of the Trinity.

God the Father is the lover, God the Son is the beloved, and the Holy Spirit is the love between the two. Augustine pointed out that love cannot exist on its own: it needs someone to give it and someone to receive it. Love therefore needs to be in three parts – just as the Trinity is three persons united together in love.

This analogy is based on 1 John 4:16, which states that 'God is love'. It reminds Christians of the **goodness** of God. St Augustine said that God's love is not just shared between the three persons – it pours out into the hearts and lives of believers.

The Jewish perspective

Jews do not share the Christian belief in the Trinity. They believe in the oneness of God as stated in the Ten Commandments, and consider belief in the Trinity to be contrary to this. Jews believe that God has various different attributes, but not that he consists of three distinct persons.

Useful terms

denomination – a branch of Christianity, such as Catholicism
doctrine – a Church teaching
monotheistic – believing in one God
Council of Nicaea – the first full 'meeting' of the Church that took place in the fourth century to clarify particular beliefs

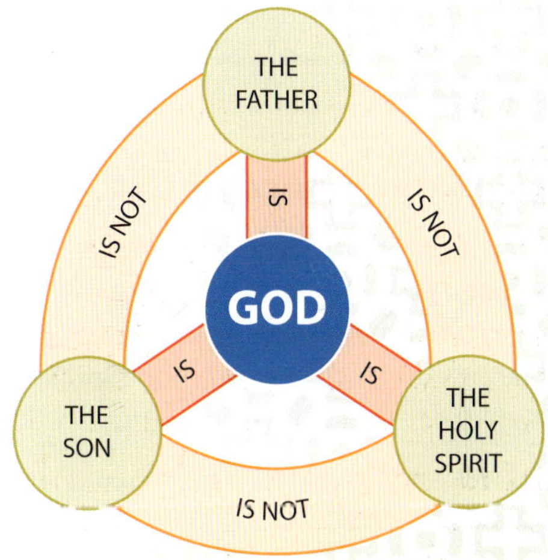

The relationship of the Trinity, showing that each person is fully God and also separate from each other

Knowledge recall

1 Define the following concepts: goodness, Incarnation, suffering. (You can find these definitions on page 41.)
2 Summarise the Christian belief in the Trinity.
3 Explain one characteristic of each person of the Trinity as mentioned in the Nicene Creed.

Evaluation practice

4 Do you think St Augustine's explanation of the Trinity as lover, beloved and love is useful? Explain why.
5 Why might someone disagree with you? Give two reasons why.

The Incarnation

What is the Incarnation?

Belief in the **Incarnation** is fundamental for all Christians. Incarnation means 'became flesh', and refers to God the Son becoming a human being in Jesus Christ.

For Christians this does not mean that Jesus is partly God and partly human; Jesus is fully God and also a full human being. Jesus has all the godliness of God – for example he has the power to perform **miracles**. At the same time, Jesus experiences all of the emotions of a human being. He feels anxiety before his death; he feels physical pain; and he knows what it feels like to have a loving family.

The importance of the Incarnation

The Incarnation is an important Christian belief because through it Christians can understand God better. They believe Jesus is God walking and talking on earth, and so his actions and teachings enable them to learn more about God. Jesus teaches Christians how they should live their lives so they might achieve salvation.

Christians also view the Incarnation as the ultimate demonstration of God's selfless love for human beings. God sent his only son to earth to endure **suffering** so that humans might know him better and have the promise of eternal life.

Christians believe that through the Incarnation, God has endured the challenges and difficulties that humans go through in life. This helps Christians to relate to God all the more, knowing that he can empathise with them about their hardships in life.

The nature of Jesus in the Bible

An important passage in the Bible that teaches Christians about the nature of Jesus is the start of John's gospel:

> '**In the beginning was the Word, and the Word was with God, and the Word was God.** He was in the beginning with God. All things came into being through him, and without him not one thing came into being. What has come into being in him was life, and the life was the light of all people. **The light shines in the darkness**, and the darkness did not overcome it... **And the Word became flesh and lived among us**, and we have seen his glory, the glory as of a father's only son... No one has ever seen God. It is God the only Son, who is close to the Father's heart, **who has made him known.**'
> *John 1:1–18 (NRSV)*

Specification focus

Incarnation: The meaning and significance of the belief in Jesus as Incarnate Son, divine Word, fully God and fully human; its scriptural origins with reference to John 1:1–18 and the kenosis hymn (Philippians 2:5–11); the importance of the doctrine in framing Catholic responses to the problem of evil, with reference to Pope John Paul II, *Salvifici Doloris* 13 and 23.

Nativity scene images often reflect the idea of Jesus as a 'light'

- John refers to Christ as **the Word**.
- He uses this metaphor to show that Christ was sent as a living example to all. Christ goes beyond words on a page: he is God's word made flesh.
- John's chapter mirrors the start of Genesis by using 'In the beginning...'. In Genesis, God's word brings about creation; in John's gospel, human beings are given a new start through the Incarnation of Christ.
- John refers to Jesus as a 'light'. He uses this metaphor to show that Jesus guides Christians along the right path, and because Jesus overcame the darkness of sin and death.
- John makes it clear that God the Son is equal to God the Father: '...and the Word was God'.

Another passage that explains Jesus' Incarnation is the 'Kenosis hymn' in Philippians 2:5–8:

> Let the same mind be in you that was in Christ Jesus,
> who, though he was in the form of God,
> did not regard equality with God
> as something to be exploited,
> **but emptied himself**,
> **taking the form of a slave**,
> being born in human likeness.
> And being found in human form,
> **he humbled himself**
> and became obedient to the point of death
> even death on a cross.

- Kenosis is a Greek word meaning 'emptying'. Paul writes that Christ emptied himself of his equality with God and became a human being. This does not mean that Jesus lost his divinity but that he assumed a role which was humbling.
- Paul says that Christ actually lowered himself below humanity by accepting a degrading death.
- Paul refers to Christ as a 'slave'. Despite his divinity, Christ places himself at the service of humankind so that through him, humans might know God more fully. This humility serves as an example to all people.

The Bible describes how Jesus showed fear and sadness – as any human would do – as he prayed in the Garden of Gethsemane before his death

The Incarnation and the problem of evil

The problem of **evil** is an argument that some Atheists put forward to show that God does not exist. The argument is that an all-loving and all-powerful God would not allow evil and suffering to take place in the world that he created. For Catholics, Jesus' Incarnation helps to solve the problem of evil for the following reasons:

- Jesus' very existence gives Catholics hope that God exists.
- Jesus' teachings and resurrection show Catholics that the suffering experienced in this life is only temporary. Jesus gives hope of life after death. For example, he says to the criminal dying on the cross next to him: 'Truly I tell you, today you will be with me in Paradise' (Luke 23:43).
- Jesus explains that those who suffer in this life will be rewarded in the next, for example through the parable of the rich man and Lazarus.
- Jesus himself suffered when he was crucified which makes it easier for Christians to endure their own suffering: they believe that Jesus understands their pain.

Useful terms

miracle – an event that cannot be explained by the laws of science
the Word – another name for Jesus to describe the idea that he is God's word made flesh

Read more about the problem of evil on page 48.

Knowledge recall

1 Define the following concepts: Incarnation, goodness, suffering. (You can find these definitions on page 41.)
2 Identify two points that John makes about the Incarnation at the start of his gospel.
3 Identify two points about the Incarnation in the Kenosis hymn.

Evaluation practice

4 Do you think for Catholics the Incarnation solves the problem of evil? Explain why.
5 Why might someone disagree with you?

The origin of evil

Natural and moral evil

In Christian teaching there are two types of **evil**: **natural** and **moral**.

- Natural evil includes any evil that has been caused by nature or anything other than human action, such as earthquakes, tsunamis and childhood cancers.
- Moral evil is evil that has been created by humans using their **free will** to make bad choices. Examples include murder, shoplifting or war.

Catholic teaching says that moral evil exists because God gave humans free will – and because humans have inherited **Original Sin**, they have a tendency to use their free will to do bad. Original Sin brought disorder into humanity but also into nature, which helps to explain the existence of natural evil too. The account of the Fall in Genesis represents the time when the whole of creation was thrown off balance.

What is Original Sin?

Original Sin is an important concept in Catholicism. It refers to the idea that all humans have a natural tendency to sin because they have inherited this trait from the first human beings: Adam and Eve. Genesis 3 tells how Adam and Eve disobeyed God and ate the only forbidden fruit in the Garden of Eden. God had given them everything they needed but they were tempted by the serpent. God then punished Adam and Eve for having disobeyed him. This story shows that human beings have a natural inclination that can lead them to do bad. This is where the concept of Original Sin (or the 'first sin') comes from.

The Catholic Church teaches that this story is metaphorical and portrays the moment when human beings first turned away from God. This action is referred to as 'the Fall' as humans fell from grace with God. Jesus' life and death repaired the damage caused by Original Sin and gives human beings the opportunity to be free from its effects. This happens through Baptism: an important sacrament that absolves a person of Original Sin. For many Catholics, it would be important to baptise their baby fairly quickly so as to ensure they are free from this inherited sin.

St Augustine and the Enchiridion

In his book *The Enchiridion*, written in the fifth century, St Augustine argued that God created a perfect world. Fallen angels (angels expelled from heaven) and human beings used their free will to turn their back on God. Natural evil came about as a result of the disorder that this brought to creation; moral evil is a result of Adam and Eve's disobedience.

St Augustine argued that experiencing evil allows humans to appreciate what is good. People might not notice the good things in the world until they are compared to the bad. He also described evil as a '**privation**' of good – meaning it is an absence of good.

St Augustine used the example of disease in the body to explain his argument. He said that evil is not a tangible, real thing – it is just the absence of a good thing that should be there instead. This means that God has not created or caused evil in the world. Humans have created evil by choosing to do bad. God does not

Specification focus

Good, evil and suffering: Catholic perspectives on the origin of evil: Original Sin and evil as a 'privation', with reference to St Augustine, The Enchiridion (3.11); alternative Christian and non-Christian views on the nature and origin of evil and the difference between moral and natural evil.

Catholic teaching traces moral and natural evil back to the Fall

Useful terms

natural evil – evil caused by natural occurrences, such as an earthquake
moral evil – evil caused by the actions of humans
Original Sin – the belief that all humans have inherited sin from the first human beings

want humans to experience evil and suffering, but **suffering** can allow for people to grow and develop, and sometimes good can come from it.

> ❛For what is that which we call evil but the absence of good? ... disease and wounds mean nothing but the absence of health; for when a cure is effected, that does not mean that the evils which were present – namely, the diseases and wounds – go away from the body and dwell elsewhere: they altogether cease to exist❜
> *St Augustine. The Enchiridion 3.11*

For Catholics, Baptism is important in freeing a person from Original Sin so they are able to enter heaven when they die

Other Christian views on evil

Many Fundamentalist Christians read the creation accounts in Genesis literally, and so believe God's world would have been perfect had it not been for Adam and Eve's bad choice, the consequences of which were then passed on to future generations. Fundamentalists share the Catholic belief in Original Sin, believing that people are born into a state of sin. Many Fundamentalists would attribute all the moral and natural evil in this world to Adam and Eve's disobeyment of God. Fundamentalists such as John Calvin consider humans to be fully bad unless they accept and follow Christ.

In contrast, Liberal Protestant Christians are less likely to believe in Original Sin or view humans as being inherently bad. They believe moral evil is created by humans freely choosing to do wrong. There is also an acknowledgement that good can come from evil and suffering. For example, the philosopher John Hick argued that the natural and moral evil that happens in the world improves people's souls by encouraging them to overcome adversity and become better people.

Non-Christian views on evil

Muslims do not share the Catholic belief in Original Sin because of some differences in the creation accounts. The story of Adam and Eve in the Bible is very similar to the story of Adam and his wife in the Qur'an, except in the Qur'an, Adam is forgiven but then told to leave the Garden of Eden. There are not the same punishments which affect generations to come as in the Christian version.

However, the Qur'an also describes how Iblis (Satan) refused to bow down to Adam under Allah's order. As a result, Allah cast Iblis out of Heaven; out of revenge, Iblis vowed to spend eternity trying to tempt humans to do wrong. Iblis is therefore traditionally seen as the source of evil in Islam.

Judaism teaches that everyone is born with the inclination to do good (yetzer ha tov) *and* the inclination to do evil (yetzer ha ra). Everyone has free will and must take responsibility for their actions. During the ten days of repentance in between the festival of Rosh Hashanah and Yom Kippur, sins should be atoned for, ready to start afresh the following year.

Read more about Rosh Hashanah on page 166.

Knowledge recall

1. Define the following concepts: goodness, free will, privation. (You can find these definitions on page 41.)
2. Summarise St Augustine's teachings about evil.
3. Explain the concept of Original Sin.

Evaluation practice

4. Do you think all humans should be held to account for Adam and Eve's sins? Explain why.
5. Why might someone disagree with you?

God's goodness

Specification focus

Good, evil and suffering: Catholic beliefs about the relationship between God's goodness and the goodness of the created world; philosophical and non-religious challenges posed by belief in God's goodness, free will and the existence of evil and suffering.

God's goodness in creation

Christianity teaches that God is omnibenevolent. This idea that God is good can be seen in the first creation story in Genesis, where the phrase 'God saw what he had made and it was good' is repeated for several different days of creation. All that God creates is good, reflecting his own **goodness**. God is a good creator who has created everything *ex nihilo* out of love for human beings.

Some people use the term **numinous** to describe the sense of awe and wonder inspired by God's creation. When a person marvels at something wonderful in nature such as a clear night sky, the view from the top of a mountain, or even a newborn baby, Catholics would say that this reflects the goodness of God.

Catholics believe that God's goodness is reflected in his creation

God's goodness can also be witnessed in how he sustains creation and is **immanent** in the world. Catholics do not believe God created the world and then just sat back and watched it from a distance. For Catholics, the miracles and answered prayers that people experience today are examples of how God is a force for good in the world.

As well as creating the world for human beings to enjoy, Catholics believe that God has also given humanity the gift of his son Jesus. God becomes man in order to teach people how to achieve eternal life. This is also a sign of God's goodness.

God's goodness in scripture

'For you love all things that exist, and detest none of the things that you have made; for you would not have made anything if you had hated it.'
Wisdom 11:24

This verse speaks of the love that God has for his creation (including humans).

'The LORD is gracious and merciful, slow to anger and abounding in steadfast love.'
Psalm 145:8–9 (NRSV)

This psalm talks of God's qualities, saying that God is omnibenevolent towards all.

'No one is good but God alone.'
Mark 10:18 (NRSV)

This is Jesus' answer to a man who calls him good. It reaffirms the idea of God's goodness.

Challenges to God's goodness

Various philosophers have put forward arguments about the problem of believing in an omnibenevolent God. This is known as the problem of **evil**, which refers to the difficulty of believing in an omnibenevolent and omnipotent God while there is evil and **suffering** in the world.

J. L. Mackie was an Australian philosopher and an Atheist who made the following points:

- Humans should not need an imperfect world in order to learn. If God created the world, then he should have made it perfect to begin with. We do not need the level of suffering there is in the world in order to know goodness.
- An all-loving God would not allow people to make choices that lead to suffering. Mackie argues that humans could have been given **free will** that only allows them to make choices which do not lead to suffering.
- Suffering does not bring out the goodness in people. For example, people can easily become bitter and resentful because of the suffering they have endured. Suffering does not have a good purpose and so a good God would not allow it.

David Hume was a Scottish philosopher who also rejected belief in God on account of the problem of evil. He referred to the problem of evil as the 'rock of Atheism', meaning that this is the greatest argument against the existence of God and one that has led to many people becoming Atheists.

Hume was the first person to put forward the '**inconsistent triad**'. This is the argument that the following three things cannot all be true at the same time: God is omnibenevolent; God is omnipotent; evil exists. Because:

- if God is omnibenevolent and wants to prevent evil but cannot, then he is not all powerful
- if God is omnipotent and can prevent evil but does not want to, then he is not all loving
- If God is omnibenevolent and omnipotent, then evil would not exist.
- evil does exist, which means that either God is not omnibenevolent or omnipotent or he does not exist.

Read about the Catholic response to the problem of evil on page 50.

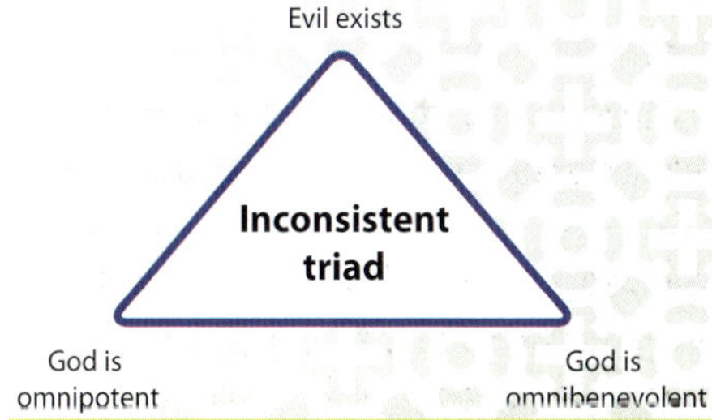

The inconsistent triad

Useful terms

numinous – a sense of awe and wonder at God's creation
immanent – God is close to his creation and involved with the world so that he can make himself known
inconsistent triad – an argument that questions how an omnibenevolent, omnipotent God can exist while there is evil and suffering in the world

The Jewish perspective

The Jewish view about God's goodness is much the same as the Catholic view. God is the only creator and all that he has created is good, as shown in Genesis. God's goodness is evident in the way he protects his creation. For example, in the Torah there are many stories of God protecting his people from those persecuting them. The parting of the Red Sea is one such example, where God rescues the Israelites in their time of need. This points to an omnibenevolent God.

Knowledge recall

1. Define the following concepts: free will, goodness, evil. (You can find these definitions on page 41.)
2. Describe two ideas about God's goodness that can be found in the Bible.
3. Explain how one might challenge the idea of God's goodness.

Evaluation practice

4. Do you agree that goodness in the world is evidence of God's existence? Explain why.
5. Why might someone disagree with you?

The Catholic response to the problem of evil

Specification focus

The importance of the doctrine of the Incarnation in framing Catholic responses to the problem of evil, with reference to Pope John Paul II, *Salvifici Doloris* 13 and 23.

Catholic views on evil and suffering

The existence of **evil** and **suffering** in the world is an argument that many Atheists use to say that an omnipotent, omnibenevolent and omniscient God cannot exist. Catholics might argue in return that an all-loving and all-powerful God can still exist while there is evil and suffering for the following reasons.

The Catholic philosopher Brian Davies argues that if God had not allowed the possibility of evil and suffering, then it would have meant that humans were not really free. One example of this is the '**free will**' defence, which argues that ultimately it is better for humans to make their own decisions freely even if this sometimes leads to moral evil in the world. Humans without free will would be little more than pre-programmed machines. With free will, people can choose to do good freely and this makes it a more valuable act.

The Protestant philosopher John Hick argued that there needs to be evil and suffering in the world to provide people with an opportunity to improve themselves. People would never be called on to do charitable acts or to show **agape** if not for the suffering that others endure. Jesus' teachings are all about showing love to others. How would it be possible to do that in a genuine way if there was no suffering? Other people argue that without evil it is not possible to have good: the two depend on each other, meaning that evil is necessary for good to exist.

John Hick argued that suffering encourages people to respond with empathy and compassion

Two important Catholic theologians, St Augustine and St Aquinas, argued that evil is not a separate 'thing' but simply a lack of **goodness**. This reinforces the goodness of God, in that it suggests God has in no way created evil. Evil is simply a **privation** (an absence of good). This reminds Catholics that human beings can freely choose to do good but sometimes they do not.

St Augustine argued that humans abused their free will and brought about moral evil. Natural evil is sent as a punishment for the moral evil that humans have committed. These ideas are referenced by the Catechism of the Catholic Church when it says 'Because of man, creation is now subject "to its bondage to decay"' (*CCC 400*).

The American philosopher William Alston argued that as humans cannot fully understand God, they are limited in how far they can question God's existence based on the presence of evil in the world. Alston believed the problem of evil is beyond human comprehension as it is impossible to know the whole truth.

Useful term

agape – love or selfless charity

This approach is illustrated in the Bible by the story of Job. Job is a good man who is tested by Satan. He experiences a series of terrible events including the loss of his seven sons and three daughters. But his faith in God is never shaken, and he does not question why such bad things have happened to him. For Christians this is a good example of how they should respond when faced with evil and suffering that they cannot fully understand.

Pope St John Paul II argued that the mystery of suffering should not undermine the belief that God loves all people

Pope St John Paul II's *Salvifici Doloris*

In 1984, Pope St John Paul II wrote the letter *Salvifici Doloris* to discuss the meaning of suffering.

> ‘But in order to perceive the true answer to the "why" of suffering, we must look to the revelation of **divine love**, the ultimate source of the meaning of everything that exists. Love is also the richest source of the meaning of suffering, which always **remains a mystery**: we are conscious of the insufficiency and inadequacy of our explanations Christ causes us to enter into the mystery and to discover the "why" of suffering, as far as we are capable of grasping the sublimity of divine love...
>
> Suffering, in fact, is always a trial – at times a very hard one – to which humanity is subjected... **together with the working of God's love**... The more he shares in this love, man **rediscovers himself more and more fully in suffering**; he rediscovers the "soul" which he thought he had "lost" because of suffering.’
> *Salvifici Doloris 13 and 23*

- The main idea that is repeated through *Salvifici Doloris* is the importance of God's love for humanity, as shown by Christ's sacrifice on the cross. Pope St John Paul II is arguing that the suffering endured in this life is something of a 'mystery', but people should trust in the depth of God's love.
- Pope St John Paul II recognises that the suffering that some people go through in this life is very hard to handle.
- He reminds Catholics that they might improve their souls and better themselves through suffering personally or witnessing the suffering of others.

Knowledge recall

1 Define the following concepts: suffering, privation, free will. (You can find these definitions on page 41.)
2 Describe what Catholics can learn about suffering from *Salvifici Doloris*.
3 Give one way that Catholics might respond to the problem of evil.

Evaluation practice

4 Do you agree with John Hick that the existence of evil and suffering in the world is necessary? Explain why.
5 Why might someone disagree with you?

The Catholic response to suffering

Specification focus

The meaning of suffering and Catholic ambivalence towards it, with reference to the significance of Christ's suffering and death and Isaiah 53.

The Catholic view on suffering

Many Catholics approach the idea of **suffering** with ambivalence, which means they have mixed feelings towards it. Within the Catholic tradition, there is a strong emphasis on helping those in need to try to reduce their suffering, for example by working towards social justice.

However, while the Catholic Church teaches that it is important to try to lessen suffering, there is also a recognition that suffering can be purposeful. It is believed that the suffering endured in this life does not go unnoticed by God. Jesus said:

> 'Blessed are the poor in spirit, for theirs is the kingdom of heaven, Blessed are those who mourn, for they will be comforted.'
> *Matthew 5:3–4 (NRSV)*

Through this teaching, Jesus makes it clear that those who have particularly hard lives will have a greater chance of happiness in the next life. They have already paid to some extent for their sins because of what they have endured in this life.

The Catholic Church teaches that suffering enables people to develop empathy for others and to demonstrate love of neighbour. If no one ever suffered then it would not be possible to show **agape**. The Christian concept of **free will** would also become futile if there was no suffering in the world. **Evil** needs to exist so Christians can freely choose to do good; free will also means that humans can freely choose to do wrong and this will bring about suffering.

The Catholic Church works hard to try to reduce suffering while also recognising that it is a necessary part of the world

The significance of Christ's suffering and death

The Bible describes how Christ experienced immense physical suffering in the final hours of his life. He also suffers emotionally in the Garden of Gethsemane the night before his death because he is so anxious about what is to come: 'In his anguish he prayed more earnestly, and his sweat became like great drops of blood falling down on the ground' (Luke 22:44).

Christianity teaches that this suffering is something that Jesus chose freely, knowing what lay ahead of him, because in the end it would be for the good of humankind. The significance of his suffering and death is greater because it was freely chosen.

Catholics believe that when they suffer, they can find comfort in knowing that God understands their suffering because he has experienced physical and emotional pain through Christ. In Luke 9:23, Jesus says his followers should 'take up their cross daily and follow me'. A Catholic might face hardships throughout their life, but this is to be expected as a follower of Christ, and they can take comfort in the belief that Christ walks alongside them in their pain.

The following passage is taken from Isaiah in the Old Testament. Christians have come to see this passage – which describes a suffering servant – to be **prophesising** the death of Christ.

Useful terms

agape – love or selfless charity
prophesising – making a prediction about something that will happen in the future
transgression – an act against a rule or law

‘He was despised and rejected by others;
a **man suffering** and acquainted with infirmity;
and as one from whom others hide their faces
he was despised, and we held him of no account...
But **he was wounded for our transgressions**,
crushed for our iniquities;
upon him was the punishment that made us whole,
and by his bruises we are healed...
He was oppressed, and he was afflicted,
yet he did not open his mouth;
like a lamb that is led to the slaughter,
and like a sheep that before its shearers is silent,
so he did not open his mouth.’
Isaiah 53:3–7 (NRSV)

- Here the idea that Jesus is 'despised and rejected' refers to how he was treated by the end of Holy Week, in complete contrast to the warm welcome he received on his entry into Jerusalem on Palm Sunday. By Friday, the crowds were cheering for Barabbas to be saved over Jesus when they were given the choice.
- The belief that Jesus sacrificed his life for humanity's sins is referred to in the phrase 'wounded for our **transgressions**'. The Catholic Church teaches that Christ's suffering and death would not have been necessary if humans had not sinned.
- The passage also refers to the mild and meek way in which the suffering servant receives his punishment. There is no retaliation or anger. The image of a lamb is used to show the gentleness of the one who is being so severely punished. This reflects the descriptions in the New Testament of Jesus' final hours, where Jesus intends to accept what lies ahead of him without complaint.
- For Catholics, Jesus is the ultimate example of how to endure suffering. When Catholics suffer, they aim to not be resentful, bitter or vengeful.

Many Catholics believe that suffering brings them closer to Christ as they can share in his pain

The Jewish perspective

In Judaism, there is an acceptance that certain aspects of life or God will never be fully understood by humans. Suffering is one such example. It can be hard to comprehend but it is simply part of life and part of God's plan. Jews recognise the role of free will and how this enables people to freely choose bad, but consider it wrong to question why God has sent suffering.

As in Catholicism, there is an emphasis in Judaism on performing charitable acts and helping others to reduce their suffering.

Knowledge recall

1. Define the following concepts: evil, free will, suffering. (You can find these definitions on page 41.)
2. Describe why Catholics are ambivalent towards suffering.
3. Explain what Isaiah says about the 'suffering servant'.

Evaluation practice

4. 'Knowing that Christ himself suffered makes suffering more bearable for Catholics.' Do you agree? Explain why.
5. Why might someone disagree with you?

Jesus as a moral authority

Specification focus

Jesus and moral authority: The example and teaching of Jesus as the authoritative source for moral teaching, with reference to Jesus as the fulfilment of the law in Matthew 5–7.

Jesus as a source of moral authority

Christians believe that Jesus is the ultimate source of **moral authority**. As one of the persons of the Trinity, he has equal authority to God the Father. Yet as a human being, he is able to communicate his teachings effectively to humanity.

When Jesus was alive, many were unsure about what authority he had. There were already laws in place in the Torah and to question these laws was considered to be a great sin.

However, Jesus himself said 'Do not think that I have come to abolish the law or the prophets; I have come not to abolish but to fulfil' (Matthew 5:17). Catholics believe that Jesus built on **the Law** given to Moses in the Old Testament. He 'fulfilled' the Law by following it himself, by explaining its true meaning and by teaching people how to obey it as God would want.

Catholics believe that as the Incarnate Son of God, Jesus has the authority of God. He has the authority to pass judgement on and even update the laws in the Torah. Through his teachings and example, Catholics can learn how to treat each other and how to behave as God wants them to. For these reasons, Jesus is a hugely important source of moral teaching.

'This is my Son, the Beloved; with him I am well pleased; listen to him!'
Matthew 17:5 (NRSV)

This command from God the Father to the apostles shows the authority that Jesus has in moral matters.

The Sermon on the Mount

The Sermon on the Mount is a speech that Jesus gave to his followers as described in Matthew 5–7. This speech covers many different topics and includes some of Jesus' best-known teachings. It begins with the **Beatitudes**. This is a list of sentences which start with the phrase 'Blessed are the…'. For example:

'Blessed are the meek, for they will inherit the earth.

Blessed are those who hunger and thirst for righteousness, for they will be filled.

Blessed are the merciful, for they shall receive mercy.

Blessed are the pure in heart, for they will see God.

Blessed are the peacemakers, for they will be called children of God.'
Matthew 5:5–9 (NRSV)

The eight blessings teach Catholics what characteristics will be rewarded by God. It is clear that those with a good heart or those who have suffered in life through no fault of their own will be blessed by God. The emphasis is not on following rules but on having a gentle nature and doing the right thing.

Later in the sermon, Jesus refers to the 'righteousness of the Pharisees and scribes' and tells how others must not follow their example if they are to go to heaven. In the gospels, the Pharisees were overwhelmingly concerned with upholding the Law even when this was at a cost of demonstrating love towards other people. In Jesus' sermon, he is emphasising the importance of having a good soul over following rules.

Useful terms

moral authority – having the capacity to teach others right from wrong
the Law – the rules given by God to Moses teaching people how to behave and worship
Beatitudes – a list of people, given by Jesus, who God will look on favourably because of their actions
Golden Rule – one of Jesus' main teachings which summarises all of his others: treat others as you would want to be treated

There is also a list of phrases in the sermon that begin 'You have heard it said…,' 'but I say…'. This is significant because Jesus is quoting scriptures from the Old Testament and then adding his own moral teaching. For example:

> ❛You have heard that it was said, "You shall not commit adultery." But I say to you that everyone who looks at a woman with lust has already committed adultery with her in his heart.❜
> *Matthew 5:27–28 (NRSV)*

Here Jesus is extending the teaching to say that of course adultery is wrong, but so too is the intention behind it – not just the act itself. For God, having the desire to commit adultery would be as immoral as actually committing adultery. People should try to develop a good nature as this will in turn lead to good actions.

Jesus also taught the Lord's Prayer during the Sermon on the Mount. This is the only formal prayer that Jesus gave his followers. Part of the prayer asks people to show forgiveness to others in order to receive forgiveness themselves. This is similar to the **Golden Rule**, which is also among the teachings of the Sermon on the Mount: 'In everything do to others as you would have them do to you; for this is the law and the prophets' (Matthew 7:12).

The Sermon on the Mount covers many topics, but focuses throughout on the idea of not just blindly following laws but having the right attitude and treating others well – for example through showing kindness, mercy and love.

During the Sermon on the Mount, Jesus gave some of his best-known moral teachings

Jesus' teachings vs the Old Testament

There are times when Jesus' moral teachings seem to contradict those in the Old Testament. The most well-known place where this seems to be the case is in the Sermon on the Mount. For example, here Jesus makes reference to the teaching on retaliation in Exodus: 'You have heard that it was said, "An eye for an eye and a tooth for a tooth." But I say to you… if anyone strikes you on the right cheek, turn the other also' (Matthew 5:38-39). Jesus is not contradicting but completing the old law. The original 'eye for eye' rule was a limit on vengeance in an age when disproportionate acts of vengeance were common. Jesus is not removing the limit, but extending it – just as in the case of adultery. Jesus is updating this teaching on justice to encourage forgiveness and mildness.

However, Jesus himself states that the commandments of the Jewish Torah (even the minor ones) will remain in full force 'until heaven and earth pass away' (Matthew 5:18). Jesus does not tell his followers to ignore the laws of the Old Testament. Instead he questions the importance of certain laws and asks believers to see the humanity of the whole situation. He wants people to have pure hearts and not just abide by a list of rules because they have to.

Knowledge recall

1. Define the following concepts: conscience, goodness, suffering. (You can find these definitions on page 41.)
2. Identify two of Jesus' teachings from the Sermon on the Mount.
3. Explain why the Sermon on the Mount is important to Catholics today.

Evaluation practice

4. Do you think Jesus is a good source of moral authority?
5. Why might someone disagree with you?

Natural Law and the development of the virtues

Specification focus

Jesus and moral authority: The existence of the Natural Law and conscience as evidence of God's goodness and the role of suffering in the development of the virtues.

Aquinas and Natural Law

Natural Law is a theory that was mainly developed by St Thomas Aquinas, who was an influential theologian in the thirteenth century. For many Catholics, his teachings on **conscience** and Natural Law point towards God's **goodness**.

Aquinas argues that everyone can use their **reason** and conscience in a difficult situation to work out what is the right thing to do. God gave humans **free will** in order to make free choices. When a situation is complex and there does not seem to be a straightforward teaching from the Catholic Church to follow, Aquinas argues that the conscience is a valuable source of authority.

Natural Law is the idea that there are moral principles and values that humans naturally follow. Catholicism teaches that because God has created humans in his image and likeness, humans have an instinctive knowledge of what it is to be good. People can use their conscience to intuitively do the right thing. Natural Law is not something that a person has to be explicitly aware of – people will automatically follow Natural Law if they use their conscience and ability to reason in the right way.

Aquinas argues that everyone should 'pursue good and avoid **evil**' when they make moral decisions, and this is what humans are naturally inclined to do anyway. For Catholics today, a strength of Natural Law is that it is applicable to all people of all times. It means that everyone has the capacity to work out what the right thing to do is in a given situation, including all of the modern-day dilemmas that Jesus never had the opportunity to speak about.

St Thomas Aquinas (1225–1274AD) was a Dominican friar whose work has been very influential on Catholic teaching

The primary and secondary precepts

Aquinas taught that the **primary precepts** are five areas of moral conduct which people naturally strive for as human beings:

- Preservation of life
- Ordering of society
- Worship of God
- Education of children
- Reproduction

People can then use their reasoning and conscience to develop secondary precepts that are based on the primary precepts. For example, a person might feel that on a particular road when there are few cars around that it might be safe to break the speed limit. But the primary precept of having an 'ordered society' would tell them that this is not a morally good thing to do. From that primary precept, a person might decide that a secondary precept which follows from it could be 'to drive safely'.

God's goodness and Natural Law

Catholics consider Natural Law to be evidence of God's goodness. Usually humans know, for example, that murder is wrong. Catholics believe that we know this because humans have a God-given conscience and are made *imago Dei*. The innate goodness that humans have is a reflection of the goodness of God.

Useful terms

reason – the ability to think logically
primary precepts – five purposes that humans naturally strive towards
virtues – morally good characteristics

The metaphor of Natural Law being written on the heart of every person is used by St Paul too: 'When Gentiles, who do not possess the law, do instinctively what the law requires… They show that what the law requires is written on their hearts' (Romans 2:14–15). Here St Paul is pointing out that Gentiles (non-Jews) often act in the same way as Jews when it comes to moral issues, which suggests that all human beings have access to Natural Law regardless of what they have been taught through their religion.

'The natural law which is inscribed by the Creator on the heart of every person consists in a participation in the wisdom and the goodness of God. It expresses that original moral sense which enables one to discern by reason the good and the bad.'
CCC 416

Developing the virtues through suffering

The Catholic Church teaches that a person who uses their conscience and applies Natural Law is developing their **virtues**. Someone who is concerned with doing the right thing morally is striving to be more virtuous.

In 1 Corinthians 13:13, St Paul talks of faith, hope and selfless love as being particularly important virtues that bring a person closer to God. These are known as the 'theological virtues'. Four other important virtues in Catholicism are the 'cardinal virtues', which summarise most of Jesus' teachings:

- Prudence – making good decisions.
- Justice – being fair to others.
- Fortitude – having the bravery to do the right thing no matter what the consequences might be.
- Temperance – showing moderation and not being excessive.

Many Catholics would argue that **suffering** can help to develop each of these virtues. For example, someone might exercise more prudence as they learn from their previous mistakes. When someone experiences injustice this could persuade them not to be unjust towards others. When someone witnesses the suffering of others, this encourages them to show selfless love to help. The ups and downs experienced in this life allow people to learn and grow and ultimately develop their virtues.

The Catholic Church teaches that suffering can encourage people to be more virtuous

This is similar to philosophical arguments (such as those posed by John Hick) that the evil and suffering experienced in this life helps to develop a person's soul. This world is all to do with 'soul making' because the evil and suffering that people go through – and the way they respond to it – helps to prepare them for the afterlife.

Read more about John Hick on page 50.

The Jewish perspective

Like Catholicism, Judaism teaches that each person has free will and the ability to make moral decisions. The moral decisions that a person makes is influenced by a balance of their two inclinations: their inclination to do good (yetzer ha tov) and their inclination to do bad (yetzer ha ra).

Jews believe God provided them with the mitzvot as a moral guide, to encourage them to do good rather than evil. In general, Orthodox Jews believe following the mitzvot as closely as possible is very important, while Reform Jews believe they can be adapted for modern society and informed by their conscience.

Read more about the mitzvot on page 144.

Knowledge recall

1. Define the following concepts: Natural Law, conscience, free will. (You can find these definitions on page 41.)
2. Describe how Natural Law is used by Catholics.
3. Explain how someone might consider Natural Law to be evidence of God's goodness.

Evaluation practice

4. 'We know right from wrong because of our upbringing and not because of Natural Law.' Do you agree?
5. Why might someone disagree with you?

Catholic sculptures and statues

Specification focus

Sculpture and statuary: The meaning and significance of various sculpture and statues to Catholic tradition and worship.

The use of sculptures and statues

Sculptures and statues are widely used in Catholicism as a focus for worship and prayer, and a reminder of Christian beliefs and teachings. They are visible in all Catholic churches and in other places such as Catholic schools and homes. There will always be a **crucifix** in a Catholic church and usually a statue of Mary. There might also be a statue of the **patron saint** of the parish.

Catholic schools are often named after a saint so will probably have a statue of that saint somewhere. Usually there will be crucifixes in most of the classrooms and the main hall too. Many Catholics also have statues in their homes, such as a statue of Mary or the **Sacred Heart**. In some Catholic countries, it is common to see a statue outside people's homes in the garden or by the road.

Diverse Christian attitudes towards statues

One of the Ten Commandments is 'You shall not make for yourself an idol' (Exodus 20:4). During the Reformation in the sixteenth century, this was one of the issues that divided the Church. Protestants interpreted the commandment to mean that sculptures and statues should not be used as this constituted worshipping false idols or gods. Today, many Protestant churches (such as Baptist churches) still tend to be less ornate than Catholic churches and are likely to not display statues.

Catholics would respond to this by arguing that they are not worshipping the statue itself; they are only using it as an aid to prayer. It is easier to concentrate on prayer if there is something visual to focus on.

Statues and sculpture also portray emotions and concepts that can be hard for people to comprehend or put simply in words. The Catholic Church supported the use of statuary in the document *Sacrosanctum Concilium*, saying that the fine arts 'achieve their purpose… as they are directed the more exclusively to the single aim of turning men's minds devoutly towards God'. For Catholics, the presence of religious statues and sculptures can act as a reminder of their faith and help to make sure their mind is never too far away from God.

Useful terms

crucifix – a cross which displays the dying Christ
patron saint – a saint to which a parish, country, school or cause is dedicated
Sacred Heart – a statue of Jesus where his heart is clearly visible

Common Catholic statues

The Sacred Heart

This is a statue of Jesus where his heart is clearly visible and circled by a crown of thorns. Other reminders of his Crucifixion are also shown, such as holes in his hands from where he was nailed to the cross. The Sacred Heart statue demonstrates the **goodness** of God because it emphasises Christ's love for humanity. The crown of thorns and other signs of the Crucifixion remind Catholics of the **suffering** that Jesus endured for their sakes. There are often flames coming out of the heart too to symbolise Jesus' burning love for all people.

Mary

Statues of Mary are commonly used in Catholicism; as the mother of Jesus many Catholics believe she deserves special respect. Mary will usually look gentle and kind, often with her palms facing outwards in an open manner, as a sign that she welcomes and accepts all that God sends. Mary's special relationship with God reminds Catholics of what God wants humans to be like. He chose a meek, mild and faithful person to be mother to his son; these qualities are reflected in statues of Mary, reminding Catholics of how they should strive to behave.

The crucifix

The crucifix is one of the most common ways that Jesus is portrayed in Catholicism. Christ's wounds are usually visible and the physical pain that he endured as he died on the cross is evident. This is a reminder for Catholics of God's love for them, as Jesus freely submitted to this pain and suffering to save humanity from its sins.

Stations of the Cross

The Stations of the Cross are a series of 14 images (or sculptures) that depict the final stages of Jesus' life. They form a devotional exercise that is often practised during Lent. Catholics walk between the Stations and say a prayer at each one as they reflect on Jesus' suffering. It is seen as a way to accompany Jesus on his final journey and to share in his suffering as a sign of gratitude. Most Catholic churches will have a set of Stations of the Cross; well-known pilgrimage sites such as Lourdes or Knock Shrine have life-sized versions which are created using sculptures.

The Jewish perspective

Statues or images of God are forbidden in Judaism, and depictions of humans or animals are discouraged. This is because of one of the Ten Commandments: 'You shall not make for yourself an idol' (Exodus 20:4). For this reason synagogues will often be decorated with Jewish symbols (such as the Star of David), abstract patterns and religious inscriptions.

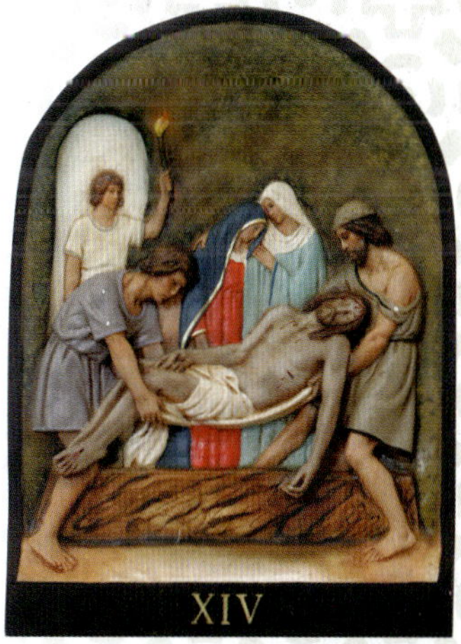

Knowledge recall

1 Define the following concepts: goodness, suffering, privation. (You can find these definitions on page 41.)
2 Identify two statues commonly found in Catholic churches.
3 How do those statues remind Catholics of Christian beliefs and teachings?

Evaluation practice

4 Do you think Christians should use statues and sculptures?
5 Why might someone disagree with you?

Michelangelo's Pieta

Specification focus

Sculpture and statuary: The importance of sculpture and statuary as an expression of Catholic beliefs about God's goodness and the meaning of human suffering, with reference to Michelangelo's *Pieta*.

What is Michelangelo's *Pieta*?

The word '**pieta**' comes from the Latin word for holiness; in Italian it means 'piety' or 'compassion'. A pieta is a piece of art depicting Mary holding Jesus' body after he was taken down from the cross. In 1499, the Italian artist Michelangelo completed what has become known as the most famous pieta. It was carved out of marble and shows Mary cradling Jesus after his Crucifixion. Today it is displayed in a small side chapel in St Peter's Basilica in Rome.

How God's goodness is seen in the *Pieta*

- The sculpture depicts the sacrifice made by God – his only son is now lying dead for the sake of humanity.
- Mary shows acceptance and not anger. God chose Mary for her goodness and it is clear here in the way she shows no resentment or anger over her son's death. This in turn points towards God's goodness and what he values.
- The pain and suffering of the crucifixion are no longer visible; both Mary and Jesus look peaceful. This suggests there is heavenly peace after this life and gives hope to Catholics who suffer of better things to come.
- The statue shows the love that a mother has for her son, which is a reflection of the love that God has for his children.

How human suffering is seen in the *Pieta*

- While Mary looks accepting of what has happened, there is great sorrow at witnessing a mother cradling her son after his death.
- Jesus appears vulnerable as he lies across his mother. This position is similar to that of a little child on their parent's lap. Just as a small child is comforted by their parents in their suffering, so too is Jesus being comforted in death.
- Christ is only wearing a small cloth and in reality it is quite possible that he would not even have had that. This is a reminder of how he was humiliated in the hours up to his death.
- Christ appears smaller and less powerful than in life. His fragility and humanity are more apparent. This is a reminder that Jesus was fully human and experienced extreme human suffering – which makes his death on the cross an even more powerful sacrifice and reminds Catholics of the depth of God's love.

Useful term

pieta – a painting or sculpture of Mary holding Jesus after his death

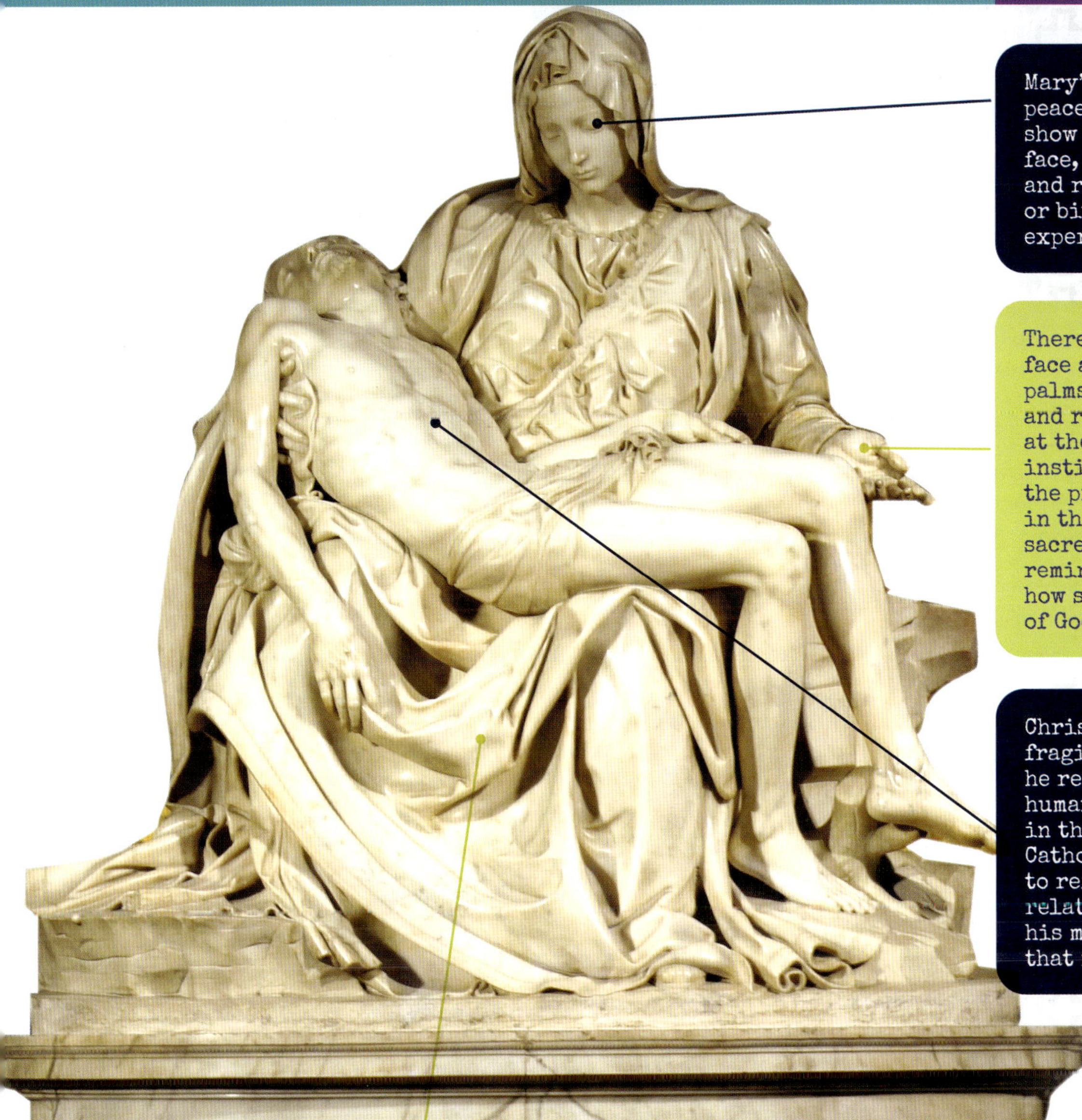

Mary's face is youthful and peaceful. Some other pietas show anguish and pain on Mary's face, but here she looks calm and resigned. There is no anger or bitterness at having to experience such suffering.

There is a goodness in Mary's face and posture. Her open palms show her openness to God, and reflect images of Christ at the Last Supper when he instituted the Eucharist. Today the priest also opens his hands in this way during the most sacred times at Mass. It is a reminder of Mary's holiness and how she mirrors the goodness of God.

Christ's lifeless body seems fragile and vulnerable as he rests on his mother. The humanity of Jesus comes through in this sculpture, and for Catholics it may be comforting to reflect on the close human relationship between Jesus and his mother, which is something that many can relate to.

Michelangelo sculpted a much larger Mary than Jesus to be able to have Jesus – a fully grown man – resting on his mother's lap. It is almost as if she is cradling the baby Jesus again, which reminds us of her strong motherly love for Jesus and thus the intense suffering she must have experienced after his death. When Jesus is presented in the Temple as a baby, Simeon prophesises to Mary that 'a sword will pierce your own soul too' (Luke 2:35).

Knowledge recall

1 Define the following concepts: Incarnation, suffering, goodness. (You can find these definitions on page 41.)
2 Describe how Michelangelo's *Pieta* shows God's goodness.
3 Give two reasons why Michelangelo's *Pieta* is popular with Catholics.

Evaluation practice

4 Do you think Michelangelo's *Pieta* depicts the suffering that Christ endured?
5 Why might someone disagree with you?

Pilgrimage to Lourdes

Specification focus

Popular devotion: The meaning and significance of pilgrimage for Catholics as a response to human suffering, with particular reference to Lourdes.

The importance of pilgrimage for Catholics

A pilgrimage is a journey to a holy site for religious reasons. The Bible describes how Jewish people would journey to Jerusalem on pilgrimage, and indeed this pilgrimage was undertaken by Christ and his family. As the Christian Church gained influence, more people started travelling to the Holy Land to visit the places where Jesus had lived and taught. Later on, other pilgrimage sites also became popular, such as those connected to the apostles or saints, or sites where someone had experienced a **vision** of Mary (as at Lourdes).

Pilgrimage is important in Catholicism for several reasons. Often it gives pilgrims a sense of **spiritual renewal** and helps them to feel closer to God. It is an opportunity to leave behind the everyday distractions of life and focus on one's faith. Some might go on pilgrimage to seek forgiveness or spiritual or physical healing. Organised pilgrimages often build in opportunity for prayer, personal reflection and attendance at Mass. Pilgrims who join these groups can enjoy the companionship of people who share the same faith. Pilgrimages provide an opportunity to meet and pray with other believers, creating a sense of unity and belonging to a wider Church.

Pilgrimage to Lourdes

Lourdes is a popular Catholic pilgrimage site in the south of France. It became famous after a 14-year-old girl called Bernadette Soubirous saw 18 visions of the Virgin Mary. In these visions, Mary told Bernadette to dig for water and when she did, a spring appeared. Since this event in 1858, many people have bathed in the waters of the spring, which is believed to have miraculous powers.

Several thousand people have claimed to experience a healing **miracle** in Lourdes, but only 70 of these claims have been verified by the Catholic Church. If a miracle is verified then usually a sudden healing has occurred which the International Medical Committee of Lourdes has studied and decided cannot be explained through science or medicine.

The most recent miracle to have been verified in Lourdes involved a French nun, Sister Bernadette Moriau, who had suffered spinal complications that meant she had to walk with a splint. After she visited Lourdes in 2008 she was able to walk unaided for the first time in years, and other medical problems were also suddenly resolved. The International Medical Committee of Lourdes investigated the recovery and could find no scientific explanation. It was therefore declared a miracle.

Lourdes has around six million visitors a year. Most pilgrims visit the grotto – the cave where Bernadette is said to have had the visions of Mary. Mass is celebrated here and streamed online so that others might join from around the world. Most days there are two processions: the Blessed Sacrament Procession followed by the Torchlight Procession, where pilgrims carry candles and say the Rosary as they process. Many pilgrims will visit the Baths and immerse themselves in water taken directly from the spring in the hope of physical and spiritual healing.

The grotto at Lourdes where Bernadette is said to have seen visions of Mary attracts millions of visitors each year

Useful terms

vision – seeing a religious figure when in a dream or trance
spiritual renewal – reinforcing or restoring a person's religious faith
miracle – an event that cannot be explained by scientific laws

Pilgrimage as a response to suffering

Many pilgrims who visit Lourdes are sick or disabled. A number of Catholic dioceses in the UK arrange yearly trips to Lourdes where well-abled (often young) people accompany those who are sick or disabled. It is an opportunity for those in good health to experience the **suffering** faced by others and to volunteer their help.

The 70 verified cases of people who have gone to Lourdes and experienced a healing miracle gives many Catholics hope that God responds to human suffering. Answered prayers and miracles are religious experiences that deepen many people's faith. Pilgrimage sites such as Lourdes give Catholics hope that despite the **evil** and suffering humans endure, God is immanent and active in the world out of his love for humanity.

Lourdes is popular with sick and disabled pilgrims as the water is believed to have healing powers

In a less obvious way, St Bernadette's own story can give hope to Catholics who are suffering. St Bernadette came from a poor family. She had bad health from a young age and also struggled in school. Many did not believe her when she started to tell people about the visions. For Catholics, it is significant that Mary chose to appear to an unassuming girl who had suffered through her life and perhaps needed this reassurance more than others. Mary's promise to Bernadette of happiness in the next life would have given her hope and courage for what was to come, despite the suffering to be endured in this life. To this day, pilgrims travel to Lourdes in the hope that their story will mirror that of Bernadette's to some degree.

> ‘I do not promise to make you happy in this world but in the other.’
> *Mary to St Bernadette*

The Jewish perspective

In the Torah, there is an instruction in Deuteronomy to go to Jerusalem three times a year during Pesach, Shavuot and Sukkoth. Since the destruction of the Temple 2000 years ago, Jews have not been able to fulfil the commandment to go on a pilgrimage. Jews pray for the Temple to be rebuilt and the opportunity to fulfil their religious duty. As a substitute, many Jews will go to pilgrimage to Jerusalem to pray at the Western Wall (the only part left of the original Temple). The Temple is considered to be the place on earth where God's presence is most closely felt, so pilgrimage to Jerusalem brings Jews closer to God.

Read more about the Temple on page 135.

Knowledge recall

1. Define the following concepts: suffering, evil, Natural Law. (You can find these definitions on page 41.)
2. Explain why the story of St Bernadette gives hope to Catholics who are suffering.
3. Identify three things that a person is likely to do on a Catholic pilgrimage.

Evaluation practice

4. Do you think it is important for Catholics to go on a pilgrimage?
5. Why might someone disagree with you?

The Rosary

Specification focus

Popular devotion: Popular piety, such as the Rosary as a reflection on the meaning and significance of the Incarnation with particular reference to the Sorrowful Mysteries.

What is the Rosary?

Popular piety describes the most common (or popular) ways that Catholics show devotion to God outside of church services. Examples of this type of worship include group prayer, pilgrimage, praying the Stations of the Cross and praying the Rosary.

The Rosary is a form of devotion that is very important to Catholics. It is a collection of prayers that have to be said in a set order, with some of the prayers being repeated many times. To help keep their place, a Catholic will use a set of **rosary beads** to count off each prayer. It can take around 20 minutes or more to say the full Rosary.

Some individuals or families might pray the Rosary on a daily basis at home. Others might say it before or after Mass at church, when a member of the parish volunteers to lead it. There are also occasions or times of the year when the Rosary is prayed more frequently. For example, families often pray the Rosary around the body of a deceased relative. If an individual has something particularly important happening in their lives, such as an exam, then a family member might offer up a Rosary for that person. The Rosary is likely to be prayed more during October – the month of the Rosary – and May – the month of Mary (as the Rosary is dedicated to her).

The Rosary remembers key events in the life of Jesus. Mary was present at many of these events and so the Rosary is a prayer that celebrates their relationship. It is a devotion that **venerates** Mary and provides Catholics with an opportunity to ask Mary to intercede for them and communicate their prayers to Jesus.

The Rosary is dedicated to Mary and celebrates her relationship with Jesus

Praying the Rosary

The Rosary is divided into sets of prayers called decades. One decade is:

- one Lord's Prayer
- ten Hail Marys
- one Glory Be.

When a person prays each decade, they try to reflect on a different Mystery. There are four sets of Mysteries that focus on different events in the life of Jesus or Mary, called the Joyful, the Glorious, the Sorrowful and the Luminous Mysteries.

For example, the Sorrowful Mysteries focus on Christ's death (Matthew 26–27). They are:

- the agony in the garden
- the scourging at the pillar
- the crowning with thorns
- the carrying of the cross
- the crucifixion.

Before a person prays each decade, they will 'announce' one of these Sorrowful Mysteries and meditate on this as they pray the decade.

Useful terms

popular piety – a commonly practised type of worship or devotion that is not part of the official liturgy of the Church
rosary beads – a string of beads used as an aid to prayer
venerate – show honour and respect

There are also additional prayers to start and end the Rosary. So, a full Rosary will look like this:

1 The person makes the Sign of the Cross.
2 They recite the Apostles' Creed.
3 They say the Our Father, followed by three Hail Marys and the Glory Be.
4 They announce the first Mystery. For the Sorrowful Mysteries, this is the agony in the garden. This is followed by another decade of ten Hail Marys.
5 The Glory Be will then be said, often followed by the O my Jesus prayer.
6 They announce the other four Mysteries and say a decade after each one.
7 They finish with a Hail Holy Queen prayer and then make the Sign of the Cross.

Catholics focus on different Mysteries on different days of the week, as suggested by Pope John Paul II. For example, they focus on the Joyful Mysteries on Monday and Saturday, and the Sorrowful Mysteries on Tuesday and Friday.

Rosary beads mean Catholics do not have to focus all their attention on where they are in the Rosary, freeing them to reflect more deeply on the Mysteries

The Sorrowful Mysteries and the Incarnation

The Sorrowful Mysteries focus on the final events in Jesus' life as described in the Bible:

- The agony in the garden. This is when Jesus prayed the night before his death that he might be spared the **suffering** he was about to endure. Jesus' humanity is shown in his anxiety about what is to come.
- The scourging at the pillar. This is when Jesus was whipped. He would have suffered a substantial amount of physical pain during this torture.
- The crowning with thorns. In order to mock Jesus, the soldiers created a crown of thorns for him to wear (to mock his title as the King of the Jews). Jesus suffered emotionally as well as physically as people tried to humiliate him.
- The carrying of the cross. Jesus was made to carry his heavy cross to Golgotha. He fell down three times on the way.
- The crucifixion. Jesus was nailed to the cross and left to die. He spoke to his mother as he was dying.

The repetitious nature of praying the Rosary encourages Catholics to meditate on these important events.

Praying the Sorrowful Mysteries reminds Catholics of all that Jesus went through for the sake of humanity. God humbled himself by becoming man, suffering substantially and dying on the cross to save humans from their sins and give them eternal life after death. Catholics value Christ's sacrifice all the more knowing and reflecting on the suffering he went through.

For many Catholics, it is a great comfort to believe that Jesus understands any hardships they go through because he himself has been through unimaginable pain. Likewise, Catholics appreciate that God became flesh and suffered so they can understand and know him better through the teachings and example of Jesus. Praying the Sorrowful Mysteries allows Catholics to reflect on and give thanks for all that God has done for them, and can bring them comfort and hope when they are suffering themselves.

Knowledge recall

1 Define the following concepts: Incarnation, conscience, suffering. (You can find these definitions on page 41.)
2 Give two examples of when Catholics are more likely to pray the Rosary.
3 Explain what the Sorrowful Mysteries are.

Evaluation practice

4 Do you think it is important for Catholics to pray the Rosary regularly?
5 Why might someone disagree with you?

Skills practice

On these exam practice pages, you will see example answers for each of the exam question types: **a**, **b**, **c** and **d**. You can find out more about these on pages 8–9.

Question *(a)*

Question ***(a)*** *tests your knowledge and understanding. You will always be asked to* ***define a key concept*** *in this question. You can find a list of the concepts at the beginning of the chapter.*

(a) What do Catholics mean by 'conscience'? [2]

Student response

An inner voice that guides us.

Improved student response

An inner voice that guides us when making moral decisions. It is God-given and causes us to do what is right and avoid bad.

What went well

The candidate has started to accurately define the word.

How to improve

You must give enough detail to ensure that the word is defined fully.

You should learn the exam board's definition for the word at the start of this chapter.

You could give an example to help explain your definition.

Tip

If you learn the exam board's definition then you know you will definitely get full marks for this question.

Over to You! Try to answer this question:

(a) What do Catholics mean by 'free will'? [2]

Helpful hints

Use the check list below to make sure that you include the most important points:

- Define what 'will' means, then say how a will can be 'free'.
- You could give an example of how a person might use their free will.

Now give yourself **two minutes** to answer this question by yourself:

(a) What do Catholics mean by 'Incarnation'? [2]

Question *(b)*

Question ***(b)*** *tests your knowledge and understanding. It will always ask you to* ***describe*** *a belief, a teaching, a practice or an event that is included in the specification.*

(b) Describe what St Augustine taught about the origin of evil. [5]

Student response

St Augustine said that evil is the absence of good. He said that evil was a punishment from God because of our sins.

What went well

The candidate has made two valid points about the teachings of St Augustine.

How to improve

You must use key concepts such as 'privation' in your response.

You should give more detail about Augustine's teachings.

You could aim to use the wording of the question in your answer to make sure you have remained focused on the question.

Improved student response

St Augustine wrote about evil in the Enchiridion. He said that God created a perfect world and natural evil was caused by fallen angels who chose to do wrong. Moral evil was caused by the first human beings – Adam and Eve – choosing to do wrong and disobeying God by eating the forbidden fruit. This is known as the Fall and it is what caused Original Sin.

Augustine used the word 'privation' to say that evil is the absence of good. It is not a thing in itself. He said that evil and suffering exist as a result of our abuse of free will – God did not create evil. The concept of evil being a privation emphasises the idea that God has not actively put evil into the world; human beings bring this about themselves when they do not do what is good.

Tip

The best answers will refer to the following teachings:
- God created the world perfect.
- Humans have abused their free will.
- Evil is not a thing in itself – it is a privation of good.

Over to You! Try to answer this question:

(b) Describe the difference between moral evil and natural evil. [5]

Helpful hints

Use the check list below to make sure that you include the most important things:

- **Describe** what moral evil is.
- Give an **example** of moral evil.
- **Repeat** the above process for natural evil.
- Point out any main **differences** between moral evil and natural evil.
- Perhaps use a **source of wisdom** such as St Augustine or Genesis to support your points.

Now give yourself **five minutes** to answer this question by yourself:

(b) Describe **two** of the Sorrowful Mysteries of the Rosary. [5]

Question *(c)*

*Question **(c)** tests your knowledge and understanding. You need to give detailed evidence and reasoning to support your explanation of the topic. For the Foundational Catholic Theology paper, you will always be asked to **explain two different viewpoints**, but you don't need to evaluate which is the better view.*

> *(c)* Explain, from **either** Catholic Christianity and Judaism or **two** Christian traditions, beliefs about the Incarnation. [8]

Student response

Incarnation means in the flesh. This is the belief that God came in the body of a human being, Jesus Christ. Christians believe that God uses the body of Jesus to communicate with us and that God worked through Jesus.

Christians believe that only through the Incarnation has God been able to communicate with us. They would say that the Incarnation was necessary because human beings had sinned.

What went well

'Incarnation' is partly defined and there is some explanation of what this means. There are some valid points about the implications of the Incarnation.

How to improve

You must write about beliefs from two different traditions.

You should use examples to explain your points more fully.

You could refer to a key text from the specification, such as the Kenosis hymn.

Improved student response

Incarnation means 'made flesh' and it is the belief that God became a human being through Jesus. For Catholics, this means that Jesus is both fully human and fully divine. He is fully human so he can feel pain like other humans. But he can also perform miracles and this is because he is divine.

Catholics believe God loved humans so much that he sent his only son to guide us and save us from sin. The Kenosis hymn refers to Jesus emptying himself of his divinity to become an example to humans of how to behave. The Kenosis hymn points out that Jesus 'humbled himself', which reinforces the idea that God came to Earth as a human being and even suffered a humiliating death so as to save people of their sins.

In Judaism, Jesus is seen as a historical figure – a man who walked on earth – but he is not considered to be divine or the Son of God. This means that Jews do not accept the Incarnation at all.

Tip

Here the candidate has used specific examples and sources of wisdom to support their explanation, such as giving examples of how Jesus is fully human and fully divine, and referring to the Kenosis hymn.

Over to You! Try to answer this question:

> *(c)* Explain, from **either** Catholic Christianity and Judaism or **two** Christian traditions, beliefs about Jesus as a source of moral authority. [8]

Helpful hints

Use the check list below to make sure that you include the most important points:

- Include **two** beliefs from either Catholicism and Judaism *or* from two traditions within Christianity (for example, Catholic and Protestant).
- For each belief, give a **source of wisdom** to support it (e.g. scripture, Church law, the Catechism, a papal statement, the Tenakh).

- Explain **why** each of the religions or traditions believe this (e.g. how they are influenced by other teachings about the nature of Jesus).
- Explain **how** this affects the actions of believers today (e.g. following Jesus' teachings or spreading the Good News).

Now give yourself **eight minutes** to answer this question by yourself:

(c) Explain from **either** Catholic Christianity and Judaism or **two** Christian traditions, beliefs about One God in three persons (Trinity). [8]

Question *(d)*

Question ***(d)*** *tests your ability to* ***evaluate****. This means you need to show you have considered more than one point of view and that you have referred to religion and belief. You will need to be able to make judgements that are supported by detailed reasoning and argument.*

(d) 'Suffering makes you a better person.'
Discuss this statement showing that you have considered more than one point of view. (You must refer to religion and belief in your answer.) [15]

Student response

Some people think that suffering can make you a better person. If you experience suffering you are more likely to be able to empathise with others. You will also appreciate your own life more. There are lots of examples of suffering in the Bible. For example Mary suffered a lot in her life by seeing her son die on the cross but she never complained and Catholics consider her to be one of the best examples of a good person. Some people might disagree as it is very difficult to say 'suffering makes you a better person' to someone who is experiencing terrible suffering like a famine. If the suffering results in someone losing their life then how can it make you a better person? It seems very unfair that some people experience far greater suffering in their life compared to others. Some people might also think that it does not matter what suffering a person experiences in their life, they are born bad and will never be a good person.

What went well

The candidate has given two different views in their answer and made some valid arguments about suffering. They have included a biblical reference and some examples to explain their points further.

How to improve

You must include evaluative and analytical comments. For example, explaining why a particular argument is strong or weak and then making an overall judgement.

You should have a clear line of argument running throughout your answer. Include various perspectives where appropriate but be clear on your own judgement.

You could learn some quotes that you can include in your writing.

Improved student response

Many people, such as Catholics, would agree that suffering can make someone a better person. Isaiah 53 ('The suffering servant') talks of how Jesus was 'despised and rejected', and this suffering for Catholics is the ultimate sacrifice which allows us to become better people. Through the Incarnation and then the suffering that Jesus endured, Catholics believe that humanity is saved and given the chance to redeem themselves morally.

Jesus referred to his followers 'taking up their cross', which suggests that through life there will be difficulties but we should follow his example and rise to the challenge of this. If you experience suffering then you are more likely to be able to empathise with others. For example, some people who have overcome addictions choose to work with others who have similar problems. This is a strong argument because suffering can

The candidate uses wording from the question and gives a Catholic response.

A source of wisdom from the specification is used to make a relevant point.

The candidate gives a specific example to support a point.

give you a different perspective on life and make you appreciate the good points in your own life more. There are many examples of suffering in the Bible. For example, Mary suffered a lot in her life by witnessing her son dying on the cross, but she never complained and Catholics consider her to be a great role model.
Others, especially Atheists, might disagree as it is very difficult to say 'suffering makes you a better person' to someone who is experiencing terrible suffering such as famine. David Hume is one example of a famous Atheist who put forward the inconsistent triad argument to disprove the existence of God. J. L. Mackie also agreed with the inconsistent triad argument and rejected the idea that evil helps us to become better people. He pointed out that suffering can make someone bitter and angry and can have the opposite effect of 'making you a better person'. However, this is a weak argument as even many Atheists would argue that 'what doesn't kill you makes you stronger'. Although in response, one might argue that if the suffering results in someone losing their life then how can it make you a better person? It seems very unfair that some people experience much greater suffering in their life compared to others.
While there are valid arguments for suffering not making someone a better person, I would argue that the fact that many religious people and also many Atheists see the benefit of suffering means that it can make you a better person. Suffering encourages people to show compassion and empathy towards others (what Christians would call agape). It can also make a person stronger and more able to cope with what life throws at them. So overall suffering is more likely to make you a better person.

The candidate explains why this is a strong argument, showing good analysis skills.

A contrasting view is given.

The candidate refers to specific thinkers and arguments rather than just making general points.

There is an overall conclusion which is in keeping with the line of argument given throughout the response.

Over to You! Try to answer this question:

(d) 'Suffering is not always evil.'
Discuss this statement showing that you have considered more than one point of view. (You must refer to religion and belief in your answer.) [15]

Helpful hints

- Decide on your own view from the beginning and argue this point throughout, but make sure to acknowledge other perspectives or counterarguments.
- Use the wording from the question in your response.
- Use phrases such as 'this is a strong/weak argument because…' to analyse the points you have made.
- Use examples and sources of wisdom to illustrate your points.

Now give yourself **fifteen minutes** to answer this question by yourself:

(d) 'The only authority we should follow is our own conscience.'
Discuss this statement showing that you have considered more than one point of view. (You must refer to religion and belief in your answer). [15]

Tip

Use the wording of the question in your opening and closing paragraphs to keep yourself focused on what the question is asking.

COMPONENT 2:
Applied Catholic Theology

Chapter 3: Life and death

Introduction

Some of humanity's biggest questions revolve around death, as it is the ultimate unknown. However, for Catholics, faith in Jesus' resurrection brings hope of eternal life. This does not mean that life on earth is unimportant – Catholics view it as a gift from God to be cherished and protected from the moment of conception to natural death. This has an impact on Catholic views about euthanasia.

In this chapter you will consider Catholic beliefs about life after death, what constitutes a 'good death' and a range of opinions on euthanasia. You will also learn about how Catholic teaching on all matters is formed (including contemporary issues like euthanasia) and how the Church has responded to the needs of the changing world. You will consider the ways in which artefacts and music are used to try to help people understand beliefs surrounding death and new life, and how symbolism and prayer are used in the Catholic funeral rite. You will also consider the importance of prayer for Catholics, not only for the dead but also as a way to enrich a relationship with God.

Things to remember:

- Make sure you know your key concepts well, so you can write with clarity and avoid confusion.
- There are overlaps with your learning about the sanctity of life from Chapter 1. Use the overlaps to your advantage, but don't confuse abortion and euthanasia.
- There are lots of issues covered here that you might have very strong personal views on. Make sure you balance your opinions with learning the content of the course. If well supported with evidence and reasoning, your own views can help to form your answer to the evaluation *(d)* question.
- Take time to learn the key ideas from the sources of authority and make sure you understand how you can use these sources of authority to support the themes they are associated with.

Concepts

Death – the end of physical life. When the physical body ceases completely to function

Eternal life – the term used to refer to life in heaven after death. Also, the phrase Jesus uses to describe a state of living as God intends which leads to this life in heaven

Heaven – those who have accepted God's grace and forgiveness in this life will enjoy an eternal existence in God's presence in the next life. This face-to-face encounter with God is what we call 'Heaven'

Hell – those who through the exercise of their own free will ultimately reject God's grace and forgiveness, will have chosen to live eternally outside of God's presence. This total lack of God for all eternity is what we call 'Hell'

Judgement – the belief that each individual will be held to account by God for the things they do, or fail to do, during their lives

Magisterium – the teaching authority of the Church, exercised by the bishops in communion with the Pope. The Magisterium is given grace by the Holy Spirit to faithfully interpret the Scriptures and Tradition

Resurrection – the raising of the body to life again after death. Christians believe that Jesus has already experienced resurrection and that all people will experience it at the end of time

Soul – the eternal part of a human being given at conception which lives on after the death of the body. Also a name for a human being's rational nature – their mind

Catholic beliefs about the meaning of death and dying well

Specification focus

Death and the afterlife: Catholic teaching on the meaning of death, the importance of dying well and the importance of palliative care with reference to Catholic teaching on assisted suicide and euthanasia.

The meaning of death

Catholics believe that there is life after **death**. This faith comes from Jesus' **resurrection** and his promise of life after death. This means that while dealing with death is difficult, Catholics hope that the person who has died will be in God's presence for eternity. This belief can bring comfort and strength, as well as offer hope that when someone dies, their suffering ends and is replaced with peace. This belief may also help a Catholic to live well, so they are prepared for their **judgement** before God.

When writing about belief in resurrection in his first letter to the Corinthians, St Paul stated that death is a change in life but not the end of life. He explains the Christian belief that physical bodies die and are replaced by spiritual bodies after death. St Paul believed that because Jesus' death and resurrection brought the chance of **eternal life**, death was no longer something to feel defeated by.

> 'Where, O death, is your victory? Where, O death, is your sting?'
> *1 Corinthians 15:55 (NRSV)*

Read more about Catholic beliefs about life after death and St Paul's teachings on page 74.

Catholics believe that Jesus' death and resurrection made eternal life possible

The importance of dying well

Most people will have some concerns about dying and death. However, many people agree that it is possible to have a 'good death' that maintains the person's dignity until their physical life ends. Dying well could include the following:

- Dealing with important practical matters. This might include making financial arrangements, like organising a will. It could also include discussing plans for the funeral.
- Spending time with loved ones. This may involve giving care to a relative or friend who is dying, or spending time together building memories. It could even include trying to resolve conflict from the past, to create peace and happier memories.
- Preparing spiritually for death. The Catholic Church offers the sacrament of the sick to Catholics who are unwell or at risk of death. This sacrament is a reminder of Jesus' concern for those who suffered illness, as well as his promise of life after death. It offers the dying person the chance to receive **absolution** and **viaticum** before their death. Family and friends may pray or read the Bible with the dying person, and a priest or chaplain may reassure them by reminding them of the Christian belief in life after death. Once the person has died, the liturgy surrounding the funeral will emphasise the belief in the resurrection.
- Ensuring that the dying person remains pain-free and maintains dignity. This may involve the use of painkilling drugs and specialist care in a **hospice**, hospital or at home, from specialist teams who will care for the physical, spiritual and emotional needs of the person who is dying. All of this is done without trying to hasten or bring about death and the person is able to die in peace, at the end their life ends naturally.

Useful terms

absolution – the assurance that God has forgiven the person's sins after their confession

viaticum – the holy communion received during the sacrament of the sick if the person is physically able to receive it. It means 'food for the journey'

hospice – a place that provides care for people with life-limiting or terminal illness

palliative care – symptom and pain management given to a person who is seriously unwell

Evangelium Vitae – an encyclical (letter) written by Pope St John Paul II in 1995 about the sanctity of life. The title means 'the gospel of life'

Catholic teaching on assisted suicide and euthanasia

The Catholic Church opposes any form of euthanasia, as it teaches that all stages of life are sacred and holy. Catholics recognise that in Genesis 1, God created human life in his image and likeness (Genesis 1:27). The prophet Jeremiah spoke of God's plan for every human life (Jeremiah 1:5). In the Ten Commandments, it states 'You shall not murder' (Exodus 20:13). Catholics interpret these teachings to mean they do not have the right to take another life, since it is given by God and blessed by him.

Pope St John Paul II recognised that a person may be given painkilling drugs as they move towards death and that these drugs may unintentionally shorten a life, but warned that ending a person's life deliberately was completely wrong.

> 'I confirm that euthanasia is a grave violation of the law of God, since it is the deliberate and morally unacceptable killing of a human person.'
> *Pope St John Paul II, Evangelium Vitae*

The sacrament of the sick can help someone to feel spiritually strengthened through illness and bring them comfort if they are facing death

You can read more about the different arguments surrounding euthanasia on pages 80–81.

Palliative care

The word palliative comes from the Latin word 'pallium', meaning 'cloak'. **Palliative care** is care which wraps around an ill person to bring them comfort. Pain relief and symptom management are both key to palliative care. This is to ensure that the patient is as comfortable as possible, even if their illness is very advanced. Palliative care is often associated with end of life care, when it is focused on helping the person to have the greatest quality of life possible until their natural death.

The Catholic Church encourages palliative care. In ***Evangelium Vitae***, the methods of palliative care are described as attempts 'to make suffering more bearable in the final stage of illness and to ensure that the patient is supported and accompanied in his or her ordeal'. The Catechism of the Catholic Church describes it as 'disinterested charity', meaning that palliative care is unselfish help of someone in need. As palliative care is focused on the dignity and care of the person, and does not hurry death, it expresses the Church's teaching on the sanctity of life. A person's life is sacred so caring for them when they are sick and dying is a moral duty and a way in which to demonstrate love and solidarity. The Church teaches that 'Those whose lives are diminished or weakened deserve special respect' (CCC 2276). Palliative care is a good way to show this special respect since it is entirely focused on the needs of the person who is unwell.

Knowledge recall

1. Define the following concepts: death, eternal life, resurrection. (You can find these definitions on page 71.)
2. What key beliefs about death does St Paul express in 1 Corinthians 15?
3. List four ways in which a person could be helped to die well.

Evaluation practice

4. Give one argument for and one argument against the idea that it's possible to have a 'good death'.
5. Which argument do you most agree with, and why?

Catholic beliefs about resurrection

1 Corinthians 15

1 Corinthians 15 is part of a letter that St Paul wrote to the people of Corinth in about 56AD, around five years after he had spent time there building up a Christian community. After he left, there were disagreements about different Christian beliefs and so St Paul wrote this letter to encourage unity, by helping the community to understand a number of Christian beliefs, including **resurrection**.

He made the following key points:

- Jesus died to save humanity from sin and was raised on the third day. A number of people saw him following his resurrection, including the 12 disciples and 500 others.
- Christ's resurrection is the central belief in Christianity. If people reject belief in resurrection, then they also reject Christ's resurrection and Christ himself.
- Jesus is the first to have risen (he is described as the 'first fruit'). He died a human **death** to save humans from sin and his resurrection has made **eternal life** possible for humans.
- The physical body is weak and limited and so will die.
- At the end of time, all people will be governed by God; the dead will be raised in eternal, perfect, spiritual bodies; and death will be overcome.

St Paul suggests that Baptism makes no sense if there is no resurrection, since Christians believe that when they are baptised, they share in Jesus' death and resurrection. He also asks why Christians would (himself included) continue their faith when they face severe punishment on earth if the resurrection was untrue.

Catholic belief in the resurrection

Catholic teaching is that the **soul** continues to live once a body has died and that when a person dies, they face **particular judgement** where their soul is sent to **heaven**, **hell** or purgatory. The dead body remains in the ground.

The Church also teaches that at the end of time, the body will be raised and united with the soul and a **Final Judgement** will be made. The faithful and those in purgatory will go to heaven, and those who have turned away from God and sinned mortally will go to hell. This faith is expressed in the Nicene Creed with the words 'I look forward to the resurrection of the dead, and the life of the world to come.'

Catholics believe in the resurrection of the body because Jesus rose from the dead. The gospels agree that on the third day, Jesus rose from his tomb and then physically appeared to many people. As Jesus was the 'first fruit' (1 Corinthians 15:20), the Church teaches that humans will also be resurrected.

The survival of the soul

Catholics believe that the soul is the non-physical, spiritual element of a person. This is in contrast to the body, which is the physical and time-limited element of a person. Humans are a combination of body and soul.

Specification focus

Death and the afterlife: Catholic beliefs about life after death, with reference to 1 Corinthians 15; Catholic belief in resurrection of the body in contrast to popular beliefs about survival of the soul.

> 'For if the dead are not raised, then Christ has not been raised. If Christ has not been raised, your faith is futile and you are still in your sins. Then those also who have died in Christ have perished.'
> *1 Corinthians 15:16–18 (NRSV)*

> 'Just as we have borne the image of the man of dust, we will also bear the image of the man of Heaven.'
> *1 Corinthians 15:49 (NRSV)*

Read more about heaven, hell and purgatory on page 76.

Useful terms

particular judgement – the judgement of an individual following their death
Final Judgement – the judgement of the whole human race at the end of time
survival of the soul – the belief that the soul does not die

Catholics believe that the soul is given by God at conception. Because it is not physical, it does not die when the body dies. The soul is an important component of life after death – it is what continues to live between bodily death and Final Judgement.

Within Christianity, there are different ideas about the soul and eternal life. In Jesus' time there were two main beliefs which are still seen in Christian thought today:

- The soul lives on after death.
- The resurrection of the body.

Catholics believe that the soul lives on after death and that it is reunited with the body for the Final Judgement, when resurrection of the body (combined with the soul) will occur.

Some Christians believe that only the soul will survive death – the body will remain dead but the soul will continue to live on. They might believe this because of the teaching of St Paul that 'What I am saying, brothers and sisters, is this: flesh and blood cannot inherit the kingdom of God, nor does the perishable inherit the imperishable' (1 Corinthians 15:50).

In Luke 23:43, Jesus comforted the criminal who was crucified beside him, telling him 'Truly I tell you, today you will be with me in Paradise.' Some Christians interpret this to mean that the soul goes to its final resting place at death.

Some Christians believe that the entire person remains dead in the grave until the end of time – that the soul does not live independently of the body, but they die and rise together. This viewpoint might be based on teaching such as John 5:28–29, where Jesus says 'Do not be astonished at this; for the hour is coming when all who are in their graves will hear his voice and come out – those who have done good, to the resurrection of life, and those who have done evil, to the resurrection of condemnation.'

The belief in the immortality of the soul was a popular belief in Jesus' time. Philosophers such as Plato taught that the soul continued after death, only to be reborn into a new body to guide the new body forward. Eastern religions such as Hinduism also believe in reincarnation or the rebirth of souls from body to body. These religions see the body as a temporary home for the soul, meaning that the body is not reunited with the soul after death – the soul is housed in a new body instead. This belief shows the importance and goodness of both the soul and the body, which God created all people to have.

The Catholic Church combines belief in the immortality or **survival of the soul** with belief in the resurrection. This forms their teaching on life after death. The key reasons for this are Jesus' resurrection, his teaching on judgement and the end of time, and the understanding that a person is both physical and spiritual.

> 'But "soul" also refers to the innermost aspect of man, that which is of greatest value in him, that by which he is most especially in God's image: "soul" signifies the spiritual principle in man.'
> *CCC 363*

> 'Each man receives his eternal retribution in his immortal soul at the very moment of his death, in a particular judgment that refers his life to Christ: either entrance into the blessedness of heaven – through a purification or immediately – or immediate and everlasting damnation.'
> *CCC 1022*

Jesus promised the repentant criminal that he would go to Paradise

Knowledge recall

1 Define the following concepts: soul, eternal life and Magisterium. (You can find these definitions on page 71.)

2 Identify three key ideas expressed by St Paul about belief in resurrection.

3 Write down Catholic beliefs about what happens to the soul after death.

Evaluation practice

4 Give two reasons why Catholics believe in resurrection of the body.

5 Which reason do you think is the most convincing and why?

Eschatology

Catholic beliefs about life after death

Eschatology is the study of the four 'last things': **death**, judgement, heaven and hell. Catholics believe in two forms of judgement:

- Particular judgement: this is the individual judgement that happens soon after death and will determine whether the person's **soul** goes to **heaven**, **hell** or purgatory.
- Final Judgement: this is the judgement that Catholics believe will come at the end of time and will be of all the living and dead. Jesus taught that those who show love to others (which in turn is showing love to God) will be rewarded in heaven and those who do not will go to hell (Matthew 25:31–46).

The Catechism of the Catholic Church describes heaven, hell and purgatory in the following ways:

Heaven:

'Those who die in God's grace and friendship and are perfectly purified live for ever with Christ.'
CCC 1023

Purgatory:

'All who die in God's grace and friendship, but still imperfectly purified, are indeed assured of their eternal salvation; but after death they undergo purification, so as to achieve the holiness necessary to enter the joy of heaven.'
CCC 1030

Hell:

'We cannot love God if we sin gravely against him, against our neighbour or against ourselves... we shall be separated from him if we fail to meet the serious needs of the poor and the little ones who are his brethren. To die in mortal sin without repenting and accepting God's merciful love means remaining separated from him for ever by our own free choice. This state of definitive self-exclusion from communion with God and the blessed is called "hell".'
CCC 1033

The discussion of whether a good God would allow people to go to hell is on pages 112–113.

Specification focus

Eschatology: Catholic teaching on heaven and hell with reference to the parables of judgement (Matthew 18:21–35, Luke 16:19–31); Catholic teaching on purgatory with reference to 1 Corinthians 3:11–15.

Michelangelo depicted the Final Judgement in this fresco, which is found in the Sistine Chapel in Rome

- Heaven is the perfect union with God for all those who have chosen God by loving him and repenting of their sins.
- Purgatory is the process where those who are on their way to heaven are made perfect and ready to enter God's presence.
- Hell is the eternal punishment for those who have freely rejected God, by living a sinful life and refusing to be sorry for it. The Catechism teaches that God does not send people to hell – they take themselves there.

St Paul's teaching on purgatory

Purgatory is a Catholic belief that is not shared by other Christians. Catholics might use the teaching of St Paul in 1 Corinthians 3:11–15 to support their belief. St Paul writes that Jesus is the foundation for life – to live a good life, one must live by Jesus' example and teaching. He makes an analogy of someone putting up a building on this foundation. The building is the life a person lives. Testing the building 'by fire' is the test of how well the person lives their life.

St Paul was emphasising that purification is necessary before entering into heaven, so that a person is completely prepared for eternal life with God. Catholics believe this purification happens in purgatory.

Jesus' parables of judgement: the unmerciful servant

In the parable of the unmerciful servant (Matthew 18:21–35), Jesus explains the importance of being merciful and forgiving of others, in order to be forgiven ourselves.

- Jesus uses the example of a servant and his master to explain the importance of always offering forgiveness to others.
- The master is merciful to the servant and pardons his debt.
- However, the pardoned servant will not pardon another man who is in debt to him.
- When the master finds out about this, he punishes the servant for his lack of mercy.
- Jesus warns that this is an example of what divine judgement will be like – if people cannot pardon others, they cannot expect to be pardoned themselves.

Jesus' parables of judgement: the rich man and Lazarus

In the parable of the rich man and Lazarus (Luke 16:19–31), Jesus reinforces the message of showing mercy to others as well as meeting their needs and makes clear that God's judgement after death cannot be changed.

- Jesus describes a wealthy man and a poor beggar named Lazarus, who lies by the rich man's gates.
- Both men die. Lazarus goes to be with Abraham in heaven but the rich man goes to **Hades**, where he is in such discomfort that he asks Lazarus to help him.
- Abraham reminds the rich man that he received the good things in his life but that Lazarus did not, so the beggar would receive comfort in heaven.
- Abraham makes clear that heaven and hell are separate and it is impossible to cross from one to the other.
- The rich man pleads for Lazarus to warn his five brothers to change their ways to avoid hell. But Abraham says that Moses and the prophets gave all the teaching that they need, so a dead man rising to tell them to change will not make any further difference.

Useful terms

venial sin – a minor sin which need not separate a person from God in heaven
mortal sin – a grave sin which means a person will be separated from God unless they repent for it
Hades – another name for hell

> 'If what has been built on the foundation survives, the builder will receive a reward. If the work is burned up, the builder will suffer loss; the builder will be saved, but only as through fire.'
> *1 Corinthians 3:14–15 (NRSV)*

> 'Then Peter came to him and asked, "Lord, if another member of the church sins against me, how often should I forgive? As many as seven times?" Jesus said to him, "Not seven times, but, I tell you, seventy-seven times."'
> *Matthew 18:21–22 (NRSV)*

Knowledge recall

1 Define the following concepts: judgement, death, hell. (You can find these definitions on page 71.)

2 State the differences between heaven, hell and purgatory.

3 Summarise what both parables of judgement teach about God's judgement of humans.

Evaluation practice

4 Give one argument for and one argument against the idea that purgatory is necessary.

5 Which argument do you most agree with, and why?

Alternative viewpoints on life after death

Specification focus

Death and the afterlife: Contrasting views about death as the end of personal existence.

Did Jesus rise from the dead?

St Paul was clear that Jesus had risen from the dead and he wrote about people who had witnessed Jesus' **resurrection**. However, over recent centuries, suggestions have been made (largely by Atheists) that Jesus did not rise from the dead, because at **death** a person ceases to exist, and resurrection cannot occur. The Catholic Church does not accept these suggestions.

One alternative explanation to Jesus' resurrection is known as the 'swoon hypothesis'. This refers to suggestions that Jesus did not actually die on the cross. For example, some suggest that the pain of the crucifixion caused Jesus to go into a coma, then when he was placed in the cool tomb he regained consciousness. The argument is that the disciples mistakenly believed he had risen from the dead.

However, St John was very clear that Jesus had died and that this was verified by the guards who crucified him.

> 'Then the soldiers came and broke the legs of the first and of the other who had been crucified with him. But when they came to Jesus and saw that he was already dead, they did not break his legs. Instead, one of the soldiers pierced his side with a spear, and at once blood and water came out.'
> *John 19:32–34 (NRSV)*

Medical experts might argue that it is hard to believe Jesus would not have died given his ordeal. The gospels talk about the scourging and the long walk to Calvary that Jesus struggled with as he fell carrying his cross. His body was very weak even before it was put on the cross. The trauma of being nailed to the cross added to this level of suffering and would have certainly resulted in death.

Another explanation is that Jesus' body was stolen from the tomb by the apostles or others. When the body wasn't there, the explanation was that Jesus had risen from the dead. This idea of a plot to steal Jesus' body is raised and rejected in St Matthew's Gospel, where guards were placed by Jesus' tomb to prevent Jesus' body being stolen.

All gospels report the tomb being found empty

> ❛Pilate said to them, "You have a guard of soldiers; go, make it as secure as you can." So they went with the guard and made the tomb secure by sealing the stone.❜
> *Matthew 27:65–66 (NRSV)*

Presumably with soldiers guarding the tomb, the body of Jesus could not have been stolen. It was the guards in Matthew 28 who saw that Jesus had risen from the dead, and later in Matthew 28, the guards are reported to have been bribed into giving the excuse that the body was stolen while they slept, to cover up the resurrection.

Non-religious explanations of life after death

Atheists and Humanists hold a range of views about death as the end of personal existence. Many do not believe in any being who will guarantee life after death. Others point to non-religious reasons why they believe there could be some form of life after death.

Many Atheists and Humanists believe the only way in which a person could continue after death is through the memories that others have of them, through the ways they have influenced the world or biologically through their children. Some might suggest that belief in life after death is just to help people deal with the unknown.

However, some Atheists believe there is non-religious evidence for belief in life after death, such as remembered lives. For example, it is claimed that as a toddler James Linegar identified as an American fighter pilot from World War II. The details he knew seemed to match the details of a pilot who had died during the war named James Houston, whose family were convinced was in some way living again through James Linegar.

Belief in the supernatural, such as ghosts and hauntings, might cause some people to believe that a person's **soul** can live on and be experienced by others after death.

Near-death experiences also cause some people to think there might be life after death. Dr Sam Parnia worked with patients who were revived after heart attacks. He gathered accounts of what happened when they were clinically dead, and found that some reported still having awareness of what was happening beyond their physical death, leading him to suggest that there is some consciousness that continues after death, at least in the short term.

Useful terms

near-death experience – an experience a person has as they are dying, which they are then able to recount to others

Read about Jewish beliefs on life after death on page 146.

Knowledge recall

1. Define the following concepts: heaven, soul, judgement. (You can find these definitions on page 71.)
2. Give details of the 'swoon' and 'stolen body' theories.
3. Write down two reasons why someone might not believe in life after death.

Evaluation practice

4. Give one reason for believing in life after death and one for not believing in life after death.
5. Which reason do you think is the most convincing and why?

The debate about the right to die

Specification focus

Death and the afterlife: Contrasting views on quality and sanctity of life and the right to die.

What is this debate about?

The right to die refers to the belief that people should be free to choose when they die. This is used to support assisted suicide and euthanasia. There are strongly held views on both sides of this debate.

The sanctity and quality of life

The sanctity of life refers to the belief that life is precious and blessed since it is created by God. It is a belief reinforced through the Bible and Church teaching. Usually, people who hold this viewpoint believe that assisted suicide and euthanasia in any form is wrong, since it is destroying God's precious creation and is a sin. Catholics and other religious people believe in the sanctity of life.

The quality of life refers to the belief that life should be worth living. This might consider to what extent a person can do everyday activities independently or the amount of pain they are in. If a person feels they have a poor quality of life, then some would argue that assisted suicide and euthanasia might be acceptable as their life does not have enough positives to make it worth living. The quality of life argument is often a non-religious viewpoint, but some religious people in favour of assisted suicide and euthanasia might also refer to it.

'You shall not murder.'
Exodus 20:13 (NRSV)

Lord Carey spoke out in favour of euthanasia and assisted suicide in 2014

The right to die

This is a controversial and emotive topic for many people since it deals with some of the most difficult human experiences: suffering, **death** and loss. The Catholic Church is opposed to euthanasia and assisted suicide. Many people from different backgrounds disagree with **assisted suicide**, **voluntary** and **non-voluntary euthanasia**.

It is illegal to assist someone to die in the UK. In September 2015, MPs voted against the Assisted Dying Bill proposed by Lord Falconer in 2014. The Bill proposed that doctors should be allowed to provide assistance to terminally ill patients to enable that person to end their own life. Assisted suicide is legal in some other parts of the world. For example, physician-assisted suicide is legal in Switzerland, but euthanasia is not. In Canada, both physician-assisted suicide and euthanasia are legal.

Some of the main arguments against euthanasia and assisted suicide are:

- It denies the sanctity of life. God gives life and so only God can take life.
- Medical treatments develop and improve rapidly. A decision to end a life could be made when additional treatment could soon become available.
- Those who are disabled, sick or elderly may feel pressured into choosing to die as they feel they are a burden to their relatives and care-givers.
- Specialist palliative care can maintain the dignity of a person without ending their life before a natural death.

However, there are many people who agree with euthanasia and assisted suicide and say that it is the kindest possible response to a person's suffering.

Useful terms

assisted suicide – providing an ill person with the means to end their own life
voluntary euthanasia – ending a person's life at their request
non-voluntary euthanasia – ending a person's life when they are unable to request this for themselves

Some of the main arguments for euthanasia and assisted suicide are:

- It offers a person who is suffering and facing death some control over their situation.
- It maintains a person's dignity since they can choose to die before their condition deteriorates to a point where their suffering would be at its greatest.
- If a person has a very poor quality of life, they may feel that life is no longer worth living.
- The former archbishop of Canterbury, Lord Carey, cited the case of Tony Nicklinson who was paralysed from the neck down following a stroke and who wanted to be helped to end his own life. Carey said 'I began to reconsider how to interpret Christian theology on the subject. As I did so, I grew less and less certain of my opposition to the right to die'.

Pope St John Paul II wrote Evangelium Vitae *to teach about issues linked to the sanctity of life, including euthanasia*

The Catholic Church's views on euthanasia

Pope St John Paul made a number of important points about euthanasia in his encyclical *Evangelium Vitae*:

'Euthanasia must be distinguished from the decision to forego so-called "aggressive medical treatment".'

'To forego extraordinary or disproportionate means is not the equivalent of suicide or euthanasia; it rather expresses acceptance of the human condition in the face of death.'

There are times when a terminally ill person might be offered medical treatment that could prolong their life. However, it might cause other suffering, such as distressing side effects. Deciding not to have this kind of treatment is acceptable. This is not the same as euthanasia.

'...it is licit to relieve pain by narcotics, even when the result is decreased consciousness and a shortening of life...'

'...as they approach death people ought to be able to satisfy their moral and family duties, and above all they ought to be able to prepare in a fully conscious way for their definitive meeting with God.'

Sometimes the pain relief used to treat a terminally ill person may make them less clearheaded and shorten that person's life. This is also not the same as euthanasia. However, there is a fine line between making a person comfortable and allowing them to consciously prepare for death. Some people do not use such pain relief in order to remain fully conscious and to unite their suffering to Jesus' death. Pope St John Paul II made it clear that this was 'heroic' but not expected of all people.

'...euthanasia is a grave violation of the law of God, since it is the deliberate and morally unacceptable killing of a human person.'

'This doctrine is based upon the natural law and upon the written word of God, is transmitted by the Church's Tradition and taught by the ordinary and universal Magisterium.'

Euthanasia is against God's law. This is a teaching based on the Bible, natural moral law and the teaching and tradition of the Church through the ages.

Knowledge recall

1. Define the following concepts: death, Magisterium, hell. (You can find these definitions on page 71.)
2. What are the differences between the quality and the sanctity of life?
3. Write a short summary of the key message about euthanasia in *Evangelium Vitae*.

Evaluation practice

4. Give one argument for and one argument against euthanasia.
5. Which argument do you most agree with, and why?

3.6

The Magisterium

Specification focus

The Magisterium: The nature of the Catholic Magisterium and its exercise in both its ordinary and extraordinary forms by both popes (pontifical) and councils (conciliar) with reference to *Evangelium Vitae* (65).

The background to the Magisterium

Before we learn about the **Magisterium**, we need to first understand how the leadership of the Church came to be and why it has authority.

When Jesus was on the earth, he commissioned twelve men to follow him. They learned from his words and actions, and were with him at key moments, such as during his Passion. Jesus gave them the responsibility to take the **Good News** to others.

> ‘And Jesus came and said to them, “All authority in heaven and on earth has been given to me. Go therefore and make disciples of all nations, baptising them in the name of the Father and of the Son and of the Holy Spirit, and teaching them to obey everything that I have commanded you.”’
> *Matthew 28:18–20 (NRSV)*

Of the twelve, Jesus gave Peter a particularly important role – Jesus recognised his faith and called him the 'rock' on which the Church would be built (Matthew 16:18). Peter became the first **Pope** or leader of the Church. Today the Pope continues the succession from St Peter and the **bishops** continue the work of the twelve. This gives them a connection to Jesus' teaching that means they have authority to teach others.

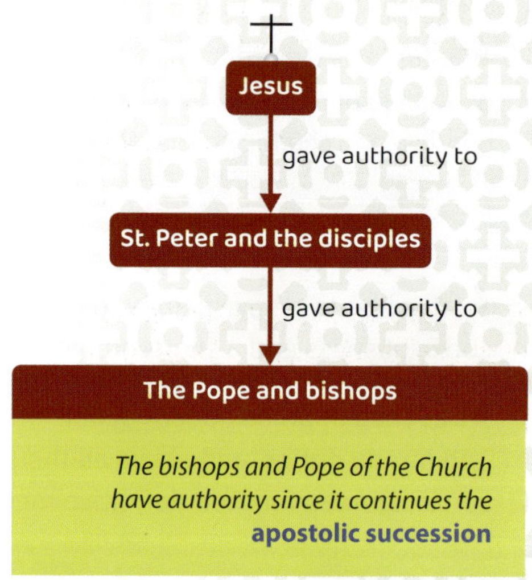

The Holy Spirit was given to the disciples at Pentecost to help them to bring the Good News to others. Jesus described the Holy Spirit as 'the spirit of truth', which will act as a 'counsellor, to be with you for ever' (John 14: 16–17). Catholics believe that the Holy Spirit gives the Church the ability to correctly interpret the scriptures and tradition about Jesus. This power is called the Magisterium and the bishops, as leaders of the Church, hold this power.

The purpose of the Magisterium

The word Magisterium comes from the Latin 'magister', which means teacher or master. The Magisterium is the work of the Pope and bishops in teaching Catholics about faith and morality. The Catechism states:

> ‘The task of giving an authentic interpretation of the Word of God, whether in its written form or in the form of Tradition, has been entrusted to the living teaching office of the Church alone. Its authority in this matter is exercised in the name of Jesus Christ. This means that the task of interpretation has been entrusted to the bishops in communion with the successor of Peter, the Bishop of Rome.’
> *CCC 85*

Here two forms of the Word of God are named:

- The 'written' form is the teaching found in the Bible.
- 'Tradition' refers to the beliefs, teachings and practices that have been passed on through the history of the Church, such as the Apostles' Creed.

Useful terms

Good News – the Christian teaching about salvation brought about by Jesus
Pope – the head of the Catholic Church, who continues the role of St Peter and has pastoral responsibility for the universal Church
bishop – the head of a local area in the Catholic Church (called a diocese), who continues the work of the apostles
apostolic succession – the unbroken connection that the bishops and Pope have with Jesus' apostles

The Magisterium, guided by the Holy Spirit, faithfully interprets these two forms of the Word of God in order to give teaching. This teaching could help to explain a long-held belief or might explain the Catholic Church's response to a particular issue that affects society at a given time.

The different forms of the Magisterium

There are three different forms of the Magisterium:

Ordinary Magisterium	These are teachings that have been passed down through the Church from its beginnings. The Ordinary Magisterium makes clear what has always been believed by the Church – it reinforces what has been taught for all time, in all places and for everyone. The Pope writes documents such as decrees or encyclicals to reinforce this teaching, to help the faithful to understand it and know how to live by it.
Extraordinary Magisterium: Pontifical	This refers to teaching that is the Pope's final say on a matter, which he has prayed about, studied and discussed. When the Pope makes a teaching '*ex cathedra*', meaning 'from the throne of Peter', he is believed by Catholics to be infallible in matters of faith and morality, meaning that his teaching in these areas is without error. In history, only two infallible statements have been made in this way: Mary as Immaculate Conception and the Assumption of Mary.
Extraordinary Magisterium: Conciliar	This refers to teaching that emerges from ecumenical councils of the Church, which are gathered to settle teaching on an issue that has emerged at that time. These are meetings of the Pope with the bishops. Sometimes others such as priests or the laity can observe, but they cannot vote on any decisions – only the Pope and bishops can. There have been 21 councils in the Church's history and they have dealt with lots of different issues, such as the divinity of Jesus (the Council of Nicaea) and the response to the Protestant Reformation (the Council of Trent). The most recent council was the Second Vatican Council in the 1960s.

The teachings from the *Evangelium Vitae* are an example of the work of the Ordinary Magisterium. There are no new pronouncements in it; instead Pope St John Paul II, having referred to the bishops, wrote to teach the faithful about the value of human life. In the encyclical, the Pope unpacks the teachings from the Bible that help to understand the belief in the sanctity of life and how these teachings apply to topics such as contraception and euthanasia. Throughout the encyclical, the Pope reminds the reader that these teachings are taught through the Ordinary Magisterium.

Catholics believe that the Holy Spirit gives the bishops and the Pope the Magisterium so that they can faithfully teach God's Word

'This doctrine is ... transmitted by the Church's Tradition and taught by the ordinary and universal Magisterium.'
Evangelium Vitae 65

You can read more about *Evangelium Vitae* on page 107.

Knowledge recall

1 Define the following concepts: Magisterium, resurrection, soul. (You can find these definitions on page 71.)

2 What are the connections between the twelve apostles, the Holy Spirit and the leadership of the Catholic Church today?

3 Create a table to help you outline the different forms of the Magisterium. In the first column, create rows for 'Ordinary', 'Extraordinary: Pontifical' and 'Extraordinary: Conciliar'. Then in the second column, write a description for each form. Finally, in the third column, write an example of its work.

Evaluation practice

4 Give one argument for and one argument against the Magisterium giving teaching to Catholics.

5 Which argument do you most agree with, and why?

The Second Vatican Council

Specification focus

The Magisterium: The nature and importance of the Second Vatican Council, its history and four key documents.

Context to the Second Vatican Council

The **Second Vatican Council** (or Vatican II) is an example of the Conciliar Magisterium – one form of the Extraordinary **Magisterium**. It was opened by Pope St John XXIII on 11 October 1962 and concluded by Pope Paul VI on 8 December 1965, following Pope St John XXIII's death in June 1963.

The purpose of Vatican II was to address the relationship between the modern world and the Catholic Church. At the opening of the council, Pope St John XXIII spoke of looking 'confidently to future times'.

> 'Illuminated by the light of this Council, the Church – we confidently trust – will become greater in spiritual riches and gaining the strength of new energies therefrom, she will look to the future without fear.'
> *Pope St John XXIII at the solemn opening of the council*

Vatican II was the Church's recognition of and response to the fact that the world had been through significant change, including two world wars. Leaders of non-Catholic Churches were invited to attend Vatican II as observers and women were invited to attend as auditors – a sign that the Church wanted to reach out to others. Sixteen documents were written in total during Vatican II, but we will focus on just four to understand the changes that they brought.

Church leaders, theologians, observers and auditors gathered in St Peter's Basilica, Rome for the Second Vatican Council

Dei Verbum (Dogmatic Constitution on Divine Revelation)

Dei Verbum means 'Word of God', and this document focuses on the belief that the Word of God is Jesus, who can be known through the Bible and the Tradition of the Church.

Catholics believe the writers of the Bible were inspired by the Holy Spirit to write what was true, but those who read the Bible must understand the literary forms used by the authors in order to best engage with the text. *Dei Verbum* emphasises the importance of tradition and the Magisterium in the interpretation of the Bible. It stresses that preaching should be based on study of the Bible and that Catholics should be guided in prayer by the Bible.

Sacrosanctum Concilium (Constitution on the Sacred Liturgy)

The *Sacrosanctum Concilium* is concerned with public worship in the Catholic Church. It reinforces the importance of the liturgy of the Mass as an expression of Jesus as the Son of God, who died and rose again to bring about forgiveness and **eternal life**.

When this document was written, it recognised that there were some elements of the Mass that could not be changed but that other features could, to enable

Useful terms

Second Vatican Council – a gathering called by Pope St John XXIII where leaders of the Catholic Church and other representatives addressed the relationship between the modern world and the Catholic Church. It ran from 1962 to 1965

laity – the members of the Church community who are not ordained

the **laity** to participate more in the Mass. Before Vatican II, the priest celebrated Mass with his back turned to the congregation and spoke in Latin, meaning that often the laity did not fully understand or see what was happening. As a result, following Vatican II, Mass was usually said in the home language, with the priest facing the congregation. This helped the congregation to see and understand the symbolism used during the Mass. The Lectionary was revised to increase the selection of readings, to further teach Catholics and enrich the liturgy.

One change established by the Second Vatican Council was that the priest faced the congregation during Mass, including the laity much more in the liturgy

Lumen Gentium (Dogmatic Constitution of the Church)

The title of this document means 'light to the nations'. *Lumen Gentium* begins by saying that Jesus is the light and goes on to say that the Church needs to bring the light of Christ to others. The Church teaches that at Baptism, a person becomes part of a priesthood of believers, meaning they have a responsibility to serve the world as Jesus did.

The document uses the analogy of the Church as a body (like St Paul does in 1 Corinthians 12). It explains that there are many parts to the Church as there are many parts to a body – the ordained clergy such as priests have a particular role and the laity also have a role. These roles are different to each other but both have great value in bringing Jesus' light to others. This document encourages the laity to live a life of service and love for others in order to bring them the Good News.

Read more about some of the teachings from *Gaudium et Spes* on page 31.

Gaudium et Spes (Pastoral Constitution on the Church in the Modern World)

Gaudium et Spes means 'joy and hope', and this document begins by expressing that the Church shares in the joys, hopes, grief and anxieties of the whole human race. It calls the Church, and the whole human race, to respond to the world as it is. At the time of the Second Vatican Council, some saw the Church as quite removed from the issues that the world faced, such as poverty and injustice, and the ways in which science and technology made an impact on people's lives. This document was a call for the Church to become more connected to the modern world. It says that one of the key ways in which the Church can engage with the world and be a source of joy and hope is through promoting peace and challenging injustice in all its forms.

Many Catholics would agree that Vatican II made a considerable difference to the life of the Church and now, many years later they can see the impact of this work.

- The laity are more involved in the Mass, not as spectators but as participants, often taking on ministries to assist the priest.
- There has been a growth in Bible study, both on a parish and academic level.
- Charities dedicated to overcoming poverty have been formed, such as CAFOD.
- Other social justice organisations have been established to encourage peace and equality in the world, such as Pax Christi and the Catholic Association for Racial Justice.

Knowledge recall

1 Define the following concepts: heaven, hell, judgement. (You can find these definitions on page 71.)
2 What was the purpose of the Second Vatican Council?
3 Summarise the key message of each of the four Vatican II documents that you have looked at.

Evaluation practice

4 Give two reasons why people might think that the Second Vatican Council made some important changes.
5 Which reason do you think had the most impact and why?

Christian sarcophagi

Specification focus

Artefacts: How Christian beliefs about eternal life influenced the iconography in Christian sarcophagi, with particular reference to the Sarcophagus with Scenes of the Passion in the Museo Pio Christiano, Vatican, Rome.

What are Christian sarcophagi?

A **sarcophagus** is a stone coffin, which is usually adorned in some way with symbolic markings, words or images. They were used across a range of cultures and religions, particularly in ancient Rome, Egypt and Greece. Christian sarcophagi have images on them which demonstrate Christian beliefs about life after **death**, to acknowledge that the person contained within the sarcophagus was a Christian.

Sarcophagus with scenes of the Passion in the Museo Pio Christiano, Vatican, Rome

Towards the end of the third century AD, wealthy Christians began to pay for carved sarcophagi to be made for themselves or their family members. They were placed in catacombs, which were underground burial chambers used in Rome by Christians and Jews. The carvings on the sarcophagi were designed to share the Christian faith of the person who had died, and to give hope for those who were mourning their loved ones.

The Sarcophagus with Scenes of the Passion dates from the fourth century and uses images from Jesus' suffering, death and **resurrection** to demonstrate key Christian beliefs about Jesus' victory over death.

① This image shows Jesus carrying the cross to Calvary, where he was crucified. He is being assisted by Simon of Cyrene – the man called on by the guards to help Jesus to carry his cross since he was so weak.

② This image shows Jesus being crowned. The gospels say that the crown was made of thorns – making a mockery of Jesus as the King of the Jews. The crown caused additional pain and suffering for Jesus. However, in this image the crown is covered in jewels rather than made of thorns, suggesting Jesus' true Kingship.

Useful terms

sarcophagus – a stone coffin, usually adorned with symbolic markings, words or images

Chi Rho – a symbol formed from the first two letters of the Greek word 'Christ'

③ This central image is full of symbolism about Jesus' death and resurrection.

Towards the top of the image is the **Chi Rho** – a Christian symbol made up of the Greek letters XP, which are the first two letters of the word Χριστος, meaning 'Christ'. The Chi Rho was used by Christians to show that Jesus is the 'anointed one' and to express the Christian faith.

The Chi Rho is circled with a laurel wreath. Laurel wreaths used to be awarded to emperors or great military leaders to demonstrate victory. The Chi Rho and the wreath together suggest the victory of Christ.

Right at the top of the laurel wreath is an eagle. Eagles were used to depict Jupiter, the giver of victory, and the birds below also represent victory. The victory in this image is over death – an empty cross is below.

④ Underneath the cross are two Roman soldiers. One looks to be thinking and the other sleeping. It looks a lot like the description of the soldiers guarding Jesus' tomb. The message is that the death and resurrection of Jesus are united events needed for salvation.

⑤ In the image on the left, Jesus is being presented before Pilate on trial.

This is followed by the image of Pilate washing his hands, which represents the fact that he did not want to execute Jesus but gave in because this was what the crowds wanted. Washing his hands was a sign of him taking no responsibility for the Crucifixion of Jesus.

Art historians note how Jesus has been presented as the hero in these images. He carries a scroll in some of the images, suggesting he was a philosopher. He is presented as calm and dignified, despite the injustice being done to him. He is the innocent victim who becomes the triumphant hero, winning victory over death.

You can read more about Jesus' death and resurrection on page 88.

Knowledge recall

1. Define the following concepts: resurrection, death, eternal life. (You can find these definitions on page 71.)
2. What is a sarcophagus and what is it used for?
3. Write a summary of the symbolism of the Sarcophagus with Scenes of the Passion. Make sure you include: carrying the cross, the crown of thorns, Jesus being put on trial, Pilate washing his hands, the Chi Rho, laurel wreath and empty cross.

Evaluation practice

4. Give two reasons why someone might feel that the artwork on the Sarcophagus with Scenes of the Passion communicates Catholic beliefs about life after death well.
5. Which reason do you most agree with, and why?

The Paschal candle

What is the Paschal candle?

The **Paschal candle** is a tall candle, lit during the season of Easter and for Baptisms and funerals. The term 'paschal' comes from the Latin word *pascha*, which refers to Easter. This is because the candle is first lit on the Easter Vigil and because it signifies the message of new life that is celebrated at Easter.

The candle has a number of symbolic features:

- It represents the light that Christ brought to the world. St John wrote about Jesus, saying: 'In him was life, and the life was the light of all people. The light shines in the darkness, and the darkness did not overcome it.' (John 1:4–5)
- The candle is made from beeswax and represents Jesus' sinless body. The wick represents Jesus' humanity and the flame represents Jesus' divinity.
- The symbols A and Ω (Alpha and Omega) are the first and last letters of the Greek alphabet. They demonstrate the belief that Jesus is the beginning and end of everything. These letters are scribed onto the candle by the priest as part of the Easter vigil ceremony.
- The cross in the middle is a reminder of Jesus' **death**, which was necessary to pay the price of human sin.
- The five studs put into the cross replicate the wounds that Jesus had as a result of his Crucifixion, which he still had after his resurrection. The studs are filled with incense as a reminder of the aromatic spices used in his burial.
- Usually the candle will also have the year it was first lit on it. This is a reminder that Jesus is present now, as he was in the past and will be in the future.

The Paschal candle and the Easter Vigil

The Easter Vigil happens during the night on Holy Saturday, the day before Easter Sunday. It is when Catholics first celebrate the resurrection of Jesus. The Paschal candle is lit for the first time every year on the Easter Vigil. The Vigil starts with the church in darkness, with a fire burning outside from which the new Paschal candle is lit. While the priest lights the candle, he prays that Jesus' resurrection will drive out darkness in people's lives.

> 'May the light of Christ rising in glory dispel the darkness of our hearts and minds.'
> *The Liturgy of the Easter Vigil*

The priest processes back into the dark church holding the candle. He sings 'the light of Christ' and the congregation responds with 'thanks be to God'. This happens three times as the priest processes to the **sanctuary**, and each time he pauses members of the congregation light the candles they are holding from the Paschal candle. The effect of this is that the light from the Paschal candle is shared, and the church becomes filled with light when before it had been dark, symbolising the belief that Jesus' resurrection overcame the darkness of sin and death.

Specification focus

Artefacts: How Christian beliefs in the resurrection are expressed by the Paschal candle as it is used in the Easter Vigil and during Catholic Baptism.

There are many important symbolic features on a Paschal candle

Useful terms

Paschal candle – a candle first lit at the Easter Vigil each year, which represents Jesus' resurrection

Sanctuary – the area surrounding the altar, which is considered to be especially holy because it is where the Eucharist is consecrated

The message of salvation continues through the rest of the Mass:

- The Easter Proclamation or Exsultet gives thanks to God for the death and resurrection of Jesus, which made salvation possible. This is usually sung by the priest, or, if necessary a cantor.
- During the Liturgy of the Word, a sequence of readings and psalms are shared which show the history of God's salvation, beginning with his gift of creation, through to freeing the Israelites from slavery in Egypt, through to the prophecies about the Messiah and finally Jesus' resurrection. These words tell the story of God's ongoing action in the world to bring people closer to him so they can receive salvation.
- The congregation renew their baptismal vows, remembering the new life that Jesus' sacrifice brought and how Baptism enables them to share in that life.
- In the Liturgy of the Eucharist, the sacrifice of Jesus is remembered when the priest uses the words and actions from Jesus at the Last Supper. The bread and wine are consecrated, which Catholics believe turns them into Jesus' body and blood. Catholics believe that the Eucharist is food for **eternal life**.

The light from the Paschal candle spreads to show that Catholics believe Jesus brought light, which overcame death and sin

Often adult converts to Catholicism are welcomed into the Church through Baptism and confirmation during the Easter Vigil. Catholics believe that becoming a member of the Church helps a person to become closer to God and so receive salvation.

The Paschal candle and Catholic Baptism

The Paschal candle is an important symbol during the rite of Baptism because it gives such a clear message of salvation and new life.

Part of the rite of Baptism is the lighting of a baptismal candle. This is a smaller candle that the baptised person can keep. It is always lit from the Paschal candle, as a sign of the light of Christ being given to the baptised person. The baptismal candle is a reminder to always walk in the light of Jesus and to keep the flame of faith burning throughout life.

The baptismal candle is lit from the Paschal candle, emphasising the connection between Jesus' death and resurrection and the new life offered in Baptism

Knowledge recall

1 Define the following concepts: soul, heaven, judgement. (You can find these definitions on page 71.)

2 Draw an image of a Paschal candle and label it clearly. Include the meaning of the symbolism.

3 Write an explanation for how the Paschal candle is connected to the belief in resurrection. Include the following words in your explanation: salvation, death, resurrection, sin, forgiveness, Easter Vigil, Baptism.

Evaluation practice

4 Give one argument for and one argument against the idea that the Paschal candle is the best symbol to represent Christian beliefs about resurrection.

5 Which argument do you most agree with, and why?

Music in the liturgy

Specification focus

Music and the funeral rite: The significance of different forms of music used in worship and how music expresses Catholic beliefs about eternal life, with reference to Fauré's *Requiem*.

Different forms of music used in worship

For Catholics, music is an essential feature of worship for lots of reasons. One reason is because music can help to communicate beliefs. Pope St John Paul II said that music and song can help worshippers to feel especially connected to the Trinity.

> '...when song and music are signs of the Holy Spirit's presence and action, they encourage, in a certain way, communion with the Trinity.'
> *Pope St John Paul II, Address to the Pontifical Institute of Sacred Music*

The Vatican II document *Musicam Sacram* says there are five different ways in which music can enhance worship:

- It helps people to pray.
- It helps people to experience the mystery of the liturgy.
- People's hearts feel united when they sing together.
- The beauty of music can raise a person's mind to heavenly things.
- The whole liturgy can feel more like a heavenly liturgy.

If there is singing at Mass, the sung parts of the liturgy are:

The Gospel **Acclamation**	The 'Alleluia' when Catholics welcome Jesus' words and teaching in the Bible.
The responses to the **Eucharistic prayer**	These are three songs of praise. The first is the Sanctus ('Holy, Holy'), the Mysterium Fidei (e.g. 'We proclaim your Death, O Lord and profess your Resurrection until you come again') and the 'Great Amen', where Catholics show they accept all the words of the Eucharistic prayer.
The Gloria	This praises the Father and Son, with the Holy Spirit.
The Psalm	Songs of praise from the book of Psalms in the Old Testament, sung between the first and second reading.
Hymns during Mass	The 'gathering hymn' draws everyone together. The 'communion hymn' can express gratitude for the Eucharist as food for **eternal life**. A hymn might be sung at the end of Mass to reflect the mission to take the Good News to others.
The Lamb of God	A prayer to express that Jesus is the Lamb of God (the sacrifice).

Other parts of the Mass can be sung too, such as the Lord's Prayer and a hymn at the **offertory**.

Catholics tend to use a variety of music in their worship. They may use very traditional music, such as ancient hymns in Latin. They might also use more modern music that is less formal in its style and words. However, all hymns should be reverent and suitable for worship.

Catholics may find that singing together helps to unite the community in prayer

Useful terms

acclamation – a prayer said or sung together to express shared belief

Eucharistic prayer – the part of the Mass where Jesus' sacrifice is remembered and the bread and wine are consecrated, becoming Jesus' body and blood

hymn – a religious song offered in praise to God, usually sung communally

offertory – when the gifts of bread and wine are given to the priest in preparation for the Eucharistic prayer

Traditional hymns	Contemporary hymns
Have been sung for many generations	Use more contemporary language, which may be easier to understand
Feels different to other music, so shows the importance and unique nature of worship	May reflect different cultures and traditions, making the music feel more inclusive
Can unite people more easily, since they are more widely known	More modern, which may help worship to feel more relevant to some people

Fauré's Requiem expresses the Christian faith in eternal life

Fauré's Requiem

The word 'requiem' comes from the Latin word for 'rest'. It is a word used in association with death, since it reflects the hope that the person is at peace once they have died. A requiem is a piece of music to be played at someone's funeral. Gabriel Fauré (1845–1924) began to write his Requiem three years after his father died, and his mother died just after it was first performed. The music is based on Christian beliefs in eternal life and unity with God following death, rather than expressing any fear or pain. Fauré described his Requiem as '… dominated from beginning to end by a very human feeling of faith in eternal rest'.

There are seven movements in Fauré's Requiem, which all are prayers asking for eternal life and mercy for the **souls** of those who have died. Unlike other requiems, Fauré chose not to include a 'Dies Ire', which is usually a terrifying piece about the **judgement** of humans before God. This is possibly because Fauré wanted to emphasise the peace and tranquillity of death.

Read about the rich man and Lazarus on page 77.

'In Paradisum', meaning 'in paradise', is the final section of the Requiem. This part of the Requiem is usually used when the coffin is carried from the church to the burial. Catholics call it the Final Commendation – a final chance to say goodbye to the deceased. The words of this section are about the angels leading the deceased to Paradise, where they will be with the martyrs and the saints. It refers to **heaven** as the place where angels welcome poor Lazarus.

Fauré uses mainly soprano (high-pitched) voices to sing the words, so that it sounds angelic. The music has a slower tempo (speed). An organ plays in the background, giving a sense of movement from this life to the next, and violins and harps are used to give a heavenly sound. The music builds to a louder and more intense point, at which we can imagine the soul passing to the peace of eternal life. Then the music gradually slows and quietens, with the word 'requiem' sung at the end to show peace has been achieved. Nadia Boulanger, Fauré's student, said that Fauré's Requiem had a 'quiet confidence' and a 'tender and peaceful expectation' of the peace that followed death.

Knowledge recall

1. Define the following concepts: eternal life, death. (You can find these definitions on page 71.)
2. Create a spider diagram showing the different ways in which music can be used in Catholic worship.
3. Create a table to remember each feature of Fauré's Requiem. In the first column, create rows for 'The words of *In Paradisum*', 'The use of soprano voices', 'The organ', 'The violins and harp', and 'The word "requiem" at the end'. Then in the second row, write what each feature represents.

Evaluation practice

4. Give two reasons why someone would say that Fauré's Requiem communicates Catholic beliefs about life after death.
5. Which reason do you think is the most effective in communicating these beliefs?

The funeral rite and praying for the dead

The Catholic funeral rite

Catholics believe that the most important action that can be done for a dead person is to pray for them, so if their **soul** has gone to purgatory then it may pass through there quickly to reach **heaven** with God. The funeral **rite** offers the opportunity for this, as well reminding the bereaved of the **death** and **resurrection** of Jesus to give them strength and hope.

There are three elements to the Catholic funeral rite:

1. The Vigil – this is often held the evening before the funeral. It might be held in a church or at home. It is a chance to prepare emotionally and spiritually for the funeral, with prayer and reflection.
2. The Funeral – this happens in the church. Catholics usually have a Requiem Mass. This is the funeral rite within a Mass, which allows the community to share the Eucharist. Family and friends are encouraged to participate in the liturgy, such as by doing the readings.
3. The Committal – this happens straight after the funeral, at the graveside or crematorium. It is where the body is buried or cremated. If the body is cremated, the ashes will be buried at a later date. The priest will lead a short liturgy.

There are a number of symbols in the funeral rite, many of which echo the baptismal rite:

- Sprinkling of holy water: shows that the person was welcomed into the Church community through Baptism, and that in Baptism they shared in Jesus' death and resurrection.
- The pall (white cloth): this is placed on the coffin to remember the white garment in Baptism. It can also be a sign that all are equal in God's eyes.
- The Paschal candle: the coffin is placed close to the lit candle, which is a reminder of Jesus' resurrection.
- Incense: used to honour the body of the dead person. Through Baptism, Catholics believe the body becomes the temple where the Holy Spirit dwells.
- A cross: placed in or on the coffin. In Baptism the person was marked with the cross and the belief that Jesus' death and resurrection meant that humans too can have eternal life.

> ❛Priest: In Baptism (Name) received the sign of the cross.
> All: May he/she now share in Christ's victory over sin and death.❜
> *The Catholic funeral rite*

- The Gospels or a Bible: these are placed on the coffin. This is to remember that the deceased lived by God's Word and in hope of eternal life. The priest says: 'In life (Name) cherished the Gospel of Christ. May Christ now greet him/her with these words of eternal life.'
- White **vestments** worn by the priest: signifies resurrection.

Specification focus

Music and the funeral rite/ Prayer within Catholic communities: The symbols, prayers and texts of the Catholic funeral rite in Britain and how these express Catholic beliefs about eternal life; the meaning and significance of the Catholic practice of praying for and offering Masses for the dead.

*There are a number of symbols of **eternal life** associated with the Catholic funeral rite*

Useful terms

rite – a religious ceremonial act with prescribed words and actions
vestments – the garments worn by the priest when he leads worship

- Readings and a psalm: these will have the theme of eternal life, such as St Paul's letter to the Corinthians (1 Corinthians 15).
- The Eucharist in the Funeral Mass: emphasises the sacrifice made by Jesus, which Catholics believe makes eternal life possible.

The prayer of commendation is said before leaving the church. In this prayer, the priest expresses the belief that there is a connection between the Church on earth and the Church in heaven. He prays that the deceased will be welcomed into heaven and raised at the end of time. He also asks for help for the bereaved to comfort one another, until all the living and dead are reunited.

There are other elements associated with a funeral, such as someone speaking about the deceased, flowers decorating the church and a gathering after the funeral. These are not part of the Catholic rite but can be ways of expressing respect, so they will usually be incorporated into the Requiem Mass.

Praying for the dead

For Catholics, prayer for the dead is a sign of love and respect. The Catholic Church encourages people to pray for their loved ones after their death. This is believed to benefit the souls of the deceased and unites the members of the Church – both living and dead – to each other and to God.

Often the dead will be prayed for in the prayer of the faithful (often called bidding prayers) in Sunday Mass. Masses are often offered in memory of a person who has died. This can happen soon after a person has died, or many years later, for example on the anniversary of their death. The person will be named and prayed for during the Mass.

The Catholic Church particularly remembers all those who have died in November. The Church celebrates All Saints' Day on 1 November and All Souls' Day on 2 November. All Saints' Day is a celebration of all the saints who are now with God in heaven, especially those ordinary saints who are not named in the books of the saints our own loved ones perhaps, who have died. All Souls' Day is for those who have died and not yet reached heaven. Catholics continue to pray for the dead for the whole of November.

One prayer that is often used when a person has died is called the 'Eternal Rest'. This prayer requests that the person enjoy eternal peace and rest in the light of Christ. It asks that all souls are able to rest in peace, calling on God's mercy.

> 'Eternal rest grant unto him/her, O Lord, and let perpetual light shine upon him/her. May he/she rest in peace. May his/her soul and the souls of all the faithful departed, through the mercy of God, rest in peace. Amen.'
> *Eternal Rest prayer*

Knowledge recall

1. Define the following concepts: death, heaven, eternal life. (You can find these definitions on page 71.)
2. Identify four elements of the Catholic funeral rite that show belief in life after death. Explain how they show this.
3. Give two reasons that Catholics might give for praying for the dead.

Evaluation practice

4. Give one argument for and one argument against the idea that the best thing to do for a dead person is to pray for them.
5. Which argument do you most agree with, and why?

Prayer

The importance of prayer

St John Damascene describes prayer as 'the raising of one's mind and heart to God' (CCC 2559). For Catholics, prayer is when a person gives themselves completely and lovingly to God, as they communicate honestly and faithfully with God and listen to him as he responds.

Prayer is often part of daily life for Catholics. They may pray at particular points of the day, such as before a meal. Prayer can also be a response to some of life's big events, such as to give thanks for something wonderful. Prayer is important to Catholics as it allows them to communicate and strengthen their relationship with God.

Jesus showed through his own example the importance of prayer, for example by praying at the start of the day (Mark 1:35), or before making an important decision (Luke 6:12). He taught the importance of authentic prayer (Matthew 6:5–15) and to trust God in prayer (Mark 11:23–26).

Different types of prayer

The Catechism identifies five different types of prayer:

1 Blessing and adoration: where people bless God for having blessed humans, and where people feel humbled in the presence and greatness of God.
2 Petition: these are personal prayers asking for something. For example, asking for forgiveness.
3 Intercession: these are prayers asking God to fulfil the needs of other people, which reinforces the sense of praying as a community.
4 Thanksgiving: these are prayers of thanks. The highest form of thanksgiving is in the Eucharist.
5 Praise: these are prayers which marvel that God is God. They are an expression of this feeling of awe.

There is a difference between formulaic and extempore prayer:

- **Formulaic prayer** is prayer that has not changed through the history of the Church. It uses words that have been passed down through generations, such as **the Lord's Prayer**, the Hail Mary or the Glory Be.
- **Extempore prayer** is prayer that is more free-form, where the words are created in the moment to match a particular need or to express a particular idea.

Formulaic prayer	Extempore prayer
Helps people to pray together, as the words are known or can be found in a prayer book.	Changing or creating a prayer to fit a particular situation helps it to feel more personal.
Sometimes it is hard to find the right words to pray, but with formulaic prayer the words are already there.	The prayer is expressed from the heart, rather than said from memory or read from a book.
With words that are already known, the prayer can become more **meditative**.	Could encourage more diverse prayers, meaning more people feel personally involved in the prayer.

Specification focus

Prayer within Catholic communities: The significance of prayer as 'the raising of the mind and heart to God', both in formulaic and extempore prayers, with particular reference to the Lord's Prayer.

Prayer is an important element of Catholic life

'In the morning, while it was still very dark, he got up and went out to a deserted place, and there he prayed.'
Mark 1:35 (NRSV)

Useful terms

formulaic prayer – traditional prayer with set words
The Lord's Prayer – the prayer that Jesus taught, which is used by all Christians
extempore prayer – prayer that is improvised by individuals to express a particular intention
meditative – a form of prayer that is often very focused and reflective

Catholics use both formulaic and extempore prayer in their lives, because each type of prayer has particular qualities that can help individuals to raise their minds and hearts to God.

The Lord's Prayer

The Lord's Prayer is of great importance to Catholics.

- It is the prayer that Jesus taught, which gives it authority. In Luke's Gospel, the Lord's Prayer is taught by Jesus when the disciples ask him how to pray (Luke 11:1–4). In Matthew's Gospel it is given as the best prayer to say in order to pray in a humble way (Matthew 6:9–13).
- It is the prayer that unites all Christians. There are slight differences to the wording at the end of the prayer between Catholics and other Christians, but the main body of the prayer is the same.
- The Catechism quotes Tertullian, who said the Lord's Prayer is the 'summary of the whole gospel' (CCC 2761), and St Augustine, who said that all the holy prayers of scripture are found in the Lord's Prayer.
- The Catechism also says that Jesus did not give the words to be said 'mechanically' and that the Holy Spirit helps people to turn to God as their Father (CCC 2766).

The table below explains the meaning of each line in the prayer.

Our Father who art in heaven	Turning to God as children and being humble and trusting in his presence. **Heaven** is not a distant place, but rather a sign of God's majesty.
Hallowed be thy name	God's name is holy. By recognising that God's name is holy, Christians are asking that God's holiness becomes a part of who they are.
Thy Kingdom come	This is about Jesus' return in the Final Judgement and God's reign over all people. It is also about God's kingdom being present in everyday life.
Thy Will be done on earth as it is in heaven	Asking God to help humans to be more united to Jesus so that salvation can be brought to the world.
Give us this day our daily bread	This is not only about physical needs but also a focus on the spiritual 'food' in the Eucharist and the Word of God.
And forgive us our trespasses, as we forgive those who trespass against us	Asking God for forgiveness and pardon, which Catholics know can only be given if they pardon others.
And lead us not into temptation	Asking God to not allow people to take the wrong path in life, which leads to sin and suffering.
But deliver us from evil	Asking to share in the victory that Jesus has gained over evil.
Amen.	Agreement with all the ideas expressed in the prayer.

Jesus taught the Lord's Prayer to his disciples

'Run through all the words of the holy prayers [in Scripture], and I do not think that you will find anything in them that is not contained and included in the Lord's Prayer.'
St Augustine (CCC 2762)

Knowledge recall

1. Define the following concepts: hell, resurrection, judgement. (You can find these definitions on page 71.)
2. Identify the five main types of prayer noted in the Catechism.
3. Write a summary of the main features of the Lord's Prayer.

Evaluation practice

4. Give two reasons why someone might say formulaic prayer is the best type of prayer.
5. Which reason do you think is most convincing, and why?

Skills practice

On these practice pages, you will see example answers for each of the exam question types: **a**, **b**, **c** and **d**. You can find out more about these on pages 8–9.

Question *(a)*

Question ***(a)*** *tests your knowledge and understanding. You will always be asked to* ***define a key concept*** *in this question. You can find a list of the concepts at the beginning of the chapter.*

(a) What do Catholics mean by the 'Magisterium'? [2]

Student response

The Pope and bishops meeting together to study the Bible.

Improved student response

The teaching authority of the Church, exercised by the bishops in communion with the Pope. The Magisterium is given grace by the Holy Spirit to faithfully interpret the scriptures and tradition.

Over to You! Try to answer this question:

(a) What do Catholics mean by the 'soul'? [2]

Helpful hints

To help you answer this question successfully, think about the advice given here:

- The Eduqas definition for this term is quite long and has two parts. Make sure you try to include both.
- If you're struggling to remember the whole definition, remember your learning from this chapter and write what you recall about the soul.

Now give yourself **two minutes** to answer this question by yourself:

(a) What do Catholics mean by 'death'? [2]

Question *(b)*

Question ***(b)*** *tests your knowledge and understanding. It will always ask you to* ***describe*** *a belief, a teaching, a practice or an event that is included on the specification.*

(b) Describe Catholic beliefs about the resurrection of the body. [5]

What went well

There is accurate detail about who is involved in the Magisterium and some of what the Magisterium does.

How to improve

You must make clear that the Magisterium does more than study – the Magisterium teaches.

You should show that the Magisterium also refers to tradition.

You could connect the work of the Magisterium to inspiration from the Holy Spirit.

Tip

Learning the definitions on page 71 is the best way to get full marks on *(a)* questions.

Student response

Catholics believe that the body will be resurrected after death. In the Bible it says that on the Final Judgement we will be raised and judged. This is why Catholics believe in life after death.

Improved student response

Catholics believe that the body will be resurrected after death. In the Bible it says that on the Final Judgement our bodies will be raised, joined with our souls and be judged on how we have treated others. Jesus' resurrection was physical – all the witnesses to his resurrection were able to see him. This is a central belief of the Catholic Church, seen in the parable of the sheep and the goats and expressed in the Creed where Catholics state 'I believe in the resurrection of the body.'

The belief in the resurrection of the body is also seen in St Paul's letter to the Corinthians where he explains how important this belief is for the Christian faith. He explains that the resurrected body is a spiritual body, which is perfect and unchanging unlike human, earthly bodies. These teachings give many Christians comfort that death is not the end.

What went well

There is clear knowledge of the Christian belief in bodily resurrection and its connection to the Bible.

How to improve

You must make more specific reference to bodily resurrection.

You should develop the impact of these beliefs on the lives and faith of Catholics.

You could make more specific references to Bible teachings where these beliefs are expressed.

Over to You! Try to answer this question:

(b) Describe Catholic teaching about the importance of dying well. [5]

Helpful hints

To help you answer this question successfully, try following this advice:

- Identify and write down one Catholic teaching about the importance of dying well.
- Describe what this action/approach would mean to the person who is dying and to their loved ones.
- Try to incorporate Church teaching, reference to a sacrament or an example from the life of Jesus.
- Choose another teaching and develop it as you did for your first point, using relevant information.

Tip

Try to use sources of authority throughout your answer to back up the points you make.

Now give yourself **five minutes** to answer this question by yourself:

(b) Describe some of Jesus' teachings on heaven and hell. [5]

Question *(c)*

*Question **(c)** tests your knowledge and understanding. You need to give detailed evidence and reasoning to support your explanation of the topic.*

(c) Explain **three** features of a Catholic funeral rite. [8]

Student response

During the Catholic funeral rite the coffin will be at the front of the church and covered with a white pall which is a white cloth that fits over the coffin. It shows purity. The priest will sprinkle holy water on the coffin to show Baptism. During the rite a friend or relative will talk about the person who has died, remembering and respecting them. This is called a eulogy.

Improved student response

One feature of the Catholic funeral rite is the covering of the coffin with a white pall and the sprinkling of the coffin with holy water. This white cloth is symbolic of the white garment worn at Baptism. The sprinkling with holy water symbolises the sacrament of Baptism. It is a reminder that when the deceased was baptised earlier in their life they were freed from Original Sin. Catholics believe that Jesus' death and resurrection opened the gates of heaven and so the congregation pray that by being baptised, the deceased will be able to go to heaven.

Another feature of the Catholic funeral rite is the prayers said for the deceased. When Catholics pray at a funeral, they are asking that the soul of the deceased person be given eternal rest in heaven. They recognise that the person's soul may need to go through purgatory first and so pray that this may be quick, so that the soul of the dead person can be with God.

A final feature of the Catholic funeral rite is the readings. Often these will be readings that emphasise Catholic beliefs about resurrection, such as St Paul's letter to the Corinthians where he encouraged Christians to have faith in resurrection and promised that when people are raised from the dead they will be given new spiritual bodies and be in God's Kingdom. This will bring comfort and hope to the bereaved.

What went well

Two of the features identified are from the Catholic funeral rite (the white pall and the sprinkling with holy water).

How to improve

You must make sure that the three features are all part of the Catholic rite (a eulogy may be shared, but this will be the case for non-Catholic funerals too).

You should ensure that you *explain* rather than describe, which means you need to give detail about why actions are done and their significance or impact.

You could make clear reference to Catholic beliefs about life after death to explain the symbolism of the Catholic funeral rite.

Over to you! Try to answer this question:

(c) Explain the importance of the Second Vatican Council. [8]

Helpful hints

To help you answer this question successfully, think about the advice given here:

- This is a broad question, so to stay focused and not end up writing too much you will need to carefully select relevant material.
- Identify one important feature of the Second Vatican Council and write it down.
- Explain why it was so important. Try to give specific detail about the teaching/change and name the relevant document if you can.
- Write about the impact that it made on people, the Church or the world.
- Do this at least one more time.

Tip

To stay focused in this kind of answer, it is useful to make sure that you identify the feature clearly in the first sentence of each paragraph. Then use the paragraph to explain the feature, showing off your knowledge about the feature and its impact, using some specialist language and a source of authority.

Now give yourself **eight minutes** to answer this question by yourself:

(c) Explain why the Paschal candle is used in the Easter Vigil and during a Catholic Baptism. [8]

Question *(d)*

*Question **(d)** tests your ability to **evaluate**. This means you need to show you have considered more than one point of view and that you have referred to religion and belief. You will need to be able to make judgements that are supported by detailed reasoning and argument.*

(d) 'Euthanasia is never acceptable.'

Discuss this statement showing that you have considered more than one point of view. (You must refer to religion and belief in your answer.) [15]

Marks for spelling, punctuation and the accurate use of grammar are allocated to this question. [6]

Student response

I agree with this because I think euthanasia is always wrong. I can't think of any situation where it would be acceptable because it's taking a life, which is wrong. Some people might disagree with me because they say that a person who is in a lot of pain and suffering, who will die anyway, should be allowed to end their life using euthanasia. It's legal in some countries showing that for some people it is acceptable. Catholics would say that euthanasia is never acceptable because the Bible teaches against it.

Euthanasia might make some ill people worried because they would be anxious about what it means for their care. I think it would be really wrong for this to happen because even if you're ill, you're still a human made in God's image.

What went well

There is clearly an understanding that there are different viewpoints about this topic. Some evidence is used to support the point in favour of euthanasia. A reference is made to the fact that Catholics base their views on euthanasia on teachings from the Bible.

How to improve

You must make sure that views that are personally held are backed up with some evidence and reasoning.

You should include some specific sources of authority, rather than just referring to 'the Bible'.

You could incorporate some judgement of the views expressed to show that you have considered their strengths or weaknesses.

Improved student response

Catholics, as well as many others, would agree that euthanasia is never acceptable because they view it as taking a life. Catholics say that God gives life and so only God can take life away. God's life-giving qualities are seen in the Genesis creation stories, and the prophet Jeremiah reminds people that God has a plan for each person. This means that Catholics would say that to take a life would be to interrupt God's plan, which is wrong.

However, there are many people who might say that in some circumstances, euthanasia might be acceptable. For example, if a person is terminally ill and already in great pain, which will increase as their condition gets worse, they may say that it is kinder to bring about that person's death sooner to prevent more suffering. Some countries allow euthanasia in these cases already, showing that it is acceptable to some people. Catholics might respond to this by saying that palliative care should include pain management and that specialists can ensure the patient is as comfortable as possible for the rest of their natural life. They might refer to the Bible which teaches 'Thou shall not kill' to back up this point, as God has given a clear teaching in the Ten Commandments not to take away human life.

I understand why some people are in favour of euthanasia, but I think the Catholic viewpoint is strongest since palliative care is designed to maintain a person's dignity, reduce their suffering and manage their symptoms without making their death quicker, which would allow dying people more time with their family and friends before they naturally die.

The answer uses of a range of sources of authority.

An alternative viewpoint has been explored, using 'however' to show that this is a different idea.

By bringing in a Catholic response, the candidate has evaluated the ideas expressed.

A judgement has been made and justified.

Also, many people who say that euthanasia is never acceptable would say that the possibility of euthanasia puts many ill and disabled people into a difficult situation, where maybe they feel under pressure from others to choose euthanasia. They might think they are being a burden on their family and friends and that euthanasia will relieve this burden. Conversely, those who think it is acceptable might argue that it offers a choice to people and that it would have lots of rules to make sure that someone chose euthanasia for the right reasons. Christians who support this view might use Jesus' teaching 'Love your neighbour' to suggest that if a person is making a choice to die, then the most loving action is to support them.

Good use of a Bible teaching.

Many Catholics would respond by saying that loving your neighbour doesn't mean taking their life and that Jesus showed the value of all people, whether they were ill, disabled or not and so this isn't a fair use of his teaching. I agree more with this perspective because as we make medical advances and find new ways of helping people who suffer, it makes euthanasia unacceptable.

Another judgement has been made and justified.

Overall, I don't think euthanasia is ever acceptable because if life is created by God *imago Dei*, it remains *imago Dei* and to damage something so precious is wrong.

Over to you! Try to answer this question:

(d) 'There is life after death.'
Discuss this statement showing that you have considered more than one point of view. (You must refer to religion and belief in your answer.) [15]

Helpful hints

To help you answer this question successfully, think about the advice given here:

- Imagine in your response that you are listening to a discussion between people who have different opinions on this theme. You need to make sure that one or both viewpoints are religious.
- Person A will give their view, and back it up.
- Person B will respond to this, showing that they have a different opinion and why.
- Person A will say what they think about person B's viewpoint and explain why.
- You will then make a judgement – which viewpoint is the strongest of the two? Why?
- Try to do this twice and, once you've written a balanced argument, with your judgements you can add an overall conclusion.

Tip

It's really important to remember to keep your arguments balanced in evaluations, especially on a topic that someone might have strong personal feelings about. Make sure you include contrasting ideas and develop them to express the reasoning behind them.

Now give yourself **fifteen minutes** to answer this question by yourself:

(d) 'There is no life after death.'
Discuss this statement showing that you have considered more than one point of view. (You must refer to religion and belief in your answer.) [15]

COMPONENT 2:
Applied Catholic Theology

Chapter 4:
Sin and Forgiveness

Introduction

How do we know what right and wrong is? This chapter will explore this question, as well as why there are punishments for criminals (including the death penalty). When people talk about getting justice they often mean revenge, but we are going to explore justice in terms of maintaining what is fair. For Christians, this goes beyond courtrooms and prison cells, because they believe that God is the ultimate judge. In this chapter you will consider the question of whether a loving God would send people to hell, and who should be saved. You will look at the ways in which the Church community is seen to be a source of salvation, and how the sacraments can help people to receive forgiveness for their sins. Christians have faith that Jesus brought salvation and they speak about this as 'Good News'. Many Christians therefore feel it is their duty to take the Good News to others. In an increasingly secular and multi-faith society this can be a challenge, though there are great benefits to living in a multi-faith society, which you will also consider.

Things to remember:

- This chapter depends on you feeling very confident about the key concepts. Make sure you learn them well.
- Some aspects of this chapter may also appear in sociology lessons. Make sure that you approach the content for this course as religious studies, so your focus is on the religious and ethical dimensions of these themes.
- Watching the news or reading a newspaper might give you some good ideas of case studies to use to develop your thoughts on these issues.
- This is another chapter where you might have strong viewpoints. Remember to back up your ideas and opinions and stay focused on the topic.

Concepts

Absolutism – the belief that there are certain actions that are always right or always wrong. The belief that moral laws exist eternally and are not just human inventions

Eucharist – meaning 'thanksgiving'. The name Catholics use to describe the rite where the bread and wine become the body and blood of Jesus and is received by the people. Also the name for the real presence of Jesus in the Sacrament of Holy Communion

Evangelisation – literally means spreading the 'good news' which we translate as Gospel. The sharing of the Gospel and life of Jesus with others

Forgiveness – the act of pardoning someone for the offences they have caused you. Overlooking a person's faults

Punishment – the consequences of a wrong decision and a penalty imposed by a person in authority on the person who has committed wrongdoing

Relativism – the belief that there is no moral law and that rules that govern what is right and wrong are human inventions and change from place to place and from age to age

Salvation – the belief that through Jesus' death and resurrection humanity has achieved the possibility of life forever with God

Sin – acting against the will or laws of God

Crime, sin, morality and punishment

Crime, sin and morality

'Crime' is a legal word that covers both actions and omissions (when something is not done) that go against the law of the land and so are punishable by law.

'**Sin**' is a religious word that covers actions and omissions that go against laws from God and are punishable by God. Christians believe that sin entered the world at the Fall, when Adam and Eve disobeyed God by eating from the forbidden tree in the Garden of Eden. All sin requires **forgiveness**.

Some actions are both sinful and criminal, such as murder and theft. **Blasphemy**, **idolatry** and adultery are sins, but they are not illegal. Families such as the Ten Boom family who hid Jews during World War II to save them from death broke the law of the land, but did not sin.

'Morality' refers to the principles by which humans understand the difference between good and bad behaviour. When a person makes a decision to avoid or commit a crime or sin, this is a moral choice. Sin and crime can have a negative impact on human relationships. Catholics believe that sin also damages a person's relationship with God.

People approach morality in different ways. Some people think that what is right or wrong depends on the situation and other people believe right and wrong are fixed.

- **Absolutist** morality: moral rules never change. They apply in the same way in every situation and cannot be altered. Morality is a standard independent of humans, yet is discovered by humans.
- **Relative** morality: moral rules can change. They depend on the context or circumstance of the moral action.

For example, people are often divided as absolutist and relativist regarding abortion.

- An absolutist view is that abortion is always wrong since it is taking a life. No one can make a decision to end another life, even if it is an unborn life.
- A relative view is that there are situations where abortion is permissible, such as to save a woman's life or because the unborn child has a significant disability.

Criminal penalties

There are a variety of responses that can be made to a criminal offence.

Retribution

Retribution is an approach which suggests that the **punishment** a person receives should be equal to the crime they have committed. For example, some people may say that the death penalty is retribution for murder or that a long prison sentence is retribution for violent crime.

Strengths:

- It is an equal and fair response to the crime, as the punishment is proportionate to the crime committed.

Specification focus

Crime and punishment: The difference between crime and sin and their relationship to morality, with reference to absolutist and relativistic approaches to the morality of actions; the different rationales given for criminal penalties: retribution, deterrence, rehabilitation and a critical evaluation of the justifiability of each.

Read more about the Fall on page 46.

Theft is considered to be both a sin and a crime

Useful terms

blasphemy – using God's name in a disrespectful way
idolatry – worshipping something that is not God as if it was God

- It is consistent with the teaching of Exodus 21:23–24: 'If any harm follows, then you shall give life for life, eye for eye, tooth for tooth, hand for hand, foot for foot.' This teaching was given to make sure that punishments were fair and equal to the crime committed. Genesis 9:6 could also be seen to support retribution.

Weaknesses:

- Using the death penalty as retribution is controversial – if taking a life is wrong, then surely it is wrong to use it as a punishment?

Deterrence

Deterrence is an approach which aims to put people off committing crime. There are two ways in which deterrence could be used: an individual is given a harsh sentence to put them off offending again, or a harsh punishment is given to put others off committing the crime. The death penalty is an example of this second category.

Strengths:

- It might prevent people from engaging in criminal activity. For example, convicting and executing murderers might save many innocent lives, as someone might think twice about committing a crime with a heavy penalty.

Weaknesses:

- Some suggest that harsher punishments do not necessarily put people off offending or reoffending, meaning that it might not be an effective form of punishment. In countries that use the death penalty for murder, for example, murder is still committed.
- It might be impossible to deter someone from breaking the law, for example if they are unable to make rational decisions because of mental illness.

Rehabilitation

Rehabilitation is an approach designed to help criminals so they can move on from their criminal acts and return to society to make a positive contribution. This could mean, for example, helping prisoners to gain skills and qualifications to become more employable on release.

Strengths:

- This is a compassionate response to the criminal, recognising that people who have done wrong need to turn their lives around so they do not become trapped in a life of crime.
- This approach is consistent with the Christian belief that all people are created imago Dei and deserve to be treated with respect and dignity, as well as be given the chance to change themselves.

Weaknesses:

- In 2019, Sir Martin Narey, the former director general of the Prison Service in England and Wales, said that the rehabilitation currently offered in prisons was not enough to fix the problems that many criminals had faced in their childhoods. He argued that childhood traumas could go so deep that short courses in prison did nothing to change a person's life, and that instead prisons needed to treat prisoners with dignity and respect to help them to begin a journey of self-growth.
- Some people may feel that rehabilitation isn't a sufficient punishment for someone who has done wrong.

> 'Whoever sheds the blood of a human, by a human shall that person's blood be shed; for in his own image God made humankind.'
> *Genesis 9:6 (NRSV)*

Rehabilitation is used to help criminals to reintegrate with society and avoid crime

Knowledge recall

1 Define the following concepts: forgiveness, punishment and absolutism. (You can find these definitions on page 101.)
2 Write down the differences between absolutist and relative morality.
3 Explain each of the three aims of punishment, and write down one strength and weakness for each one.

Evaluation practice

4 Give one argument for and one argument against the opinion that 'retribution should be the aim of all punishments'.
5 Which argument do you most agree with, and why?

Christian teachings on forgiveness

Jesus' teachings on forgiveness

Forgiveness is a very important aspect of the Christian faith. Christians look to the example of Jesus who offered forgiveness to those who had offended other people or God with their actions.

- He forgave Zacchaeus who had abused his position of authority to take money from others (Luke 19:1–10), and he forgave the woman caught in adultery (John 8:1–11).
- In the parable of the prodigal son, Jesus taught that God the Father would wait for those who sinned to return, when he would welcome them back with open arms (Luke 15:11–32).
- Jesus called on God to forgive the guards who executed him (Luke 23:34).
- Christians believe that Jesus' death was for the forgiveness of human **sin**.

Christians take their lead from Jesus and try to be forgiving towards others.

Matthew 18:21–22 (the parable of the unmerciful servant)

The usual teaching from the Jewish leaders in Jesus' time would have been based on Amos 1:6 where forgiveness was offered three times, so with his suggestion of seven times Peter is trying to show that he knew people should strive to be more forgiving. Seven is an important number in the Bible that represents completion or perfection (such as the seven days of creation).

When Jesus says seventy-seven times (or 'seventy times seven' in some translations), he is not indicating that people should keep count of the number of times they should forgive. Forgiveness is not about keeping count but rather it is about love. Jesus is teaching that forgiveness should be infinite.

Matthew 6:14–15

The quotation on the right is taken from Jesus' teachings on how to live properly as people of faith, where he speaks about hypocrites who make their faith all about themselves and how others perceive them. When he taught how to pray, he taught the Lord's Prayer, which contains the idea that forgiveness from God is possible only if a person is prepared to forgive others: 'forgive us this day our trespasses, as we forgive the trespasses of others'.

Christians would say that being unforgiving is sinful. A person who will not forgive is still angry and unwilling to give someone a second chance. In his teachings, Jesus stresses that forgiveness must come from the heart. It is as much about the person who is forgiving changing their attitude as it is about the person who has sinned. A person cannot say they have forgiven when deep down they did not mean it – to be able to **repent** before God means that the person needs to live as Jesus showed.

This means it is not about a straight exchange of 'you forgive and God will forgive you'. Christians believe that God's justice is merciful, and Jesus is teaching that the same **mercy** shown by God should be in every person's heart, which makes

Specification focus

Crime and punishment: Christian teachings about forgiveness, including interpretations of teachings: Matthew 18:21–22, Matthew 6:14–15, with reference to the tension between forgiveness and punishment.

‘Then Peter came and said to him, "Lord, if another member of the church sins against me, how often should I forgive? As many as seven times?" Jesus said to him, "Not seven times, I tell you, but seventy-seven times."’
Matthew 18:21–22 (NRSV)

Read more about Jesus' moral teachings on page 55.

‘For if you forgive others their trespasses, your heavenly Father will also forgive you; but if you do not forgive others, neither will your Father forgive your trespasses.’
Matthew 6:14–15 (NRSV)

Useful terms

repent – to feel sorry for wrongdoing
mercy – compassion shown by someone who has the power to punish

a person want what is right but also have compassion for those who have done wrong. By forgiving others, a person allows God's mercy to work through them. This is harder than it sounds and so is a challenge for Christians to live by.

Forgiveness and punishment

It might seem like **punishment** is not needed if there is forgiveness, because the person who has hurt has been forgiven. However:

- A person may choose to forgive without the person who hurt them repenting.
- Punishment may reinforce what is right and wrong, which helps a person to change themselves.

For Christians, forgiveness and punishment can work together to ensure that justice is done. Justice does not mean getting revenge or being overly harsh to a person but instead restoring what is right. For Christians, what is right is that a person is in a positive relationship with God and other people, and so justice refers to the way that this is brought about.

This idea can be seen in the way parents respond to their children's wrongdoings. A parent may give a punishment to help their child to learn right from wrong, but will also forgive them for their wrongdoing.

Case study

In 1986, Jill Saward was brutally raped by two men from a gang who had broken into her family home. During the ordeal, her father and boyfriend were tied up and assaulted by the gang who also stole items from the house.

Jill was a devout Christian who believed not only in forgiveness but also in justice.

The prison sentences given to the men who raped her were short as the judge felt that her trauma had not been enough to justify a longer sentence. Jill decided to give up her right to anonymity to challenge the way in which rape was dealt with in the courts, to make it much fairer for other victims and to make sure that justice was properly done. She campaigned for this until she died in 2017.

Jill forgave the men who did this to her. She did this because she knew that not forgiving and remaining angry would destroy her even more. She forgave because she wanted to be worthy of God's forgiveness. She said 'I believe forgiveness gives you freedom. Freedom to move on without being held back by the past.'

Jill Saward demonstrated that forgiveness and punishment can work together to bring about justice

Knowledge recall

1. Define the following concepts: sin, forgiveness, punishment. (You can find these definitions on page 101.)
2. Identify the main teaching about forgiveness in Matthew 18:21–22.
3. Write down why Jesus taught that people should forgive others.

Evaluation practice

4. Give one reason for and one reason against the idea that Christians should always forgive those who have sinned against them.
5. Which reason do you think is the most convincing, and why?

Catholic teaching on capital punishment

Specification focus

Crime and punishment: The development of Catholic teaching on capital punishment with reference to St Augustine, Letter 134 (4) and 153 (3) to Macedonius and Pope John Paul II, *Evangelium Vitae* 56.

What is capital punishment?

Capital punishment refers to the death penalty. The death penalty has been used throughout history to punish the most serious crimes. It was abolished in the UK in 1969 but is still used in some other parts of the world.

Capital punishment is a controversial matter that people have very strong views about. The Catholic Church has given teaching about it over the years in order to help Catholics reconcile their belief in justice with mercy. This teaching has evolved over time with a changing understanding of the aims and purposes of **punishment** and the nature of the world in which we live. Most recently Pope Francis has said that it must not be used, which is a development from earlier teaching.

St Augustine in Letter 153 (3) to Macedonius

St Augustine lived between 354 and 430 AD. As well as being a theologian he was also a Catholic bishop with responsibilities towards the people in his pastoral care. Here we will look at extracts from two letters he wrote – one to Macedonius (who oversaw the legal administration of an area in Africa) and one to Apringius (who was a proconsul or governor). Both men were Catholic Christians in the Roman Empire, which used the death penalty. St Augustine recognised the legal arguments for the death penalty but wanted to emphasise the spiritual arguments against it.

‘…we pity the person, but hate the offence or **transgression**. In fact, the more we dislike the vice in question, the less do we want the offender to die without correcting his vices.’

Here St Augustine separates the person from the **sin**, echoing the popular saying 'hate the sin, love the sinner'. In other words, the criminal should be pitied and treated with compassion. He says that the worse the crime, the more we want to help that person to change before they die.

‘Therefore, if you take action against the crime in order to liberate the human being, you bind yourself to him in a fellowship of humanity rather than injustice.’

St Augustine argues that punishing the crime helps a person to move on from their crime and become a better person. This is a way to recognise the dignity of the person, rather than acting unjustly.

‘Moreover, there is no space to reform character except in this life. After that, each person will have whatever he has won for himself here. That is why we are forced to intercede for the guilty, out of love for the human race. For otherwise punishment will end this life for them, and once it is ended, they will not be able to bring their punishment to an end.’

- A person cannot change once they are dead and so needs to be given every chance to change while they are alive.
- Once a person dies, they will face the consequences of their actions on earth, which is why it is important to help them to change before they die. Augustine believed that otherwise they would face eternal punishment.

St Augustine in Letter 134 (4) to Apringius

‘Now if there were no other established method of restraining the hostility of the desperate, then perhaps extreme necessity would demand the killing of such people.’

Augustine says there are other ways of punishing the most dangerous criminals which should be used instead of the death penalty. The death penalty is an extreme measure and it is more merciful to use a different punishment.

Useful terms

transgression – an act against a rule or law

penal system – the justice system; the way in which crime is punished

> Even then, as far as we are concerned, if nothing milder could be done, we would prefer to have them set free than to have the sufferings of our brothers avenged by shedding their blood.

It is preferable to set a criminal free than to be responsible for their death. Here Augustine is showing how strongly he disagrees with the death penalty.

Pope St John Paul II was opposed to the death penalty in all but the most extreme circumstances

Pope St John Paul II, *Evangelium Vitae* 56

Pope St John Paul II wrote *Evangelium Vitae* in 1995 to articulate Catholic teaching on a wide range of matters of life and death. Like St Augustine, he taught that the death penalty should be avoided but believed there are times where it is the only option to keep society safe.

In *Evangelium Vitae* 56, Pope St John Paul II begins by writing about the purposes of punishment for criminals:

- To restore justice and order.
- To be an adequate punishment for the crime.
- To keep society safe.
- To give the criminal the chance to change their life for the better.

To achieve these purposes, Pope St John Paul II says that:

> ...punishment must be carefully evaluated and decided upon, and ought not go to the extreme of executing the offender except in cases of absolute necessity: in other words, when it would not be possible otherwise to defend society. Today however, as a result of steady improvements in the organization of the **penal system**, such cases are very rare, if not practically non-existent.

> In any event, the principle set forth in the new Catechism of the Catholic Church remains valid: "If bloodless means are sufficient to defend human lives against an aggressor and to protect public order and the safety of persons, public authority must limit itself to such means, because they better correspond to the concrete conditions of the common good and are more in conformity to the dignity of the human person."

Here he makes the point that a punishment should be carefully considered. He says the death penalty should not be used unless it is the only way in which society can be kept safe. In other words, it is absolutely the last resort for the most dangerous criminals.

Pope St John Paul II cites the teaching in the Catechism that not using the death penalty is preferable since it helps to maintain the dignity of the criminal. The punishments given should be 'bloodless' wherever possible.

Pope Francis developed Catholic teaching on the death penalty in 2015. Read about it on page 109.

Knowledge recall

1 Define the following concepts: evangelisation, forgiveness, punishment. (You can find these definitions on page 101.)
2 State the key points made by St Augustine about capital punishment.
3 Summarise the main message from Pope St John Paul II about capital punishment.

Evaluation practice

4 Give one argument for and one argument against the idea that Catholics should never accept capital punishment.
5 Which argument do you most agree with, and why?

Arguments for and against capital punishment

Specification focus

Crime and punishment: Arguments for and against capital punishment within Christianity, with reference to Genesis 9:6, Exodus 21:24 and Matthew 5:38 and non-religious views.

Arguments used by Christians in favour of the death penalty

Christians have differing views about capital punishment. Often these views come from reading the Bible and interpreting what its message means for society today. Christians who support the death penalty often refer to Genesis 9:6 and Exodus 21:24 from the Old Testament.

> 'Whoever sheds the blood of a human, by a human shall that person's blood be shed; for in his own image God made humankind.'
> *Genesis 9:6 (NRSV)*

This verse refers to the belief that human life is created *imago Dei*. Therefore taking a human life is destroying something sacred and made by God. It is a serious crime that deserves an equally serious **punishment**.

> '...eye for eye, tooth for tooth, hand for hand, foot for foot.'
> *Exodus 21:24 (NRSV)*

- This is the idea of retribution – whatever a person does to someone else is done to them. The examples here are of a body part being taken, so if a person takes out someone's eye in an assault then the punishment is to have their own eye removed.
- The thinking behind this logic was to make the punishment equal to but not greater than the crime committed (for example to prevent someone being put to death for injuring a person's foot).

Some Christians might also use these other arguments:

- One of the Ten Commandments is 'do not kill'. Often the death penalty is used as a punishment for murder and so some Christians would say that using the death penalty to punish murder emphasises the importance of this commandment.
- Pope St John Paul II taught that the death penalty could be used in the most extreme circumstances.

Arguments used by Christians against the death penalty

> 'You have heard that it was said, "An eye for an eye and a tooth for a tooth." But I say to you, Do not resist an evildoer. But if anyone strikes you on the right cheek, turn the other also.'
> *Matthew 5:38–39 (NRSV)*

- This passage is from the Sermon on the Mount, where Jesus interpreted the Law of Moses and set a higher moral standard without undermining the teaching of the Law.
- Jesus taught that people should not stoop to the lowest level of someone else's behaviour, but rather rise above it and use a peaceful resolution. Turning the other cheek means not retaliating.

Read more about the Sermon on the Mount on page 54.

Some Christians might also use these arguments:

- Jesus offered **forgiveness** and a fresh start to sinners, such as Zacchaeus (Luke 19:1–10). It is not possible to offer this to someone if they have been executed for their crime. The message of forgiveness is at the heart of Christian belief.

Useful term

human rights – the basic rights and freedoms that all people have, no matter who they are

- The Commandments teach 'Do not kill' and so taking a life is wrong, even as punishment.
- Pope Francis has recently updated Catholic teaching on capital punishment, saying that capital punishment goes 'against the inviolability of life and the dignity of the human person, which contradicts God's plan for man and society'. Pope Francis is referring to the belief in the sanctity of life and that humans are made *imago Dei*. This means that all forms of taking a life are wrong, since all life is created by God and blessed by him.

In 2015, Pope Francis taught that capital punishment was wrong as it denies a person's dignity

Non-religious arguments in favour of the death penalty

There are many 'non-religious' arguments about capital punishment too, which are used by religious and non-religious people alike. Such arguments that support the death penalty include the following:

- In the case of crimes such as murder, the most severe form of punishment is justified: if someone has murdered another person, they deserve to die because they have shown they do not respect life. The death penalty is also a strong deterrent, meaning it might stop someone from committing murder.
- It costs a lot of money to keep a person in prison for their whole life. This money should be used instead to help other people in society who need greater support, rather than it being spent on people who have committed serious crimes.
- The death penalty being given as punishment might force the criminal to reflect more carefully on their actions. It could help that person to realise the seriousness of their crime, change themselves and if possible make amends for their wrongdoing before they die.

Non-religious arguments against the death penalty

Non-religious people might argue against the death penalty for the following reasons:

- There is a risk that the wrong person is executed. There have been cases, such as the execution of George Kelly in 1950, where later it was found that another person had committed the crime and an innocent person had been put to death.
- A popular saying is that 'two wrongs don't make a right'. If the response to a wrong action is another wrong action then there is no good resolution.
- The wait a person faces before they are put to death is unacceptable – it is a type of emotional or psychological torture because the person is waiting for their death.
- All people deserve to have their lives and **human rights** protected (including people who have committed crime). The death penalty is seen as a human rights offence by many people who campaign to end it.

Death row: a time to reflect and seek forgiveness or psychological torture?

Knowledge recall

1 Define the following concepts: relativism, absolutism, Eucharist. (You can find these definitions on page 101.)

2 Write a summary statement for each of the following teachings: Genesis 9:6, Exodus 21:24 and Matthew 5:38. Indicate whether the teaching can be used in favour of or against capital punishment.

3 Create a table of arguments for and against capital punishment, including both religious and non-religious teachings.

Evaluation practice

4 Give two reasons why a Catholic Christian might be opposed to the death penalty.

5 Which reason do you think is the most convincing, and why?

Catholic beliefs about salvation

What is salvation?

When Catholics talk about **salvation** they are referring to their belief that Jesus saved humanity from the consequences of **sin**, which are a damaged relationship with God and the prospect of separating themselves from God's love and goodness for eternity.

Catholics believe that God's love meant that he was prepared to send his son Jesus, to live amongst humanity and show them how to live as God's people before dying on the cross to overcome sin.

Catholics believe that humans sin because they have free will and have a natural tendency to sin. Catholics believe that God gave the gift of free will to humanity, meaning that humans were made with the ability to choose their behaviour – both good and bad. Free will also means that humans can reject God and his efforts to save humanity completely.

Catholics believe that those who accept God's gift of salvation will be able to go to heaven after death. Catholics believe that Jesus' life, death, resurrection and ascension all helped to redeem, or free them from sin. Catholics hope that if they have kept faith in God and lived well, they will be saved through Jesus' sacrifice on the cross and be with God in heaven eternally.

The Catholic Church teaches that Jesus' death was a **sacrifice** made for the sake of human sin, so that humanity's relationship with God could be restored again. Jesus' death on the cross was the action that brought **redemption** from sin: it paid the price for sin and repaired the relationship with God.

However, the event of Jesus' death was not the only way in which Jesus offered salvation: he taught about how to gain salvation in his life too. In this sense, Jesus' death was the event that offered salvation and Catholics believe they can choose to accept this salvation by following Jesus' teachings and living a life inspired by him. In the parable of the sheep and the goats, the people who go to hell are the ones who did not show true faith in Jesus or help others, meaning they did not choose to accept salvation. These events at the end of Jesus' life are known together as the Paschal Mystery.

The Paschal Mystery

Good Friday: Christians believe this is the day when Jesus was crucified. They view his death as a sacrifice made for the whole of humanity that made salvation possible.

Easter Sunday: Christians celebrate Jesus' resurrection. The Gospels describe how in the morning, his tomb was empty and Jesus had risen. Witnesses spread the news of the resurrection to others. Christians see this as Jesus' power over sin and death (Jesus 'defeated' sin and death by rising back to life; his resurrection also defeated sin and death for everyone else too, making it possible for anyone to enter heaven).

Specification focus

Redemption: The meaning and significance of the term 'salvation' for Catholics and the role of grace and human freedom in redemption. How do Catholics believe the life, death, resurrection and ascension of Jesus saves them?

Catholics believe Jesus' death on the cross redeemed humans and saved them from sin

Useful terms

sacrifice – to give up something valuable for the sake of someone or something else

redemption – the belief that Jesus paid the 'ransom' to free humans from sin by dying on the cross

covenant – a promise or agreement between two parties. Covenants were made between God with Noah, Abraham and Moses

The ascension: Christians believe that Jesus went up to heaven forty days after his resurrection. It is a reminder of Jesus' divinity, since he rose to be on the right hand of God the Father. It also gives Catholics hope that they too can be in heaven with God if they accept salvation. Before ascending, in the Great Commission (Matthew 28:16–20) Jesus asked his apostles to continue his work and promised them the Holy Spirit, which they received ten days later at Pentecost (Acts 2:1–13). When the apostles and Mary received the Holy Spirit, they spread the Good News about Jesus so that others could be saved from sin too.

Salvation history

The Paschal Mystery is part of a bigger picture called 'salvation history', which refers to the times throughout history when God worked to save his people.

Christians believe that when God created the world he made it perfect, and that humans spoilt God's creation through sin. By sinning, humans damaged their relationship with each other and with God.

In the Old Testament, God responded to this through the **covenants**. For Catholics, the covenants are a reminder that God loves his people and wants to be in a relationship with them.

Read about the covenants with Abraham and Moses on pages 138–141.

The New Testament describes how God sent Jesus as the Incarnation to live among people and help them to become God's people again. Jesus is presented as the new and everlasting covenant (Luke 20:20). During Jesus' life on earth, he showed people how to love and serve others, the value of **forgiveness** and what the Law meant. He showed people how to live in order to achieve salvation.

Catholics view Jesus as a sacrificial lamb. It was usual in Jesus' time to make animal sacrifices to show love to God and to seek forgiveness. However, to seek forgiveness for the whole human race, rather than offering an animal, Jesus' life was given. Catholics remember this sacrifice in the **Eucharist** where they believe that the bread and wine become Jesus' body and blood.

Catholics therefore believe that Jesus' life, death, resurrection and ascension are vital for salvation and are part of God's plan to save his people. They believe that all of these events worked together to bring about a new relationship between God and humans.

Salvation and grace

Catholics believe that God's actions to save humanity were a result of his love. This love is often called 'grace'. Just as parents have unconditional love for their children, no matter what their behaviour, Catholics believe that God loves his children (humans) even though they sin and turn against him. This means he continues to freely choose to love them and he offered them the chance to be saved by sacrificing his only son, Jesus. Grace is therefore a very important concept when talking about salvation since it emphasises both God's love and the ends to which God was prepared to go for his creation.

Catholics believe that God's grace can also be experienced through the sacraments – St Augustine described them as the 'outward signs of an invisible grace', meaning they are the ways in which Catholics can receive God's complete love through celebrations such as Baptism or the Eucharist. Catholics believe that by accepting and embracing God's grace, they can be saved.

Knowledge recall

1 Define the following concepts: sin, salvation, evangelisation. (You can find these definitions on page 101.)
2 Write down what happened on Good Friday, Easter Sunday and the Ascension and how they are connected to salvation.
3 Why do Catholics believe that God sacrificed Jesus?

Evaluation practice

4 Give one argument for and one argument against the idea that Jesus' death and resurrection were more important than his life on earth.
5 Which argument do you most agree with, and why?

Catholic beliefs about hell

Specification focus

Redemption: The compatibility of a belief in Hell and a belief in the unconditional love of God and the universal nature of God's mercy.

Free will and the problem of hell

Catholicism teaches that:

- God is omnibenevolent (all loving).
- God's love is unconditional (humans do not have to do anything to receive it).
- God is merciful (he has limitless compassion and **forgiveness** which is universal – it is offered to all).

Many people would conclude that if God has all of these qualities then it is hard to believe that hell exists, or that God would allow for people to go to hell. Mainstream Christian teaching is that hell is total separation from God for eternity. In the parable of the rich man and Lazarus (Luke 16:19–31), the rich man goes to hell because of his selfishness and then realises he is stuck there and cannot move to heaven.

Hell is traditionally depicted as a place of fire and torment, but today is more commonly viewed as total separation from God

There are different ways to answer this dilemma. Many Catholics would respond based on the idea of free will. Humans spend their lives making free choices. When they make choices that are based on love either for others or for God, they become closer to God. When a person makes a selfish, hateful or arrogant choice either in terms of how they treat others or how they respond to God, they remove themselves from God.

When a person dies, they have already made the choices that have either taken them closer to God (heaven) or removed them from God (hell). By this logic, a person is not sent to hell by God: rather they take themselves to hell through their own choices.

> 'The affirmations of Sacred Scripture and the teachings of the Church on the subject of hell are a call to **the responsibility incumbent upon man to make use of his freedom in view of his eternal destiny**. They are at the same time an **urgent call to conversion**: "Enter by the narrow gate; for the gate is wide and the way is easy, that leads to destruction, and those who enter by it are many. For the gate is narrow and the way is hard, that leads to life, and those who find it are few."'
> *CCC 1036*

Read more about the how people's choices have an impact on life after death on pages 76–77.

The Catechism reminds Catholics that humans should use their free will well during life on earth, while thinking about the impact of their behaviour on their life after death. The Church reminds Catholics that if they make mistakes then they can 'convert' themselves – they can give themselves to God and live their lives for him even if they have previously acted against him. Catholics believe that God's mercy is endless and that he would give forgiveness and new life to the person who is sincerely sorry and determined to change.

In Matthew 7:13–14, Jesus teaches that it is not easy to follow the road to **salvation**. He describes the narrow and the wide gate. The wide gate is the route to hell, which is easy to follow. However, the narrow gate – the route to heaven –

is harder to follow. It requires a person to be selfless and loving, both to God and their neighbour.

Catholic teaching is that hell is not a place. Rather it is the absence of all that is good (not unlike Augustine's idea that **sin** is a privation or absence of good). Heaven is the eternal union with God and hell is the absence of that eternal union. A person who has used their free will to choose to reject God's love and salvation can therefore be said to be in hell because they are completely separate from God.

When asked in 2015 by a girl scout why hell exists, Pope Francis explained that hell is 'telling God, "You take care of yourself because I'll take care of myself." They don't send you to hell, you go there because you choose to be there. Hell is wanting to be distant from God because I do not want God's love. This is hell.'

For Catholics there has to be an alternative to heaven (the absence of heaven) in order for humans to be able to make free choices. Many Catholics would say that giving humans free will is the most loving thing that God could do.

Catholics believe that they have to live a good life, which is often more challenging, in order to be rewarded in heaven

Salvation and hell

The philosopher John Hick believed that God's love and mercy means that all will be saved. This idea is known as universal salvation. Hick believed that after death a person continues to move towards God, no matter their starting point (i.e. whether they were a good person or a sinful person), and that ultimately all are united with God. John Hick is not alone in this view – throughout history there have been others who have said that they believe God will allow all people (including those who have not repented for serious sin) to receive salvation, and this is a view held by some liberal Christians today.

However, there are many Christians who would challenge this belief, because:

- It undermines the saving work of Jesus if ultimately all people can be saved anyway.
- It undermines the idea of God's justice. If all people go to heaven and receive salvation, that means people who have committed the worst crimes will enjoy the same reward as those who have lived the most loving, charitable and compassionate lives.

The Catholic Church teaches that a person needs to respond to God's offer of salvation through having faith in Jesus and living according to his teachings in order to be saved from hell.

Knowledge recall

1 Define the following concepts: forgiveness, absolutism, sin. (You can find these definitions on page 101.)
2 Give reasons to support the belief that a person takes themselves to hell.
3 Identify the problems with the belief that all people will receive salvation.

Evaluation practice

4 Give one argument for and one argument against the belief that an all-loving God would allow some people to go to hell.
5 Which argument do you most agree with, and why?

The nature of the Church

Specification focus

Church: The nature of the Church as one, holy, catholic and apostolic and Mary as a model of the Church.

What is the Church?

There are two main meanings of the word 'Church':

- A church is a building where Christians gather to worship.
- The Church (with a capital C) is the worldwide community of believers.

Over time, people have tried to describe the character of the Church and how it is different to other institutions. When Catholics say the Nicene Creed, they profess their faith that the Catholic Church is 'one, holy, catholic and apostolic'. These are known as the four marks of the Church and are considered to be its defining features.

The Church is one

- The description of the Church as 'one' means that the Church comes from one source: God.
- The community of the Church therefore comes from one starting point.
- Catholics believe that Jesus came to earth for all people, not just some, and so 'one' also refers to the idea that all people are equally able to share in **salvation**.
- Catholics would say that all members of the Church are united in one community since they share the same prayers, traditions and beliefs. If a person were to go to Mass in a foreign country, they would recognise that it is the same as their experience at home (although in a different language!).
- Although there is diversity in the Church community, different people, cultures and traditions are all part of the one Church and so should be celebrated.

The Church is holy

- Catholics believe that God is holy and because he is God incarnate, Jesus too was holy. The Church is holy because it is Christ's body and he is its head.
- The Church was formed by his followers who were inspired by his holiness.
- The Church is holy since it is the community that is centred on Jesus and comes from Jesus. Catholics believe that all people are called to holiness.
- Catholic teaching says that when a person is baptised and enters the community of the Church for the first time, they are freed of sin and become members of Christ's body.
- Just because the Church is described as holy, it does not mean that all members of the Church are perfect: people in the Church are committed to holiness but sometimes make mistakes. They ask God for **forgiveness** so they can become better people. One of the prayers at Mass asks 'Lord, look not on our **sins**, but on the faith of your Church.'

Catholics believe that the Church is apostolic since Jesus established the apostles as the first leaders of the Church

The Church is catholic

- Here the word 'catholic' (with a small 'c') means 'worldwide' or 'universal'. The Catholic Church is open to all people, in all parts of the world.
- Part of the way in which Catholics understand this word is to recognise that they have a special role to play in making the Church catholic, since they have the responsibility to spread the Good News to all people around the world.

The Church is apostolic

- The word 'apostle' refers to someone who is a messenger, and the twelve apostles were Jesus' closest followers who saw and heard everything he did and said. Out of these apostles Jesus gave special authority to St Peter, calling him the 'rock' on which Jesus will build his Church (Matthew 16:18).
- Catholics believe that St Peter was the first Pope and that all subsequent popes are continuing in St Peter's role. Catholics also believe that the bishops today are continuing the work of the other apostles. This means that the leaders of the Church have the authority of the apostles and so the Church continues to take the Good News about Jesus to others around the world.

Mary as a model of the Church

The apostles established the early Church with Mary, Jesus' mother. The Bible describes how on the Day of Pentecost – which is considered to be the birthday of the Church – Mary was with the apostles as they received the Holy Spirit, enabling them to take the Good News to other people. Mary is considered to be a model of the Church because she embodied faith, charity and she put Christ at the centre of her life. The Church seeks to do these three things, and Catholics aspire to be like Mary.

Mary is also special to Catholics because they believe:

- She was chosen before her birth to be the Mother of God. She is vital in God's plan for salvation.
- Mary can intercede or help with their prayers.
- Jesus loved Mary and listened to her. Catholics believe she can help bring them to her son, Jesus.

Catholics show special devotion to Mary in some of their prayers, such as the Hail Mary. There are usually statues of Mary in Catholic church buildings, and the month of May is dedicated to Mary and October is dedicated to the Holy Rosary, so the Rosary is said more regularly during these months. Catholics also go on pilgrimage to places associated with appearances of Mary, such as Lourdes or Walsingham.

In her life Mary showed many qualities that Catholics try to emulate:

- When Mary was told by the Angel Gabriel that she would become the mother of Jesus, she accepted this willingly and with joy, despite knowing that society might treat her harshly. She nurtured Jesus as he grew up, was a source of encouragement and stayed by him as he went to his death.
- Mary showed charity in her life as she cared selflessly for the needs of others. For example, shortly after becoming pregnant with Jesus, she travelled to visit Elizabeth who was pregnant with John the Baptist. Her journey would have been long and difficult, particularly given that she was pregnant, yet she cared enough for Elizabeth to want to spend time with her.
- She remained associated with Jesus' apostles despite the fact this could have been dangerous.

Catholics hope to have the same level of faith in God. Sometimes it is hard to have faith, particularly when experiencing challenges and suffering, but Catholics believe that Mary shows them how to remain strong in their faith by placing trust in God.

Catholics are inspired by Mary's faith and charity

Read about the Rosary and its connection to Mary on page 64.

Knowledge recall

1 Define the following concepts: punishment, Eucharist, sin. (You can find these definitions on page 101.)
2 Write down a sentence to define each of the four marks of the Church (one, holy, catholic and apostolic).
3 Identify three ways in which Mary is a model of faith.

Evaluation practice

4 Give two reasons why Catholics would say that the Church should be like Mary.
5 Which reason do you most agree with, and why?

The Church and salvation

The Church as the Body of Christ

In his first letter to the Corinthians, St Paul spoke of the Church as the Body of Christ. He believed that the Church is made up of many different parts which are connected to one another and depend on each other, just like how a body works. Jesus is the head of the body. The analogy of the Church as the Body of Christ also communicates the following ideas:

- The Church is living, just as a body is living. Jesus is the head of the living body. Therefore, the Church is the way in which Jesus is alive in the world today. St Teresa of Avila taught that Christ has no hands, eyes and feet now except those of his followers, so the Church needs to act as Jesus did on earth.
- The **Eucharist** is also called the 'Body of Christ' and so this reminds Catholics that through receiving the Eucharist, their bonds with Jesus and the community are made stronger.
- **Salvation** comes from the Body of Christ, both in the Eucharist and through being part of the community of the Church: Catholics believe that the liturgy and the teaching of the Church can help them to achieve salvation. Catholics believe salvation was made possible through Jesus' sacrifice and they believe that Jesus is the head of the Body of Christ, meaning that salvation comes from him and flows through the whole body.
- The Church is a community made up of different parts, just as the body is made up of separate parts. Each part of the body/community has a distinct role to play, but each part also depends on the others so that the whole can function together.

The Church as the People of God

The belief that the Church is the 'People of God' identifies the Church as a community of people who are bound together by their love of God, which is seen in how they live according to his will. Anyone can join the People of God. For Catholics, becoming a member of the People of God happens through faith in Jesus and through Baptism, when a person accepts the faith of the Church for themselves.

The People of God are called to build **God's Kingdom** on earth. This entails continuing the work of Jesus – loving God and others, forgiving others, working for justice and living a life of service.

Salvation outside the Church

In *Letter LXXII*, Cyprian of Carthage (a bishop in the early Church) expressed the belief that 'Outside of the Church there is no salvation.' This means that the only way to be saved from **sin** is to be a member of the Church.

The Catechism responded to this by saying: 'Re-formulated positively, it means that all salvation comes from Christ the Head through the Church which is his Body' (CCC 846). The Catechism goes on to say that:

- Jesus is the way to salvation. To be a member of the Church is to be a member of Jesus' body.
- The Church is necessary for salvation.

Specification focus

Church: The meanings and significance of different understandings of the Church as the 'Body of Christ' and 'the people of God' and the meaning of the claim 'outside the Church there is no salvation' with reference to the Catechism of the Catholic Church 846–848.

St Paul used the analogy of a body to refer to the unity of the Church community

Useful term

God's Kingdom – when all people live as God calls them to, according to his will

- A person enters into the community of the Church through faith and Baptism.
- A person who refuses to enter or remain in the Church, despite knowing that it was founded by God through Jesus, cannot be saved.
- However, there are some people who do not know about Jesus or the Church. If they seek God and try to act as their conscience teaches them, they may also be saved.
- God can lead people who have not yet heard the Gospel to faith that is pleasing to him. Humans will not be able to understand how God does this.
- The Church has a duty to evangelise people, meaning that the Church should take the message of Jesus to people who have not yet heard it.

However, the Catholic Church also teaches that religious freedom is essential to allow for human dignity. This means that people must be free to seek and express any faith. The Church is opposed to any form of discrimination, including on the basis of religion.

> 'Every form of social or cultural discrimination in fundamental personal rights on the grounds of sex, race, colour, social conditions, language, or religion must be curbed and eradicated as incompatible with God's design.'
> *CCC 1935*

Within Christianity, there are different attitudes about whether people outside the Church can be saved or not. The three different attitudes are known as exclusivism, inclusivism and pluralism.

Exclusivists say that the message of Christianity is essential to salvation. Anyone who does not accept Jesus as the Son of God and their saviour cannot come to God the Father. They might support this view with the belief that Jesus said he was the only way to God.

> 'Jesus said to him, "I am the way, and the truth, and the life. No one comes to the Father except through me."'
> *John 14:6 (NRSV)*

However, some might argue that God's infinite love means that he would give humanity the chance to know him in many ways, not just through Jesus, so that more can be saved.

Inclusivists also believe Jesus is the key to salvation, and that his life, death and resurrection made salvation possible. However, they believe too that it is possible for people who are not members of the Church to be saved. This might be because they believe that all faiths contain truth but the full truth is in Christianity. The German theologian Karl Rahner described non-Christians who lived lives that were full of Christian values as 'anonymous Christians'.

Pluralists believe that all faiths lead to God. This means there are different routes to salvation found in different religions, so a person does not have to belong to the Christian Church to be saved. They might use Jesus' words 'In my Father's house there are many dwelling places' (John 14:2) to suggest that God gives salvation to all. However, some might argue that a Christian who believes this downplays the importance of Jesus' life, death and resurrection, reducing the importance of Jesus himself for salvation.

Knowledge recall

1. Define the following concepts: relativism, sin, salvation. (You can find these definitions on page 101.)
2. Identify what it means to say the Church is the 'Body of Christ'.
3. Outline the belief that the Church is the 'People of God'.

Evaluation practice

4. Give one reason why someone would agree and another reason why someone would disagree with the belief that 'outside of the Church there is no salvation'.
5. Which reason do you most agree with, and why?

Features of a church building

Specification focus

Buildings: How the sacred objects within a Church represent Catholic beliefs about salvation with particular reference to the altar and the font; how the orientation of Catholic churches and their architectural features facilitate Catholic worship and reflection on the mystery of salvation.

The orientation and architecture of Catholic churches

Catholic church buildings have many distinct features that reflect the belief in **salvation**.

- Traditional churches are often cruciform (cross-shaped), reflecting the importance of Jesus' death on the cross and how it offered salvation to all.
- Some newer churches may be circular to encourage a greater sense of community. It means that the congregation are gathered around the altar, to emphasise the unity of the people who share in the **Eucharist**.
- Churches might have stained glass windows, which were traditionally used to teach those who could not read about Bible stories or the saints' lives. Today they can inspire people to live in a way worthy of salvation.
- Church towers, steeples and tall ceilings give the sense that churches are pointed to the heavens, helping people who worship in them to feel connected to God.
- Traditionally churches face east, which is both the direction from which the sun rises (an image of Jesus' resurrection) and the direction of the Holy Land where Jesus lived, died and rose again. In Matthew 24:27 it is suggested that the Second Coming of Jesus will be from the east. The events of Jesus' life, death, resurrection and the belief in the Second Coming are all associated with salvation, since Catholics believe that Jesus' life and sacrifice secured salvation, and that the Second Coming is when all people will be judged on their response to Jesus' offer of salvation.

Useful terms

Communion – another term for the Eucharist; the body and blood of Jesus

host – a disc of unleavened bread used in Holy Communion

Blessed Sacrament – the consecrated host, which Catholics believe is Jesus' body. It can also refer to the consecrated wine, which Catholics believe is Jesus' blood.

Sacred objects in a church

There are a number of objects inside a church which demonstrate Catholic beliefs about salvation.

① The **altar** is a table that is made completely or partially of stone, because in ancient times stone altars were used for animal sacrifices. Traditionally, the altar is on the sanctuary at the front of the church building. In a church, the altar shows the belief that Jesus' death was a sacrifice made for human **sin** and to secure salvation. It is where the priest consecrates the bread and wine during the Liturgy of the Eucharist, using Jesus' words from the Last Supper. Catholics believe this is when the bread and wine become Jesus' body and blood which are received in **Communion**. Catholics believe that the Eucharist is 'food for eternal life': it is spiritual food which will help them to become closer to God.

② The **tabernacle** is a locked, ornate cupboard, usually found on the wall near the altar. If there are any consecrated **hosts** after Mass, they are locked into the tabernacle to be used in another Mass, or for Communion for the sick and housebound. A lamp is lit near to it when the **Blessed Sacrament** is inside the tabernacle. Catholics show respect to this by genuflecting (kneeling briefly on one knee) in front of it. For Catholics, it is very important to have Jesus present in the Church in the Blessed Sacrament as it can help them to feel closer to him.

③ A **crucifix** is also situated behind the altar. This is a cross with a figure of Jesus on it. It helps Catholics to remember Jesus' suffering and death, which they believe was a sacrificial act to bring salvation. Another reminder of Jesus' suffering and death are the Stations of the Cross, which are 14 images that tell the story of Jesus' journey to the cross. These are present all year, but particularly used during Lent as a focus for prayer.

④ There will be a **lectern** at the front of the church. This is a stand to hold the lectionary, which is a book containing the Bible readings heard during the Liturgy of the Word, read by a reader and a priest or bishop. Catholics believe the Bible readings are the Word of God and contain the teachings that can help a person to live as God wants. By hearing God's Word and acting on it, Catholics believe they can live as God's holy people, which will lead them to salvation.

⑤ The **baptismal font** is a stone or wooden basin that contains the holy water to be used at Baptism. Catholics believe that sin is washed away in Baptism. Sin forms a barrier between God and humanity and so without Baptism, that distance will remain. Catholics see a connection between Baptism and Jesus' death and resurrection, believing that in Baptism they are born to a new life in Jesus. As a result, Catholics believe that being baptised can help them to receive salvation. At the entrances to churches there are often small bowls of holy water called stoops. A Catholic who comes into the building blesses themselves with holy water as a reminder of their Baptism.

There might be small rooms called confessionals in the church. These are used for the sacrament of reconciliation, where the priest offers God's **forgiveness** to a person. This sacrament helps to remove the barrier formed by sin and to restore the bond between the person and God, bringing them closer to salvation.

Statues of the saints and Mary are often found in Catholic churches as a focal point for prayer. Catholics are inspired by the lives of the saints and Mary, and aspire to live more like them because they showed great faith and served God. Catholics hope that by living a life of faith and service, they can be worthy of salvation.

Read more about the sacraments on page 120.

Knowledge recall

1 Define the following concepts: sin, salvation, absolutism. (You can find these definitions on page 101.)

2 Describe two ways that the architecture of a church reflects beliefs about salvation.

3 For each of the following sacred objects, write down how the object is connected to salvation: altar, tabernacle, crucifix, lectern, baptismal font, confessional, statues of saints and Mary.

Evaluation practice

4 Give one argument for and one argument against the idea that the sacred objects in a church building are effective symbols of salvation.

5 Which argument do you most agree with, and why?

The sacraments

The sacramental nature of reality

Catholics believe that through the sacraments they are able to receive God's **grace**. They believe the sacraments were instituted (started) by Jesus and were given to the Church to bless and strengthen the faith of God's people.

Sacraments are often described as 'outward signs of an inward grace'. This means that signs and symbols, which are visible (outward), are used to communicate about the invisible (inward) way in which God's grace is given to humans.

The Catholic Church teaches that the whole of reality is sacramental because the whole of creation is infused with God's presence and love. Just as Jesus is the sacrament (or sign) of God's presence on earth, so the whole of reality can be seen as a sacrament of God's love.

The seven sacraments

The Catholic Church recognises seven sacraments, which can be grouped into sacraments of initiation, healing and vocation.

Sacraments of initiation are Baptism, Confirmation and **Eucharist**. Through these a person becomes a full member of the Church community.

Sacrament	Meaning and effect	Connection to salvation
Baptism	Entering into Christ's family. Water and white garments symbolise the washing away of Original Sin and new life in Jesus. Baptismal promises show signs of faith in God. Anointing with the Oil of Chrism represents being called into the universal priesthood, and the Oil of Catechumens gives strength in the struggle against evil.	**Sin** is washed away, bringing the baby or person closer to God. They begin a new life as a disciple of Jesus and a member of his Church.
Confirmation	Being strengthened by the Holy Spirit. The laying on of hands symbolises the bishop giving the gifts of the Holy Spirit to the person being confirmed. This person renews their baptismal promises and is again anointed with chrism to signify that they will share their faith in Jesus with others.	The person is strengthened to live out their faith, sharing the Good News of Jesus with others. This will help others to grow closer to God and receive salvation. The Holy Spirit also enables the person to serve God and increase in holiness.
Eucharist	Sharing in Jesus' sacrifice. Bread and wine are consecrated by the priest using the words that Jesus said at the Last Supper. Catholics believe that through **transubstantiation**, the bread and wine become the body and blood of Jesus.	The Eucharist is spiritual food which sustains Catholics in their faith. Catholics believe that Jesus died as a sacrifice and by remembering this and sharing in the Eucharist, they hope to be worthy of **salvation**.

The sacraments of healing are Reconciliation and the Anointing of the Sick, which grant God's **forgiveness** and peace.

Specification focus

Sacraments: The Catholic belief in the sacramental nature of the whole of reality and its connection to the seven sacraments: their names, meanings and effects; the meaning and significance of sacraments for a Catholic understanding of salvation, the meaning and significance of the Eucharist as 'the source and summit' of Christian life and the role it plays in Catholic understanding of salvation.

Read more about grace on page 111.

Useful terms

grace – the freely given love of God
transubstantiation – the belief that through the power of the Holy Spirit, bread and wine become the body and blood of Jesus
absolution – the assurance that God has forgiven the person's sins after their confession

Sacrament	Meaning and effect	Connection to salvation
Reconciliation	Confessing and being forgiven for sins. A person reflects on when they have sinned. The priest hears the confession *in persona Christi*, meaning that the **absolution** granted is Christ's forgiveness.	The person is granted forgiveness for their sins. Forgiveness is essential in order to receive salvation.
Anointing of the Sick	Healing and peace when in poor health. The priest will hear a confession and give Holy Communion if this is possible. He will anoint the person with the Oil of the Sick to strengthen them, and perform the laying on of hands to confer God's blessing on them.	The person is granted forgiveness. Their suffering is united with Jesus' suffering, which Catholics believe he bore to bring salvation.

The sacraments of vocation are Matrimony and Holy Orders, which express God's call to serve him.

Sacrament	Meaning and effect	Connection to salvation
Matrimony (marriage)	Joining a couple as one, to serve one another and others. Vows are made to one another and wedding rings are blessed and exchanged.	The couple's love for each other reflects the love that Christ has for the Church. This love strengthens them to serve one another and others to bring them closer to God and salvation.
Holy Orders	Becoming a deacon, priest or bishop in order to bring others closer to God. The man is anointed with chrism to show that he has been called to a life of service. The laying on of hands shows that he is given authority to minister to others.	Deacons, priests and bishops can help people to form a deeper relationship with God, such as through the sacraments, which will help them to achieve salvation.

The Eucharist

For Catholics, the Eucharist (or Holy Communion) is the ultimate expression of thanksgiving to God. It is celebrated during every Mass. Mass is important because it is when Catholics gather to pray together, hear God's Word from the Bible and celebrate the Eucharist. These are all important ways for Catholics to strengthen their faith and to increase in holiness. It is for this reason that the Catholic Church says it is an obligation to attend Mass on Sundays and particular holy days.

The Eucharist is described as the 'source and summit' of Christian life. It is seen to be the beginning and end of everything – it reminds Catholics of the belief that salvation starts with God (source) and brings them to God (summit). The Eucharist is a source of God's love, hope and strength which connects Catholics to God, who is love, hope and strength.

The Eucharist is important for Catholics since through it:

- The Church is united, spiritually nourished and strengthened.
- The sacrifice of Jesus is remembered and made real again for those who celebrate. The priest speaks Jesus' words from the Last Supper when he spoke of his body being broken and his blood being poured out. He instructed the disciples to 'Do this in memory of me'. (Luke 22:19–20).
- Jesus is really present. Catholics believe that in Mass the bread and wine become Jesus' body and blood and that through this sacrament, Jesus continues to be with his Church always, as he promised (Matthew 28:30).

For Catholics, the Eucharist is the 'source and summit' of Christian faith

'Then he took a loaf of bread, and when he had given thanks, he broke it and gave it to them, saying, "This is my body, which is given for you. Do this in remembrance of me." And he did the same with the cup after supper, saying, "This cup that is poured out for you is the new covenant in my blood."'
Luke 22:19–20 (NRSV)

Knowledge recall

1 Define the following concepts: Eucharist, salvation, evangelisation. (You can find these definitions on page 101.)
2 What does it mean to say that the sacraments are 'outward signs of an inward grace'?
3 For each sacrament, identify the main effect of the sacrament and how it brings salvation.

Evaluation practice

4 Give two reasons why the Eucharist is important to Catholics.
5 Which reason do you think is the strongest, and why?

Evangelisation

What is evangelisation?

> ❛Go therefore and make disciples of all nations, baptizing them in the name of the Father and of the Son and of the Holy Spirit, and teaching them to obey everything that I have commanded you.❜
> *Matthew 28:19–20 (NRSV)*

Catholics believe that the **Good News** of Jesus' life, teachings, death and resurrection need to be shared with others, so they can be given the chance to believe in it too. This is **evangelisation**.

Before he ascended to heaven, Jesus gave his disciples the mission of going out into the world, to bring people to faith in him and to baptise them. This mission is still the mission of all people in the Church community. The earliest Christians often risked their lives by taking the Good News to others and, over time, the focus moved to bringing the Good News to people and places which had not yet heard the Christian message. Evangelisation today is both focused on sharing the Good News with those who have never heard it, and reintroducing it to communities which have become more secular.

Evangelii Gaudium

In 2013 Pope Francis wrote *Evangelii Gaudium*, which means 'The Joy of the Gospel'. Pope Francis wrote this document to encourage Catholics to become involved in evangelisation, recognising that everyone in the Church community can take the Good News to others. He does not see the Good News as something that should only belong to select groups. He wants the Church to move from being in a 'comfort zone' to engaging with the world in the way that Jesus did – by showing love for all people and challenging the status quo when it allows people to suffer. In *Evangelii Gaudium*, the message of evangelisation is connected with the work that Catholics are called to do to bring about greater social equality and promote solidarity with those who suffer.

Pope Francis makes the following points:

- The first role of evangelisation is to teach people who do not know Jesus about his Good News. This is called missionary work, which is the first and foremost task of the Church and also the greatest challenge.
- The first people to hear the message of the Good News should be 'the poor and the sick, those who are usually despised and overlooked' (*Evangelii Gaudium* 48).
- The Church needs to engage with all people even though this might be hard. But that hardship is preferable to ignoring the needs of the poor.
- God chose for Jesus to be born into a poor family and this shows his love for the poor. Despite Mary's poverty, her faith transformed human history. Therefore, the Church should be poor and be for the poor.

Specification focus

Mission and Evangelisation: Catholic teaching on the imperative to evangelise and the forms this should take, with reference to Pope Francis' *Evangelii Gaudium* 15, 48–49, 197–198, 264–265; how Catholic beliefs about the relationship between faith and salvation influence attitudes to mission and evangelisation locally, nationally and globally.

Pope Francis uses Twitter to reach out to the whole world

> ❛I prefer a Church which is bruised, hurting and dirty because it has been out on the streets.❜
> *Evangelii Gaudium 49*

Useful terms

Good News – the Christian teaching about salvation brought about by Jesus

interfaith dialogue – engagement between those of different faiths and no faith to bring about positive outcomes such as respect, tolerance and social harmony

- Catholics evangelise because they love Jesus and want others to love Jesus too. Sharing faith in Jesus is a precious gift.
- The Good News of Jesus is so profound that Catholics should share it with others even if they do not realise they need to hear it. Pope Francis writes 'We have a treasure of life and love which cannot deceive, and a message which cannot mislead or disappoint' (*Evangelii Gaudium* 265).

Local, national and global evangelisation

Catholics believe **salvation** is so important that they should share their faith in salvation with others. This means that in order to help others achieve salvation, Catholics have a duty to help others to find faith and ultimately be saved from **sin**. Evangelisation can take many different forms.

Local

The parish community shares God's love through worship and the sacraments. Catholics gather together for Mass, which strengthens their faith and the bonds of the community. Non-Catholics are welcome to attend Mass too, where they can learn more about the faith. Parish churches work to reach out to the whole community, to help and support people such as through charitable work or social activities. Within parishes, a person can explore their faith and learn more about Catholicism.

National

The Bishops' Conference in England and Wales helps the Catholic Church to share its faith with others, for example through providing educational resources or promoting **interfaith dialogue**. Every year the Catholic Church celebrates 'Home Mission Sunday', which aims to inspire Catholics to share their faith with others. In 2020, the Bishops' Conference launched 'The God Who Speaks' initiative to encourage a focus on scripture. This is supported by events and resources to encourage all people to find out more about the teachings in the Bible.

Global

The Catholic Church has the mission of bringing the Gospel to all parts of the world. Pope Francis is well known around the world not only for his inspirational teaching, but also for his use of Twitter to share the Gospel message.

There are global initiatives such as World Youth Day, which was first established by Pope St John Paul II in 1985 with the aim of gathering young people together to share and express their faith. Hundreds of thousands of young people travel from around the world for this event. The last was in 2019 in Panama and the next is 2023 in Lisbon.

Catholic charities such as CAFOD work globally to help the poor through practical projects, such as providing aid after a natural disaster or tools and education to help a farming community become more self-sufficient. The charity Missio works with missionaries around the world to help strengthen the Church in a range of ways, such as through working with the poor or providing resources to a Church community.

Read more about Catholic beliefs about salvation on page 110.

Missio works to strengthen the Church around the world

Knowledge recall

1. Define the following concepts: evangelisation, sin, salvation. (You can find these definitions on page 101.)
2. Write down the key points of *Evangelii Gaudium*.
3. Give an example each for how the Church evangelises on a local, national and global level.

Evaluation practice

4. Give two reasons why Catholics feel they have a duty to evangelise others.
5. Which reason do you think is most convincing, and why?

Evangelising in Britain

The benefits and challenges of evangelising in Britain

Britain is a Christian country with a long Christian heritage. It is also a multi-faith society, meaning that people of many religious faiths or none live side by side. The religious identity of British society is changing all the time. The human right of religious freedom – meaning that people are allowed to express their faith (or lack of it) freely – is protected in Britain. This means that Catholics live in society with people who have different faiths and traditions, as well as those who do not believe in God at all. This will have an impact on **evangelisation**.

Benefits	Challenges
• Opportunities to get to know people of other faiths can help to break down prejudices and strengthen communities. • Interfaith dialogue is an important way of showing respect for other people's faiths, but also helps a person to reflect more deeply on their own faith. • Some Christians would see that the diverse mix of faiths and no faith in Britain provides an opportunity for evangelisation.	• Evangelisation could make faith communities wary of each other if they feel the suggestion is that their faith is 'inferior'. • While Christianity is still the majority religion, Church attendance is decreasing and so evangelisation is harder to achieve with fewer members and with many people choosing to turn away from Christianity.

The 2001 and 2011 censuses

There is a census every ten years in Britain. This is a survey that gathers information about different aspects of British society. One area that it explores is religious identity. The most notable observation from the 2011 census in contrast with the 2001 census is the decrease in people describing themselves as Christian, and the growth of non-Christian religions and people of no faith.

> ❛The decade 2001 to 2011 saw a fall in the number of people identifying as Christian, and an increase in those identifying with minority religious groups and those reporting no religion.❜
> *Office for National Statistics*

Here are some key changes between the two censuses:

2001 census	2011 census
41m Christians	33.2m Christians
8.5m no religion	14.1m no religion

UK laws, festivals and traditions

The Christian heritage of Britain spans back almost 2000 years. While many changes have happened over that time, Britain's Christian heritage is still evident today. The monarch is the Supreme Governor of the Church of England, which is

Specification focus

Mission and Evangelisation: Evangelising in Britain; benefits and challenges. Results of the 2011 census compared to the 2001 census, show an increase in diverse religious and non-religious beliefs and practices (including those of Christianity; Buddhism; Hinduism; Islam; Judaism; Sikhism; Humanism and Atheism), whilst also showing that over half of those who responded considered themselves Christian; UK laws, festivals and traditions are rooted in the Christian tradition. However, festivals, beliefs and cultures of other religious and non-religious traditions are also recognised and celebrated.

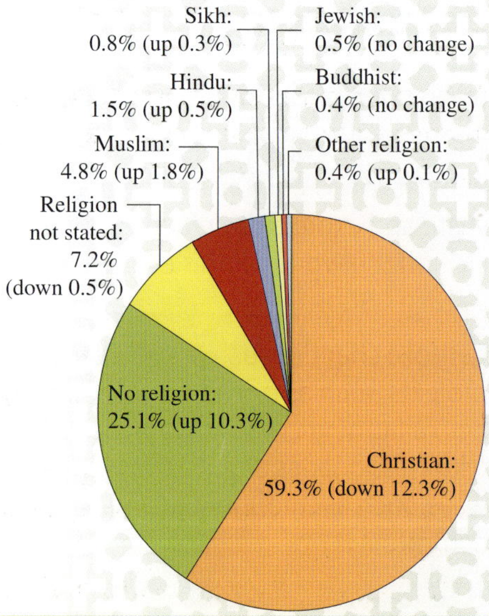

Religious make-up of Britain in 2011

the official Church of the country. The Church of England was formed following the Reformation, which was the break between the Catholic and Protestant Churches in the sixteenth century.

The Christian identity of Britain can also be seen in the following ways:

Laws	• In the House of Lords, there are two groups of members: the Lords Temporal are secular (non-religious) members and the Lords Spiritual are the twenty-six Church of England bishops. The House of Lords debates and is involved in passing laws alongside the House of Commons. This means that Christian leaders help to make decisions about British law. • Many laws in Britain show Christian heritage by being close to the Ten Commandments, such as the commandment 'Do not steal'.
Festivals	• Despite fewer people calling themselves Christian, the main festivals of Christmas and Easter are still key celebrations in British culture. Holiday leave from schools and colleges as well as in many jobs is focused on these points in the year. • For some Christians, these two celebrations are the only two times they will attend a church service each year. • Many non-Christians today celebrate Shrove Tuesday and Halloween, both of which have Christian origins.
Traditions	• For Christians, Sunday is traditionally a day of rest. Previously shops and businesses did not open on Sundays and people tended to use the day to go to church and spend time with family. In 1994 the law changed, allowing shops and businesses to open. However, opening hours are usually limited so Sunday is still different to other days. • National events such as Remembrance Day still have a Christian identity. Prayers, Bible readings and hymns feature in the national ceremony held at 11am on Remembrance Day. • The monarch must be a member of the Church of England and is crowned by the Archbishop of Canterbury.

As a multi-faith society, more and more non-Christian celebrations are seen in Britain. For example, the Diwali celebrations in Leicester are some of the biggest outside of India. People of all faiths and none gather along Belgrave Road to see the lights and to join in the celebrations. Talks, exhibitions and activities are put on to educate and include people who want to know more about the festival.

Another example is Mitzvah Day, which has been celebrated every year in the UK since it was established in 2005. It is primarily a Jewish celebration of the duties given by God. The day coincides with the UK Inter Faith Week and so it has extended to include members of other faiths too.

World Humanist Day is a non-religious celebration marked annually in June with a range of events, such as informative talks and live entertainment. It is designed to appeal to Humanists and those who want to learn more about Humanism.

People from all faith backgrounds come to Leicester to join in with Diwali celebrations

Read more about Mitzvah Day on page 145.

Knowledge recall

1. Define the following concepts: evangelisation, Eucharist, relativism. (You can find these definitions on page 101.)
2. Identify three ways in which religious identity in Britain changed between the 2001 and 2011 censuses.
3. Write down an example of how the Christian identity of Britain is seen in its a) laws, b) festivals and c) traditions.

Evaluation practice

4. Identify one challenge and one advantage associated with living in a multi-faith society.
5. Which viewpoint do you most agree with, and why?

Skills practice

On these exam practice pages, you will see example answers for each of the exam question types: **a**, **b**, **c** and **d**. You can find out more about these on pages 8–9.

Question *(a)*

*Question **(a)** tests your knowledge and understanding. You will always be asked to **define a key concept** in this question. You can find a list of the concepts at the beginning of the chapter.*

(a) What do Catholics mean by the 'Eucharist'? [2]

Student response

Holy Communion.

Improved student response

The Eucharist is another term for Holy Communion. The word means 'thanksgiving' and refers to the rite where Catholics remember Jesus' words at the Last Supper and his sacrifice on the cross. Catholics believe the bread and wine become Jesus' body and blood.

What went well

The candidate knows that the term 'Eucharist' is another word for Holy Communion.

How to improve

You must write a complete sentence to respond to the question.

You should demonstrate what Catholics believe about the Eucharist.

You could develop your response using specialist words.

Over to You! Try to answer this question:

(a) What do Catholics mean by 'sin'? [2]

Tip

Make sure you develop your response to show you fully understand the concept.

Helpful hints

To help you answer this question successfully, think about the advice given here:

- The exam board definition is quite short, so it is worth learning off by heart.
- You can add an example to your answer, even though the exam board definition doesn't have an example. This might help to show your understanding further.

Now give yourself **two minutes** to answer this question by yourself:

(a) What do Catholics mean by 'forgiveness'? [2]

Question *(b)*

*Question **(b)** tests your knowledge and understanding. It will always ask you to **describe** a belief, a teaching, a practice or an event that is included on the specification.*

(b) Describe Pope John Paul II's teaching on capital punishment. [5]

Student response

Pope St John Paul II said that the death penalty was acceptable in certain situations but not in others. He said that sometimes it was the only thing that could be done to keep society safe.

What went well

The candidate has accurately identified an aspect of Pope St John Paul II's teaching.

How to improve

You must show why Pope St John Paul II didn't always believe the death penalty was acceptable.

You should connect the teaching of Pope St John Paul II to Christian belief.

You could describe how the death penalty might keep society safe.

Improved student response

Pope St John Paul II was largely against the death penalty because punishment is not just to keep society safe from criminals, but also to give criminals a chance to change. However, he did recognise that in some extreme situations the death penalty might be the only possible way to keep society safe, such as in the case of a very dangerous criminal who was a serious threat to others. Pope St John Paul II said there was little need for the death penalty because there were other effective ways to keep society safe. He said it was important to keep the dignity of all people including criminals so 'bloodless' punishments needed to be used.

Over to You! Try to answer this question.

(b) Describe the teaching of Jesus on forgiveness. [5]

Helpful hints

To help you answer this question successfully, think about the advice given here:

- Try to be as specific as possible in your answer.
- Use sources of authority to help you to develop the points you have made.

Tip

Pope St John Paul II's teaching is quite specific, so approach your answer carefully to make sure that it is as precise as possible.

Now give yourself **five minutes** to answer this question by yourself:

(b) Describe how the altar and font represent Catholic beliefs about salvation. [5]

Question *(c)*

Question ***(c)*** *tests your knowledge and understanding. You need to give detailed evidence and reasoning to support your explanation of the topic.*

(c) Explain why the death of Jesus is important to Catholics. [8]

Student response

The death of Jesus is important to Catholics since when Jesus died, he did so for the forgiveness of human sin. Catholics believe this gives them new life.

The death of Jesus is important because he was a sacrifice. They call Jesus the Lamb of God.

What went well

There are a few relevant reasons why the death of Jesus is important to Catholics.

How to improve

You must develop each point made, showing the importance of these beliefs.

You should use a wide range of specialist language and sources of authority to show the depth of your understanding.

You could show the impact of these beliefs on Catholic life and worship.

Improved student response

Jesus' death is important to Catholics because they believe it helped to achieve salvation. They believe Jesus died to bring forgiveness for human sin. Catholics believe Jesus was an innocent sacrifice and call him the 'Lamb of God' because of this. Catholics hope that when they die, they can be with God in heaven, and that Jesus' death helps to bring the salvation that is needed for this to happen. However, Catholics also believe they must have faith in Jesus and live a Christian life in order to receive salvation.

Catholics also believe Jesus' death is important because it helped to bring God and humans closer together. Catholics believe sin distances humans from God, so when Jesus died for human sin he helped to restore the relationship between humans and God. This is seen in the Eucharist, which is called the 'source and summit' of Christian faith since salvation comes from the Eucharist and the Eucharist brings salvation.

Over to You! Try to answer this question.

(c) Explain Catholic teaching about the importance of evangelisation. [8]

Helpful hints

To help you answer this question successfully, think about the advice given here:

- You really need to know what evangelisation is in order to answer this question. Make sure you know the meaning of the word before you start writing.
- The specification has a source of authority for this theme – *Evangelii Gaudium*. You should try to refer to this in your answer.
- However, you can also use other teachings, such as the Great Commission (where Jesus told the apostles to take the Good News to others and to baptise them), and the story of Pentecost (where the Holy Spirit gave the apostles and Mary the courage and ability to spread the Good News).
- Remember to reflect on the connection between evangelisation and salvation.

Now give yourself **eight minutes** to answer this question by yourself:

(c) Explain how Catholics see Mary as a model of the Church. [8]

Question (d)

*Question **(d)** tests your ability to **evaluate**. This means you need to show you have considered more than one point of view and that you have referred to religion and belief. You will need to be able to make judgements that are supported by detailed reasoning and argument.*

Tip

Make sure you don't fall into a story-writing mode when you answer this question. It's really important that you consider the structure of your answer so that it's an explanation rather than a description.

(d) 'A loving God would not condemn anyone to Hell.'
Discuss this statement showing that you have considered more than one point of view. (You must refer to religion and belief in your answer.) [15]

Student response

I agree with this statement. If God is loving then it makes no sense for him to send someone to hell. If he loves people then he will give them the chance of eternal life even if they have lived a sinful life. God knows, because he is omniscient, that a person will suffer for eternity in hell, so to send people to hell would contradict the idea that God is all loving.

However, many Christians might argue that God doesn't send people to hell but they choose hell for themselves through their actions. God offers the chance for salvation because he is loving. However, humans are free to accept or reject the offer of salvation. If a human rejects the offer of salvation and lives in a sinful way, they have turned away from God and taken themselves to hell.

What went well

There are two clearly stated ideas that contrast with each other. There is some development in the answer using explanations to back up the points made. There is a good use of specialist words in the answer and evidence of a good level of knowledge and understanding.

How to improve

You must use some sources of authority to develop your reasoning further.

You should analyse the ideas you have expressed to show how they contrast with alternative viewpoints.

You could express why you think some arguments are more convincing than others.

Improved student response

Many people would agree with this statement. If God is loving, then it makes no sense for him to send someone to hell. If he loves people then he will give them the chance of eternal life even if they have lived a sinful life. God knows, because he is omniscient, that a person will suffer for eternity in hell, so to send people to hell would contradict the idea that God is all loving. However, some question whether an all-loving God would allow for injustice in the afterlife. If a person has sinned in this life and not asked for forgiveness, then surely it would be unfair for them to be in heaven with people who have tried to live good lives and asked God for forgiveness. God's loving nature can't allow for him to be unfair. In the parable of the rich man and Lazarus, the rich man went to hell because he had been selfish in his life – it would be unfair for him to go to heaven because of his sinfulness. However, some people might argue that the rich man realised his mistake once he was in hell, and even asked for some way to save his brothers. Wouldn't a loving God allow him into heaven once he had realised his sinfulness and shown he was sorry? I think that the belief that everyone goes to heaven is attractive but the argument that this is unfair is a strong argument because it's hard to understand why God would let people who hate him and have sinned into heaven.

However, many Christians might argue that God doesn't send people to hell, but they choose hell for themselves through their actions. God offers the chance for salvation because he is loving. However, humans are free to accept or reject the offer of salvation. If a person rejects the offer of salvation and lives in a sinful way, they have turned away from God and so taken themselves to hell. On the other hand, people might argue that in the parable of the Final Judgement, people who have not cared for others are sent to hell and that those who have cared for others are sent to heaven. This suggests that God sends people to heaven and hell. However, Christians believe that Jesus lived among humans in order to teach them how to live in order to go to heaven and that when he died, he died for everyone's sins. Therefore, if a person doesn't want to listen to this teaching and rejects the salvation brought by Jesus, they choose not to go to heaven. I think this argument is strong since God shouldn't force a person to go to heaven – that would be unloving.

Clear response to the question.

Using the word 'however' at the start of this sentence shows that an alternative viewpoint is being used, which enables evaluation to occur.

This is a source of authority from a different chapter, but it's perfectly valid to use it here.

A clear judgement about the arguments has been made.

Another line of argument has been introduced.

The use of the word 'unloving' links the answer back to the question.

In conclusion, it's a nice idea to think that a loving God lets everyone into heaven, but if God is loving he has to be fair and allowing everyone into heaven isn't fair, especially given the teaching given by Jesus on how to live a good life. A person who finds themselves in hell has made the decision to go there themselves, not God.

The conclusion shows a personal opinion and a judgement on the ideas expressed.

Over to You! Try to answer this question:

(d) 'Some actions are always wrong.'
Discuss this statement showing that you have considered more than one point of view. (You must refer to religion and belief in your answer.) [15]

Helpful hints

To help you answer this question successfully, think about the advice given here:

- This question depends on knowing about relativism and exclusivism. You will need to use examples to make your point, but choose those examples wisely.
- There could be a temptation to ramble about this topic so stay focused and make sure you show the exchange of two opinions. Make sure you show evidence of:
  - what you know and understand about this topic
  - the impact of different opinions on different people
  - specialist vocabulary
  - sources of authority (teachings from the Bible, for example)
  - judgement of the arguments you have given
  - other opinions, so that your answer isn't one-sided.

Now give yourself **fifteen minutes** to answer this question by yourself:

(d) 'Capital punishment is wrong.'
Discuss this statement showing that you have considered more than one point of view. (You must refer to religion and belief in your answer.) [15]

Tip

It's a good idea to think about your own responses to the issues you've studied well before you have to write exam answers on them. However, if you see an exam question that asks something from a perspective you'd not considered before, take a couple of moments to think through what to write, before committing pen to paper.

Chapter 5: Beliefs and teachings

Introduction

Judaism is considered to be the oldest of the world's monotheistic religions. It is founded on the belief that there is one God who has revealed himself to key prophets and created covenants with Noah, Abraham and Moses to establish laws that many Jewish people still follow today. In this chapter, you will consider core Jewish beliefs and teachings concerned with the nature of God, the Messiah, the covenants with Abraham and Moses, the value of life, the mitzvot and the afterlife. In the UK today, there is a core Jewish population of around 300,000 which is the fifth largest Jewish community in the world. Around two thirds of the UK's Jewish population live in London and its surrounding areas, and Manchester, Leeds and Glasgow also house large Jewish communities. There are Jewish communities found across the UK.

Things to remember

- There are different denominations or groups of Jews who may disagree with each other on various matters. It is important that you know how their beliefs vary and how this influences their daily lives. You should be aware of two main Jewish groups:

  Orthodox Jews – the largest Jewish group in Britain. They are traditional in their beliefs and teachings as they believe the Torah was given directly from God and its laws should be followed today as written in the Torah.

  Reform Jews – a Jewish group which believe that the Torah is a document written by humans but inspired by God, which reflects the human search for God. Due to this, Reform Jews emphasise the importance of ethical mitzvot alongside ritual mitzvot.

  In addition, there are **Secular Jews**: many of whom identify strongly with the Jewish people and express their Jewish heritage through cultural and historical connections rather than through religious practices and rituals. Additionally, there is diversity within Judaism in the UK due to ethnic divisions. The two main groups are Ashkenazi and Sephardi Jews. Traditionally Ashkenazi Jews have their ancestry mainly in Germany and France. Whilst Sephardi Jews connect their ancestry with Spain and Portugal.
- For the exam, you will need to explain different Jewish views on the core beliefs and teachings shown within this chapter. You will also need to show why you think some of these teachings are effective and accurate or why you think they are morally wrong or out of date.

Concepts

Covenant – a promise or agreement between two parties. Covenants were made between God with Noah, Abraham and Moses

Kosher – ('fit' or 'proper') foods that are permitted to be eaten according to Leviticus Chapter 11. It is also used to refer to the purity of ritual objects such as Torah scrolls

Messiah – the anointed one who Jews believe will bring in a new era or age for humankind. This will include rebuilding the Temple and bringing in an age of universal peace

Mitzvot – the term has a mix of meanings. It is often used to refer to duties (such as the 613 in the Torah) and good deeds

Shabbat – day of spiritual renewal and rest. Beginning at sunset on Friday and closing at nightfall on Saturday

Shekhinah – the place where God's presence rests and can be felt

Synagogue – house of assembly; building for Jewish public prayer, study and assembly

Torah – the five books of Moses (Genesis, Exodus, Leviticus, Numbers and Deuteronomy). Regarded as the holiest books of the Tenakh

The nature of God: One, Creator, Law-Giver and Judge

Specification focus

The nature of God: Issues of God as: One, Creator: Genesis 1:3–5; 1:26–28, The Shema; Law-Giver and Judge: Exodus 20:1–15.

God as One

Monotheism is a central belief within Judaism: there is one God who is indivisible and unique. This is shown clearly in the first line of the **Shema**, which states 'Hear, O Israel! The LORD is our God, the LORD alone' (Deuteronomy 6:4). For many Jews, the Shema is considered to be the most important prayer and many recite it three times a day. The Shema is also contained in the **mezuzah**, which Jews touch as they pass to remind them of God. The belief in one God is at the forefront of Jewish life.

In Judaism God is believed to be omniscient, omnipotent and omnipresent; this reinforces the belief there is one God who alone has these qualities. Many Jews show their respect for God by not speaking his name, instead substituting the word 'HaShem'. There are many Hebrew names for God within Judaism which are often in the masculine plural. However, Jews do not believe that God is a physical being and therefore God is neither masculine or feminine. Some may also write God as 'G-d', again as a sign of respect and honour.

The belief in one God is reinforced by the command 'You shall have no other gods besides me' (Exodus 20:3). The worship of any other gods is against God's will and therefore wrong. **Synagogues** reflect this belief by containing no images or statues of living beings, as this could lead to them being a focus for worship. God alone is to be worshipped; anything else is forbidden.

God as Creator

Judaism teaches that God created the world and all that it is in it. In Genesis 1 in the **Torah**, God is shown as an omniscient and transcendent creator. When he creates, he does so with order and design and a clear purpose. Genesis 1:3–5 outlines how God created day and night:

> ‘God said, “Let there be light”; and there was light. God saw that the light was good, and God separated the light from the darkness. God called the light Day, and the darkness He called Night. And there was evening and there was morning, a first day.’
> *Genesis 1:3–5*

These verses show how God is an omnipotent creator, who can create through his word alone. Genesis goes on to give details of the order in which God created everything, supporting the Jewish belief that the world was created by God rather than by chance.

God's final and most important creation – humanity – is introduced in Genesis 1:26–28:

> ‘God said, “**Let us make man in our image, after our likeness**. They shall rule the fish of the sea, the birds of the sky, the cattle, the whole earth, and all the creeping things that creep on earth.” And God created man in His image, **in the image of God He created him; male and female He created them.** God blessed them and God said to them, “**Be fertile and increase, fill the earth and master it**; and rule the fish of the sea, the birds of the sky, and all the living things that creep on earth.”’
> *Genesis 1:26–28*

Useful terms

monotheism – belief there is only one God
Shema – a prayer found in the Torah which proclaims belief in one God
mezuzah – a small scroll of parchment in a decorative case with the Shema written on it. Mezuzahs are attached to doorposts in Jewish homes

This passage teaches Jews that God created humans in his image and likeness and blessed them, which makes them God's most special creation. They also have a special role: to be stewards of the world, which God created and gifted to humans.

Many Orthodox Jews read the creation stories in Genesis metaphorically, and so do not believe that God created the world as described in the **Torah**. Even though it is read metaphorically, they take very important messages from the text such as God is the ultimate and sole creator of the universe. This is reflected in Orthodox prayers such as the start of the Barukh She'amar prayer: 'Blessed be He who spoke and the world came into being.' The Torah is a source of fundamental Jewish and human values, such as the equality of all humanity, stewardship and the responsibility to care for the environment so that it can be passed on for future generations.

Many Jews celebrate God's creation of the world by observing **Shabbat** – a weekly day of rest which reflects God resting on the seventh day after completing creation. Many also celebrate Rosh Hashanah each year as the anniversary of creation. Both are reminders of the gift God gave to humans.

Jews celebrate Shabbat each week to commemorate God resting on the seventh day after creating the world

God as Law-Giver

Judaism teaches that God wants humans to live in a specific way, so he revealed the Torah to Moses. This contains the 613 **mitzvot** (duties), which Moses taught to the Israelites. These duties are required for each Jew to live a good and moral life. They also help to create a society that is fair, equal and moral as God wanted. An example of these duties is the Ten Commandments (Exodus 20:2–14), which form the basis of Jewish ethics.

Read more about the mitzvot on pages 144.

Orthodox Jews try to keep all of the duties as laid out in the Torah, whereas Reform Jews believe the duties need to be adapted to fit in with modern life and society. Most Jews will always try to keep the Ten Commandments.

God shared his law with Moses by giving the Torah and the Ten Commandments (written here in Hebrew)

God as Judge

For Jews, God is a Law-Giver and therefore also a Judge: he will judge individuals on how well they follow the Torah and the duties he has given to them. As Jews believe God is omniscient, many believe that God judges every moment of their lives. Therefore, they should strive to do good and treat others well, in accordance with the mitzvot.

Judaism teaches that God is a God of justice and compassion. Each year, the festival of Rosh Hashanah is when God starts his judgement of individuals based on their actions throughout the year, balancing good actions against bad ones. As God is compassionate, he gives Jews an opportunity to atone for anything they have done wrong in the ten days leading up to Yom Kippur (the Day of Atonement). Therefore, all Jews have the chance to right the wrongs of the past year.

Knowledge recall

1. Define the following concepts: Torah, mitzvot, covenant. (You can find these definitions on page 131.)
2. Explain what Jews believe about God's creation of the world.
3. State one source of wisdom that supports the idea of God as Law-Giver.

Evaluation practice

4. Give a reason why some Jews believe God's oneness is the most important aspect of God's nature.
5. Do you think that God is the ultimate Creator? Give two reasons for your view.

The nature and significance of the Shekhinah

Specification focus

The nature of God: The nature and significance of Shekhinah (the divine presence).

The nature of the Shekhinah

Shekhinah is the term used to refer to God's presence when it rests and can be felt strongly on earth. It is sometimes referred to as the divine presence, or the idea of God **dwelling** on earth. Unlike the other characteristics of God discussed on pages 132–133 (One, Creator, Law-Giver and Judge), which are considered to show the transcendence of God, the Shekhinah is meant to show the **immanent** nature of God. Judaism teaches that God is omnipresent, but the Shekhinah represents times and places when God's presence is particularly felt and experienced as he works in the world. It is seen as a way of God reaching out and connecting with Jews. The Shekhinah is not the physical presence of God, but rather the spiritual presence of God on earth. Many Jews believe that it is important to engage with the Shekhinah in a spiritual and practical sense through prayer and pilgrimage.

Some Jews believe the Shekhinah is the feminine aspect of God and therefore is associated with feminine attributes – representing the more loving, caring and compassionate qualities of God. Some Jews believe that when the Shekhinah is felt it promotes feelings of safety, security and peace. They believe it enables a closer and more personal relationship with God.

Orthodox Jews believe they can experience the Shekhinah at the Western Wall in Jerusalem

The Shekhinah in the Tenakh

The word 'Shekhinah' does not feature in the **Tenakh**, but the Jewish scriptures do include many mentions of people experiencing God and his dwelling on earth. For example:

'They heard the sound of the LORD **God moving about in the garden** at the breezy time of day; and the man and his wife hid from **the LORD God** among the trees of the garden.'
Genesis 3:8

'The LORD **went before them in a pillar of cloud by day**, to **guide them along the way,** and **in a pillar of fire by night**, to **give them light**, that they might travel day and night.'
Exodus 13:21

'And let them **make Me a sanctuary that I may dwell among them**.'
Exodus 25:8

'When Solomon finished praying, fire descended from heaven and consumed the burnt offering and the sacrifices, and **the glory of the LORD filled the House**.'
2 Chronicles 7:1

It is clear from these quotes that the Shekhinah has been present during great moments of Jewish history. God therefore shares these significant moments with the Jewish people.

Useful terms

dwelling – a place of living or a home

immanent – God is close to his creation and involved with the world so that he can make himself known

Tenakh – the Jewish Bible, consisting of the Torah (the five books of Moses), Nevi'im (prophets) and Ketuvim (writings)

The significance of the Shekhinah

For many Jews, the Shekhinah is important as it indicates the special connection between God and the Jewish people. God is present in Jewish history and makes himself known at times of great need or significance. This means the Shekhinah represents the closeness of God and that God offers security and care when it is needed, which can give Jews hope in times of need. The Shekhinah shares the pain and suffering of the Jews and therefore some Jews believe that it offers support in times of need.

At times of great importance, such as when the **Torah** was given to Moses, the Shekhinah is often referred to as the 'glory' of God. This shows God's power and majesty, reinforcing the fact that God's presence on earth does not diminish his power or nature: rather his omnipotence is felt clearly. This glory then radiates to the Jewish people, showing that they are glorified by being in God's presence.

The Tenakh describes how when the Israelites were wandering in the wilderness, Moses constructed a tabernacle (a tent) that was a portable sanctuary where God dwelt. God's presence could be felt here and would appear as either cloud or fire. Moses would meet with God face-to-face in the tabernacle and so it was also called 'the tent of meeting'. The Ark of the **Covenant** was kept in the tabernacle, which was a chest containing the two stone tablets on which the Ten Commandments were written.

Eventually, the tabernacle was replaced by the First Temple in Jerusalem (this was later destroyed and rebuilt as the Second Temple). The Temple became the centre of Jewish life and worship. It housed the Ark of the Covenant and was where Jews believed God concentrated his presence. Today, only the Western Wall of the Second Temple still stands. Some Jews believe God's presence is no longer concentrated here due to the Temple's destruction and is more closely felt in the Jewish home. However, some Orthodox Jews believe that God's presence can still be felt at the Western Wall.

Ways Jews experience the Shekhinah today

Many Jews believe the Shekhinah can still be felt today in various ways. Examples include:

Worship	A ner tamid ('eternal light') is a light or lamp that is always present in a **synagogue** and never goes out. This is to show that God is always present. Through communal worship Jews can be in the presence of God.
Prayer	A minyan (ten adult men for Orthodox Jews, in Reform Judaism, a minyan can be made up of ten adult men and women) is required for prayers in the synagogue. The Talmud states that 'the Divine Presence dwells in any place where there are ten adult male Jews' (Sanhedrin 39a). This shows that the Shekhinah is felt in prayer.
Study	Some Jews study the Hebrew scriptures at home, in synagogue or at a yeshiva (a Jewish academy) in order to understand their faith more fully. By studying scriptures that are considered to be God's revealed word, some Jews believe they can experience God's presence.
Shabbat	During **Shabbat**, the women of the home light two candles and welcome the Shekhinah into the home, so the home becomes a holy place for the duration of Shabbat.
Pilgrimage	Orthodox Jews believe they can experience the Shekhinah when they visit the Western Wall in Jerusalem. The Western Wall is the last part of the Second Temple that is still standing. As Orthodox Jews believe the Shekhinah was fully present in the Temple, they believe it is still present here. Many Jews will go on pilgrimage to pray at the Western Wall to feel a heightened awareness of the presence of God.

Exodus describes the tabernacle as a portable tent that housed God's presence

Knowledge recall

1 Define the following concepts: Shekhinah, Torah, covenant. (You can find these definitions on page 131.)

2 One way the Shekhinah appears in the Torah is as the glory of the Lord. Give two other ways the Shekhinah appears in the Torah.

3 State one source of wisdom that supports belief in the Shekhinah.

Evaluation practice

4 'The Shekhinah is not important when trying to understand God.' Give one Jewish response to this statement.

5 Do you agree that the best place for Jews to experience God's presence is at the Western Wall in Jerusalem? Give two reasons for your view.

The nature and role of the Messiah

The nature of the Messiah

The term **Messiah** comes from the Hebrew word 'Mashiach', which means anointed. In Judaism, the Messiah is a future Jewish ruler who will be anointed in the same way that a monarch is anointed with oils to mark them as special, unique and having ability to rule with authority. There is no direct mention of the Messiah in the **Torah**, but there are passages in the Tenakh which have been interpreted as indicating the coming of a Messiah. For example:

> 'See, a time is coming – declares the LORD – when I will raise up a true branch of David's line. He shall reign as a king and shall prosper.'
> *Jeremiah 23:5*

> 'In those days and at that time, I will raise up a true branch of David's line, and he shall do what is just and right in the land.'
> *Jeremiah 33:15*

Belief in the Messiah varies between different Jewish groups, but traditional ideas about what the Messiah will be like include the following:

- The Messiah will be a human man (not God on earth, as this undermines the oneness of God).
- He will have the authority of God, to rule in the best interests of Judaism.
- He will be descended from King David, who was one of the most influential rulers of the Israelites.
- He will be a great political leader and will defend Judaism from its enemies.

Many Orthodox Jews are still waiting for the coming of the Messiah, with debate over when this might happen. Some believe the Messiah will come when Jews need him most, while others believe it will be when the world is near perfection. However, many believe that in every generation there is someone who has the potential to be the Messiah.

The role of the Messiah

The role of the Messiah is much debated within Judaism, but it is traditionally believed that he will be:

- Righteous – some Jews believe the Messiah will be a righteous king, who through his rule will spread good and justice throughout the world so that all people are united and can live equally. ('For a child born has been to us, a son has been given us. And authority has settled on his shoulders. He has been named "The Mighty God is planning grace; the Eternal Father, a peaceable ruler"' – Isaiah 9:5).
- A bringer of peace – some Jews believe the Messiah will bring about a **Messianic Age** of peace and harmony for all nations. This is also known as olam ha-ba and will signal the end of the world as it is. ('Nation shall not take up sword against nation; they shall never again know war' – Isaiah 2:4.)

Specification focus

Messiah (Mashiach): Different views within Orthodox and Reform Judaism about the nature and role of the Mashiach (Messiah); special person who brings an age of peace, ourselves, his arrival as signalling the end of the world, praying for his coming, concerned more with living life according to the mitzvot.

This is a model of the Temple – the holiest place in Judaism – which was destroyed in 70 CE. Orthodox Jews believe the Messiah will restore it to glory when he arrives

Useful term

Messianic Age – a new era or age for humankind; a time of peace

- The restorer of the Temple – some Jews believe the Messiah will rebuild and restore the Temple in Jerusalem that was destroyed in 70 CE.
- The restorer of Israel – some Jews believe the Messiah will return the Jewish people back to Israel and bring understanding of God to all people. ('I am going to take the Israelite people from among the nations they have gone to, and gather them from every quarter, and bring them to their own land' – Ezekiel 37:21).

The Messianic Age

The Messianic Age is believed by many Jews to be a new era for humankind of peace and prosperity. For many Orthodox Jews, the arrival of the Messiah will indicate the beginning of the Messianic Age. This will be followed by the resurrection of those who have died and the return of the Jews to Israel.

The Messianic Age will be a time of total peace, prosperity and justice for all, as shown in the teaching 'the wolf shall dwell with the lamb' (Isaiah 11:6). It will be a new time without pain, persecution or hatred.

Orthodox and Reform views of the Messiah

Many Orthodox Jews accept the traditional understanding of the Messiah and wait in hope for his arrival. In Maimonides' *Thirteen Principles of Jewish Faith*, the twelfth principle is 'the belief in the arrival of the Messiah and the Messianic Era'. Maimonides was an influential Jewish philosopher in the Middle Ages; his twelfth principle shows how the Messiah is a central belief for many Orthodox Jews, with many praying for him to come and redeem the world and bring about universal peace.

Many Reform Jews reject belief in a Messiah who will bring about the Messianic Age. Instead they believe the responsibility for bringing about the Messianic Age does not lie with just one person – it is the collective responsibility of all people to do good actions to bring about a new world of peace and justice. Reform Jews get their vision of the Messianic Age from the Prophets. For example, Micah 4:3 describes a time when 'nation shall not take up sword against nation; they shall never again know war'. This shows that the Messianic Age is a time of eternal and universal peace. The Prophets give descriptions of what this age will be like, with the focus on the Messianic Age, rather than an individual Messiah.

It is not always clear in Jewish tradition how the Messianic Age will be achieved. However, the Prophets indicate it requires 'only to do justice and to love goodness and to walk modestly with your God' (Micah 6:8). Therefore, Reform Jews believe that living well and doing good in the here and now will help to bring about the Messianic Age. Many Reform Jews engage in activities to promote a better, more just world and therefore the concept of Tikkun Olam is important as a means of helping to bring about the Messianic Age. Many Jews promote helping individuals, supporting environmental causes and making the world a better place due to the 'Messianic impulse' – the urge to bring about the Messiah and the Messianic Age.

'It is not your duty to complete the work, but neither are you at liberty to desist from it.'
Pirkei Avot 2:16

Knowledge recall

1. Define the following concepts: Messiah, synagogue, Shabbat. (You can find these definitions on page 131.)
2. List three traditional characteristics of the Messiah.
3. State one source of wisdom to show what the Messiah will do.

Evaluation practice

4. 'The Messiah is of central importance in Judaism.' Give one way a Reform Jew would respond to this statement.
5. Do you agree that the Messiah is an important figure in Judaism? Give two reasons for your view.

The covenant with Abraham

The covenants with the Jews

A **covenant** is an agreement between two people or groups and it usually has conditions attached to it that need to be fulfilled. Judaism teaches that throughout its history God has made covenants with key people in order to build a relationship with the Jews.

- The first covenant was made with Noah, in which God gave the Noahide Laws.
- The second was with **Abraham**, who founded Judaism and believed in monotheism. The covenant that God made with Abraham's descendants is unconditional.
- The final covenant was with Moses, who gave the Jewish people the **Torah** and the Law. This covenant made at Sinai is conditional.

The Abrahamic covenant

Abraham is considered to have founded Judaism after having made a covenant with God. He is often referred to as the first patriarch or 'Abraham our Father' by many Jews, showing that he is thought of as the father of Judaism.

For many Jews, Abraham is a role model, he is someone they look up to and try to be like in their own lives. This is because he rejected the **polytheism** that was widespread in society at the time and instead embraced monotheism. He is also seen as a model of faith and virtue as he trusted in God throughout his life, regardless of what God asked him to do. Due to these qualities, God invited Abraham into a covenant, which Abraham accepted.

The Abrahamic covenant is found in the book of Genesis, and is made up of three promises: land, descendants and blessings. In return there is one condition for the Jews, which is that males undergo circumcision (this is the 'sign of the covenant').

The first promise: land

In the first part of the covenant, God tells Abraham to leave Haran – where Abraham and his family had settled after leaving their home of Ur – and travel to the land of Canaan, which God promises will become his home and a home for his descendants to come. Abraham does as God commands, making Canaan his home and the home of his children. Abraham's grandson Jacob was also known as Israel, and his children become known as the Children of Israel, so the land came to be called the Land of Israel. Israel is often referred to as the **Promised Land** as throughout the covenant, God reiterates the promise of land so that Abraham and his descendants will have a home.

The Promised Land is central within Judaism. Israel is considered to be the Jewish homeland both historically and today. Many Jews feel a special connection with Israel due to God's promise of this land to Abraham. It is the focus of daily prayers, synagogues are oriented towards Jerusalem; at Jewish weddings a glass is broken by the groom as a memorial to the destruction of the Temple; some Jews are buried with soil from Israel to show their connection with the land. Many Jews travel to the Western Wall and gather there to remember that it was part of the Temple. Some Jews gather here in hope of the final redemption and the restoration of the Temple which some believe will be brought about by the coming of the Messiah.

Specification focus

Covenant: The meaning and significance of the Abrahamic Covenant: Genesis 12:1–3, 17:6–8, 17:11–14 including the importance of the 'Promised Land'.

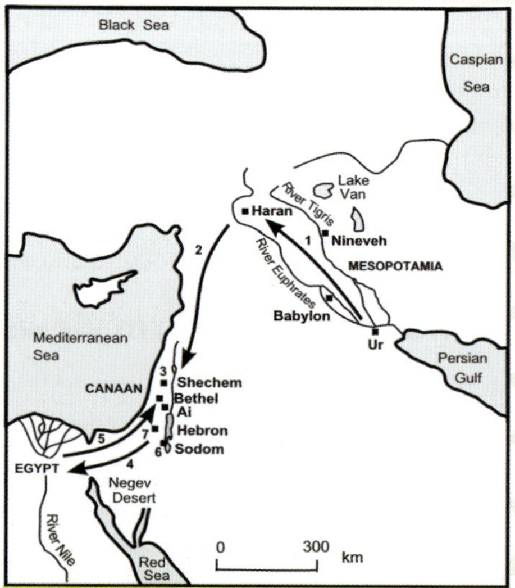

Abraham put his trust in God and travelled hundreds of miles with his family to reach the Promised Land

> The LORD said to Abram, "**Go forth from your native land** and from your father's house **to the land that I will show you.**"
> *Genesis 12:1*

Useful terms

Abraham – 'Father of many'; the founder of Judaism
polytheism – believing in many gods
descendant – a person who is related to you and lives on after you, such as a child or grandchild
Promised Land – the land God promised to Abraham and his descendants
circumcision – the removal of the foreskin from the penis

The second promise: descendants

> I will make of you **a great nation**, and I will bless you; I will make your name great, and You shall be a blessing.
> *Genesis 12:2*

God promises that Abraham will become the founder of a 'great nation', meaning that he will have many descendants who are connected to God and the Promised Land. Many Jews refer to Abraham as 'Father', showing their connection to him as his descendants.

The third promise and one condition: blessings and the sign of the covenant

> **I will bless those who bless you** and curse him that curses you: and all the **families of the earth shall bless themselves by you**.
> *Genesis 12:3*

God promises to bless Abraham and his descendants. For many Jews this reinforces their special relationship with God and the belief that they are his chosen people. Jews are considered the chosen people of God as they have been chosen to enter into and keep his covenants. They also have the obligation to keep the mitzvot, worship and practice revealed in the Tanakh.

In order to clearly mark out those who have entered into his covenant, God commands that Abraham and all of his male descendants go through **circumcision**. This is known as the sign or seal of the covenant, and it is a physical sign of entry into the covenant relationship with God.

Circumcision is still an important rite within Judaism and the ceremony where it happens is known as Brit Milah. It occurs, as commanded, when a baby boy is eight days old. The baby is also formally named at this point, and this shows that the boy is called into the covenant relationship with God.

> **You shall circumcise the flesh of your foreskin**, and that shall be the **sign of the covenant between Me and you**. And throughout **all generations, every male among you shall be circumcised at the age of eight days... Thus shall My covenant be marked in your flesh as an everlasting pact**. And if any male who is uncircumcised fails to circumcise the flesh of his foreskin, that person shall be cut off from his kin; he has broken My covenant.
> *Genesis 17:11–14*

Read more about the Shekhinah and its connection to the Temple on page 134.

> **I will make you exceedingly fertile,** and **make nations of you**; and kings shall come forth from you. I will maintain My covenant between Me and you, and **your offspring to come, as an everlasting covenant throughout the ages**, to be God to you and to your offspring to come. **I assign the land you sojourn in to you and your offspring to come**, all the land of Canaan, as an everlasting holding. **I will be their God.**
> *Genesis 17:6–8*

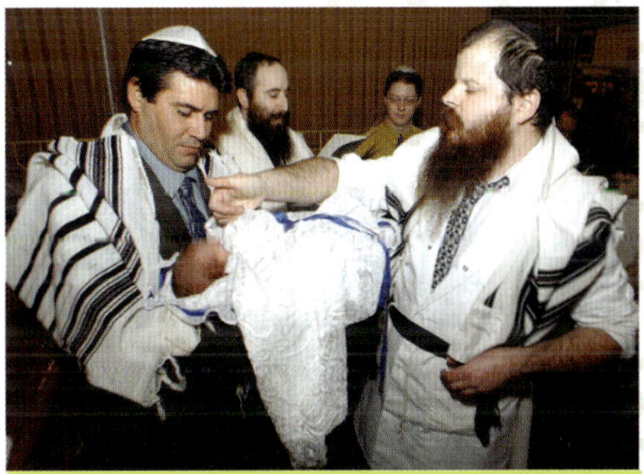

Almost all eight-day-old Jewish males are circumcised to show they have entered into God's covenant

Knowledge recall

1. Define the following concepts: covenant, kosher, mitzvot. (You can find these definitions on page 131.)
2. List the three promises that God made to Abraham.
3. State one source of wisdom to support the Abrahamic covenant.

Evaluation practice

4. 'Without Abraham there would be no Judaism.' Give one response to this statement.
5. Do you think that the Abrahamic covenant is important for Jews today? Give two reasons for your view.

5.5

The covenant with Moses at Sinai

The escape of the Israelites

In this **covenant**, God chose **Moses** to deliver the Israelites from slavery in Egypt and take them to the Promised Land. Moses is a very important figure in Judaism; he is considered to be the greatest prophet and the only person to have had a face-to-face encounter with God. Moses is also thought of as a great teacher, as after receiving the **Torah** he taught it to the Israelites, so they would know the laws of God.

God chose Moses to form a covenant with as Moses had great empathy for the Israelites. He had been born an Israelite but was brought up by Pharaoh (the ruler of Egypt) after his mother placed him in a basket and sent him down the Nile to save his life. When God gave Moses the task of freeing the Israelites, Moses was at first unsure, but God gave him courage and through him performed miracles (the ten **plagues**) that led to the Israelites being freed.

It was after the tenth and worst plague – the death of the Egyptians' firstborn sons – that Pharaoh reluctantly agreed to let the Israelites go. However, Pharaoh went back on his promise and chased the Israelites to the Red Sea. God parted the sea and when Pharaoh and his army were halfway across, he brought the sea down on top of them to destroy them all. Every year many Jews celebrate Pesach (Passover) to commemorate the actions of Moses.

> ‘But Moses said to God, “**Who am I that I should go to Pharaoh and free the Israelites from Egypt?**” And He said, “**I will be with you**; that shall be your sign that it was I who sent you. And **when you have freed the people from Egypt, you shall worship God at this mountain.**” Moses said to God, **“When I come to the Israelites and say to them, ‘The God of your fathers has sent me to you,’** and they ask me, ‘What is His name?’, what shall I say to them?” And God said to Moses “**I Will Be What I Will Be**.” He continued, “Thus shall you say to the Israelites: ‘I Will Be sent me to you.’” And God said further to Moses, “Thus shall you speak to the Israelites: The LORD, **the God of your fathers, the God of Abraham, the God of Isaac, and the God of Jacob, has sent me to you:** This shall be My name forever, this My appellation for all eternity.’
> *Exodus 3:11–15*

Receiving the Torah

Following their escape from Egypt, the Israelites went to Mount Sinai, and here God made a new covenant with Moses and the Israelites. In this covenant God reaffirmed that the Israelites are his chosen people who he will protect from harm. He also gave Moses the Torah (containing the 613 **mitzvot**), which Moses taught to the Israelites, so they could keep the covenant. God gave the mitzvot to the Israelites, so they would understand the consequences of their actions. By following the mitzvot they are doing as God wants, but by not following them they are disobeying God.

Specification focus

Covenant: The meaning and significance of the Covenant with Moses at Sinai: Exodus 3:11–15 including the continuing importance of the idea of a 'Promised Land'; importance of the Ten Commandments: Exodus 20:2–14.

Moses learned the Torah so that he could share God's Law with the Israelites

Useful terms

Moses – a prophet who led the Israelites out of slavery in Egypt
plague – a widespread disease or disaster sent by God
Ten Commandments – ten laws handed directly from God to Moses
Oral Torah – a commentary on the written Torah, giving explanation and descriptions

Within the mitzvot God gave the **Ten Commandments**, which form the core of Jewish ethics. Orthodox Jews also believe that God gave Moses the commentary on the Torah (known as the **Oral Torah**) to help them better understand it.

The importance of the Ten Commandments

The Ten Commandments (Exodus 20:2–14) are central in Judaism. All Jews are expected to keep them as they form the basis for Jewish ethical practice.

Commandment	Its importance	Who it concerns
'I the LORD am your God who brought you out of the land of Egypt, house of bondage'	A reminder of the covenant with Moses. A reason why Jews celebrate Pesach.	God
'You shall have no other gods besides Me'	Reinforces Judaism as monotheistic. A reason why there are no statues or images in **synagogues**.	God
'You shall not swear falsely by the name of the LORD your God; for the LORD will not clear one who swears falsely by His name'	A reason why many Jews will not say God's name. Many use 'HaShem' instead.	God
'Remember the sabbath day and keep it holy'	**Shabbat** must be kept as a day of rest and worship in the synagogue.	God
'Honour your father and mother, that you may long endure on the land that the LORD your God is assigning to you'	Builds respect between generations and encourages Jews to give thanks for their parents.	Humans
'You shall not murder'	Life is sacred and must be protected, which is why Jews believe in pikuach nefesh.	Humans
'You shall not commit adultery'	Sex should be between a husband and a wife, for the purpose of procreation. Adultery is never acceptable.	Humans
'You shall not steal'	Other people and their possessions must be respected.	Humans
'You shall not bear false witness against your neighbour'	It is important to be honest and fair as this builds a strong society.	Humans
'You shall not covet your neighbour's house: you shall not covet your neighbour's wife, or his male or female slave, or his ox or his donkey, or anything that is your neighbour's'	It is important for Jews to be happy with what they have as greed and envy causes conflict.	Humans

The Ten Commandments are central to Jewish belief

The importance of the Promised Land

The Promised Land is an important theme in this covenant, as Moses led the Israelites to the Promised Land after he freed them from slavery in Egypt. The Promised Land is also known as the Land of Israel and is the land that God promised to Abraham. By Moses taking the people back to the Promised Land, it demonstrates that it is their home and a place of sanctuary. It reinforces their special connection with God.

Knowledge recall

1 Define the following concepts: covenant, Torah, mitzvot. (You can find these definitions on page 131.)

2 List three reasons why the covenant with Moses is important for Jews.

3 State one source of wisdom to support the covenant with Moses.

Evaluation practice

4 'The covenant with Abraham is more important than the covenant with Moses.' Give one Jewish response to this statement.

5 Do you believe that Moses is important in Judaism? Give two reasons for your view.

The nature and importance of pikuach nefesh

The value of humanity

Judaism teaches that God is the creator and giver of life, therefore life belongs to God. In the **Torah** it states that God created humans last and differently to other life, indicating that human life is the most important of God's creations. Judaism also teaches that humans are created in the image and likeness of God, which means they have a special dignity and value which was given to them by God.

This is reinforced in Genesis 2:7, which tells how 'the Lord God formed man from the dust of the earth. He blew into his nostrils the breath of life; and man became a living being'. For Jews, this shows that God gave part of himself to create life and that within each person is a part of God (a soul) meaning that humans have a special dignity and relationship with God. God also gave humans responsibility over other creatures, again showing that humans are distinct and unique.

> 'God said, "Let us make man in our **image, after our likeness**. **They shall rule** the fish of the sea, the birds of the sky, the cattle, the whole earth, and all the creeping things that creep on earth." And God created man in His image, **in the image of God He created him; male and female** He created them.'
> *Genesis 1:26–27*

The sanctity of life

For Jews, the belief that God created humans in his image and likeness and gave them a soul means all humans have the **sanctity of life**. This belief is very important in Judaism as it underpins the idea that all human life has special and equal value, and therefore needs to be treated with the utmost reverence.

> '**It was You who created my conscience**; You fashioned me in my mother's womb. **I praise You, for I am awesomely, wondrously made**; Your work is wonderful; I know it very well.'
> *Psalms 139:13–15*

For many Jews, belief in the sanctity of life influences their approach to matters of life and death. Most Jews believe that human life is of supreme importance and therefore reject practices which prematurely end it, such as **euthanasia**. Many Jews do not agree with euthanasia because:

- God gives life and so God should choose when to end life.
- It might lead people to view those who have a lower quality of life, such as someone with a terminal illness, as less valuable.
- God knows and has a special relationship with everyone, therefore every person's life should be cherished.

Specification focus

Life on earth: Beliefs and teachings about the nature and importance of pikuach nefesh (sanctity of life): Genesis 1:26–27, Talmud B Yoma 84b, Psalm 139: 13–15, Jeremiah 1:5.

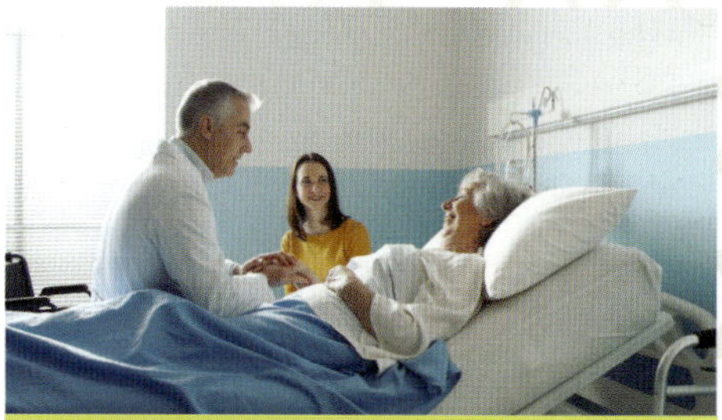

Judaism teaches that human life has great value and should be respected and protected until a person's final breath

Useful terms

sanctity of life – the belief that human life is sacred because it is a gift from God
euthanasia – the painless killing of someone who is suffering
pikuach nefesh – the obligation to save a life in need

Suicide is also considered to be wrong for similar reasons, although Judaism advocates for a sympathetic approach to be taken in these circumstances.

> ‘**Before I created you in the womb, I selected you**; before you were born, I consecrated you; **I appointed you** a prophet concerning the nations.’
> *Jeremiah 1:5*

Pikuach nefesh

Due to the belief that God created life and therefore it is sacred, most Jews believe in **pikuach nefesh**. This is the action of saving a life in need and in Judaism it is considered a moral duty as the value of human life is so high. Pikuach nefesh is so important that it is possible to break all but three **mitzvot** (incest, idolatry and adultery) to save a human life. For example, if a Jewish person is starving then it is acceptable to feed them non-**kosher** food in order to save their life. **Shabbat** is a day of rest and worship for Jews, but pikuach nefesh is so important that it is acceptable to break the rules of Shabbat in order to save life. For example, it is permitted to drive an ill person to hospital or call a doctor, even though both of these activities are normally forbidden on Shabbat. Talmud B Yoma 84b states 'one must remove debris to save a life on the Sabbath'.

The obligation to save life does not extend to saving your own life at the cost of someone else's. For example, this means that it is not acceptable to kill someone else to survive, as each life has equal value and killing for one's own benefit is wrong. If a person needs to defend themselves from harm, this is acceptable but should be proportionate to the situation. In cases where a pregnant mother's life is at risk due to the pregnancy, pikuach nefesh means that abortion may be permitted to defend the established life of the mother.

Pikuach nefesh is significant as it is a practical way of showing that all life is sacred and of equal value. It maintains the belief that all humans have a God-given right to life and to live their life in the fullest way. Many Jewish celebrations use the toast 'L'Chaim', meaning 'to life', to celebrate the joy in life and to show that life should be lived and celebrated.

Pikuach nefesh means that a Jewish doctor could work on Shabbat if it would save the life of a patient

> ‘One who saves a life, it is as if they had saved a whole world. One who destroys a life, it is as if they had destroyed a whole world.’
> *Sanhedrin 4:5*

Knowledge recall

1. Define the following concepts: mitzvot, Shabbat, Shekhinah. (You can find these definitions on page 131.)
2. List three reasons why Jews believe life is to be valued.
3. State one source of wisdom to support the sanctity of life.

Evaluation practice

4. 'Pikuach nefesh is more important than keeping the mitzvot.' Give one Jewish response to this statement.
5. Do you agree with the Jewish belief that all life is sacred? Give two reasons for your view.

5.7

The mitzvot

Specification focus

Life on earth: The relationship between free will and the 613 mitzvot (duties) between humans and with God.

The significance of the mitzvot

The **mitzvot** are very important in Judaism as they are given by God and form the basis of Jewish ethical behaviour. The word mitzvah means 'commandment', and together the mitzvot teach Jews how God wants them to behave. Within Judaism there are 613 mitzvot which instruct Jews on how to worship, how to treat other people, the food they can and cannot eat, and how to live. The mitzvot are the conditions of the **covenant** with Moses, and many Jews believe that to be fully part of this covenant it is important to keep as many of the mitzvot as possible.

Read about the covenant with Moses on page 140.

The mitzvot can be divided into two categories: positive mitzvot which explain what actions can be done, and negative mitzvot which explain what actions cannot be done. As many Jews believe the mitzvot are divine because they were given by God, they believe that by following them they can develop a closer relationship with God. Many Jews wear a tallith (a prayer shawl) with tzitzit (knotted tassels) attached to each corner as a reminder of their obligation to keep the mitzvot.

> 'That shall be your fringe; look at it and **recall all the commandments of the LORD and observe them.**'
> *Numbers 15:39*

Judaism teaches that each person is born with a balance of yetzer ha ra and yetzer ha tov. Jews should try to keep the mitzvot and do good actions to increase yetzer ha tov and become better people

Orthodox Jews believe that it is very important to keep as many of the mitzvot as possible to build a close relationship with God. They believe the mitzvot should not be changed in any way as they are divine, and they will often consider the mitzvot when they need to make decisions.

Reform Jews believe the mitzvot are important, but they recognise that it is impossible to follow some of them due to the changes that have taken place in society since Moses' time. Therefore, they believe the mitzvot need to be interpreted to fit in with modern society and contemporary issues. For example, some Reform Jews might be more relaxed about following the dietary laws when eating out. They may feel that it is most important to focus on keeping the Ten Commandments and using their conscience to make decisions.

The mitzvot and free will

Judaism teaches that God created humans with **free will** and gave them the mitzvot as a moral guide. This free will means that humans can choose to follow the mitzvot or not. This is very important in Judaism as it means that all humans can be held accountable for their actions as they are using their free will to choose how to act. God does not force anyone to keep the mitzvot as anyone who is forced to do good or evil cannot be moral when they have no control over their actions. Therefore, a person must freely decide to keep the mitzvot as it is only by doing so that the mitzvot take on moral meaning.

Judaism teaches that each person is born with both **yetzer ha tov** and **yetzer ha ra**. In the hope of encouraging people to do good rather than evil, God gave the mitzvot as an indication of right and wrong. It is down to the individual to freely follow the mitzvot to increase yetzer ha tov and their moral goodness.

Useful terms

free will – the decision making part of a person's mind is called the will. A will is free if a person is able to choose right from wrong without being controlled by other forces

yetzer ha tov – the tendency to do good actions

yetzer ha ra – the tendency to do bad actions

If a Jew uses their free will to break a mitzvah or ignore the mitzvot, this damages their relationship with God and means they need to actively repent and atone for this. Jews have ten days between Rosh Hashanah and Yom Kippur each year to atone for their sins and mend their relationship with God and other people.

Moral and ritual mitzvot

The mitzvot can be divided into moral mitzvot (those dealing with humans) and ritual mitzvot (those dealing with God). Moral mitzvot explain how people should treat each other and are important in helping to build just and fair societies. Moral mitzvot teach that all human life has equal value and all humans should be treated with respect as they are created in the image and likeness of God. An example of a moral mitzvah is 'You shall not murder' (Exodus 20:13).

Ritual mitzvot deal with how to show respect for God. They are important as they help to establish and maintain a strong relationship between the individual and God. An example of a ritual mitzvah is 'you shall have no other gods besides Me' (Exodus 20:3).

Living out the mitzvot

Many Jews try to live out the mitzvot in their daily lives, but there is one day set aside in the UK each year where Jews can show their commitment to the mitzvot: Mitzvah Day. It is a day when Jews give their time to make a difference to the community through:

- tikkun olam – this means 'repairing' or 'perfecting' the world. It manifests that Jews hope for and work towards social justice and harmony, which includes care for fellow humans and care for the environment. Jews can do this by taking steps to reduce carbon emissions, using renewable natural resources and by treating the earth, animals and natural resources with respect.
- gemilut hasadim – this means 'acts of loving kindness'. They give freely of themselves to show loving-kindness to others. The Torah states 'Love your fellow as yourself' (Leviticus 19:18). Jews can do this by doing good deeds which help individual people.
- tzedekah – this means 'righteousness' or 'justice'. This encourages Jews to work to promote social justice and equality for all people. Giving to charity is seen as an essential way of bringing this about and therefore, within Judaism, it is an obligation to give to charity and help with charitable works.

Examples of Mitzvah Day projects include cooking meals for those in poverty, litter picking in local parks, creating care kits for the homeless, or knitting fidget toys for dementia patients.

Jews live out the mitzvot each year on Mitzvah Day, when they take time to improve communities and help those in need

Knowledge recall

1. Define the following concepts: mitzvot, kosher, synagogue. (You can find these definitions on page 131.)
2. List three reasons why the mitzvot are important to Jews.
3. State one source of wisdom which shows a mitzvah.

Evaluation practice

4. 'Jews do not have an obligation to keep the mitzvot.' Give one Jewish response to this statement.
5. Do you think that tikkun olam is important for Jews? Give two reasons for your view.

Beliefs about the afterlife

Jewish beliefs about life after death

Judaism does not focus on what happens in the afterlife as there is no specific mention of it in the **Torah**. Most Jews are more focused on living a good life in the here and now and try not to worry about what may happen after death. They believe that true understanding of life after death is beyond the ability of humans and so it is only important to be concerned with what can be understood and controlled in this life.

In Judaism the afterlife is known as **olam ha-ba**, whereas life on earth is known as **olam ha-ze**. Many Jews believe olam ha-ze is preparation for what is to come in olam ha-ba, therefore it is important to live this life according to the Torah. Life should be celebrated and cherished as God gave it to be lived, so treating others well and being a good person should be at the centre of Jewish life. However, this should be done as it is the right thing to do, not out of hope for a reward in the afterlife.

'Do not be like servants who serve the master in the expectation of receiving a reward.'
Ethics of the Fathers 1:3

Some Jews believe that after death the righteous will go to heaven as they have lived a good life and followed the **mitzvot**. Heaven is often referred to as Gan Eden (the Garden of Eden). Some Jews believe those who have not lived good lives and failed to follow the mitzvot will be sent to hell (Gehenna), which is a place of suffering and torment. Some Jews also believe in Sheol, which was traditionally seen as a dark place that all would go to but has now become seen as a place of waiting and purification. From Sheol it is believed that souls will either go to Gan Eden or be destroyed.

A small number of Jews believe in **reincarnation**, and that when they are reborn they should work to make the world a better place.

'This world is like a lobby before the Olam Ha-Ba. Prepare yourself in the lobby so that you may enter the banquet hall.'
Pirkei Avot 4:21

Jewish beliefs about the immortality of the soul

Many Jews believe in the **immortality of the soul**. Genesis describes how when God created man, he 'blew into his nostrils the breath of life; and man became a living being' (Genesis 2:7). Here God gives man a soul – something fundamentally different from other animals, which means that humans have God's breath within them. As this comes from God, it is immortal. Therefore, many Orthodox Jews believe that when they die the soul will live on to be resurrected with the body during olam ha-ba. Most Reform Jews reject any form of physical resurrection or physical life after death but some do believe the soul will continue to live on after death. As a result of this, Reform Jews do not forbid cremation as there will be no physical resurrection of the body.

Specification focus

The afterlife: Orthodox and Reform beliefs and teachings about life after death, judgement, and resurrection; spiritual and/or bodily resurrection, immortality of the soul and the belief that we must focus on this life in preparation for whatever happens in the next.

Life after death is not a big focus in Judaism. It is considered better to concentrate on doing good, such as performing charity by working at food banks, rather than worrying about what might happen in the next life

Useful terms

olam ha-ba – 'the world to come'; the afterlife
olam ha-ze – 'this world'; life on earth
reincarnation – a cycle where a soul is born into a new body
immortality of the soul – the idea that the soul lives on after the death of the body
resurrection – the raising of the body to life again after death

Jewish beliefs about judgement

Judaism teaches that God is the ultimate judge and will judge all humans on how well they have lived their lives and followed the mitzvot. Some Jews therefore believe that God will hold a Day of Judgement that will take place after the arrival of the **Messiah**, when all people – living and dead – will be judged on their actions. If they have followed yetzer ha tov they will receive a good judgement from God, but if they have followed yetzer ha ra they will not: God is a merciful judge, but also a just one.

Rosh Hashanah is a very important festival within Judaism as Jews believe this is a day of judgement which occurs every year. Rosh Hashanah allows Jews to reflect on their actions of the previous year and recognise their misdeeds. God also judges their actions and then they have ten days between Rosh Hashanah and Yom Kippur to make up for their bad deeds, meaning that they go into the new year without these sins. By atoning for their sins, many Jews believe that they will receive a good judgement on the final Day of Judgement.

Orthodox Jews believe in a physical resurrection, where those who have been good and righteous will be raised to life

Jewish beliefs about resurrection

There are many different beliefs about **resurrection** within Judaism. Orthodox Jews believe in resurrection of the body, where the body will be raised from the dead and reunited with the soul. One of the Thirteen Principles of Faith is 'the belief in the resurrection of the dead'.

Orthodox Jews believe the righteous will be resurrected and that this will take place during the Messianic Age. Due to this they do not agree with cremation, organ donation or post-mortems, as the body should be left intact ready for resurrection. Cemeteries are known as Houses of Life, indicating the belief that the dead will be resurrected.

> 'Many of those that sleep in the dust of the earth will awake, some to eternal life, others to reproaches, to everlasting abhorrence.'
> *Daniel 12:2*

Most Reform Jews reject belief in physical resurrection but do believe the soul will continue to live on after death. One Jewish teaching is that a person will live on in the memories of others, so it is important they live a good life to be remembered positively when they are gone.

Read about the Messiah and the arrival of the Messianic Age on page 136.

Knowledge recall

1. Define the following concepts: Messiah, Shekhinah, Shabbat. (You can find these definitions on page 131.)
2. List three Orthodox Jewish beliefs about the afterlife.
3. State one source of wisdom to support the Orthodox belief in resurrection.

Evaluation practice

4. 'It is important to focus on this life and not worry about the afterlife.' Give one Jewish response to this statement.
5. Do you think the afterlife is important for Jews? Give two reasons for your view.

Skills practice

On these exam practice pages you will see example answers for each of the exam question types: **a**, **b**, **c** and **d**. You can find out more about these on pages 8–9.

Question *(a)*

*Question **(a)** tests your knowledge and understanding. You will always be asked to **define a key concept** in this question. You can find a list of the concepts at the beginning of the chapter.*

> *(a)* What do Jews mean by 'Shekhinah'? [2]

Student response

Represents the feminine part of God on earth.

What went well

The candidate has given a partial definition of what Shekhinah means and tried to link to God's presence.

How to improve

You must give a complete definition that fully explains the key term.

You should learn the exam board's definition of the word at the start of this chapter.

You could give an example to support your definition.

Improved student response

The Shekhinah is the place where God's presence rests and can be felt. For example Orthodox Jews believe that the Shekhinah rests and can be felt in Jerusalem at the Western Wall.

Over to you! Try to answer this question:

> *(a)* What do Jews mean by 'Covenant'? [2]

Helpful hints

To help you answer this question effectively, you could use the check list below to make sure you include the most important things:

- Include a **synonym** for the word 'covenant'.
- Give an **example** of a covenant in Judaism.

Tip

The easiest way to make sure you get full marks for this question is to learn the definitions found on page 131.

Now give yourself **two minutes** to try and answer this question by yourself:

> *(a)* What do Jews mean by 'Messiah'? [2]

Question *(b)*

*Question **(b)** tests your knowledge and understanding. It will always ask you to **describe** a belief, a teaching, a practice or an event that is included on the specification.*

> *(b)* Describe different Jewish beliefs about resurrection. [5]

Student response

Jews believe different things about resurrection. Some believe there will be resurrection of the dead as it is mentioned in some Jewish texts, but they disagree on if it will be a bodily resurrection or not. Some believe the body will be resurrected and others believe it is only the soul that will be resurrected.

What went well

The candidate briefly mentions two different beliefs on resurrection.

How to improve

You must make it clear how the beliefs differ and who holds them.

You should include how these beliefs influence those who hold them.

You could make reference to or even quote sources of wisdom or authority to support your answer.

Improved student response

Judaism does not have one clear teaching on resurrection, and Orthodox Jews differ in their opinion to Reform Jews. Most Orthodox Jews believe in the resurrection of the body as it states in the Kaddish 'He will revive the dead'. Because they believe this is a bodily resurrection, many Orthodox Jews disagree with cremation and post-mortems. Many Reform Jews reject belief in the resurrection and so all mention of resurrection has been removed from Reform prayer books. They instead believe in the immortality of the soul. Most Jews argue that it is impossible to know what happens after death as it is in the hands of God and so the focus should be living a good life on earth.

Over to you! Try to answer this question:

(b) Describe Jewish beliefs about God as Creator. [5]

Helpful hints

Use the check list below to make sure you include the most important things:

- **Describe** one of the teachings in the Torah about God as creator.
- Give an **example** or quote from the Torah to support your point.
- Then **repeat** the above process, giving two more teachings from the Torah about God as creator – for example about God as the creator of the universe, human life or the mitzvot.

Now give yourself **five minutes** to answer this question by yourself:

(b) Describe the Abrahamic Covenant. [5]

Question *(c)*

Question ***(c)*** tests your knowledge and understanding. You need to give detailed evidence and reasoning to support your explanation of the topic.

(c) Explain why Moses is important in Judaism. [8]

Tip

The best answers reference all aspects of the question. Here, the candidate talks about:

- Orthodox and Reform Jews, showing diversity of belief on the resurrection within Judaism
- what Orthodox and Reform Jews believe about resurrection and how this influences the practice of their faith
- scripture which supports one of the points made.

Student response

Moses was chosen to save the Israelites from slavery in Egypt. God appointed him with this task as they believe he had a special relationship with God. They also believe he is the only person to have seen God face-to-face. Moses was also given the Torah by God on Mount Sinai and taught how to follow it, therefore he is considered a great rabbi.

What went well

This response gives three brief reasons why Moses is considered important in Judaism.

How to improve

You must make clear links to Judaism.

You should give clear evidence of why Moses is important. Use the word 'because' to develop and provide evidence for your points.

You could include some quotes or examples from the Torah to support your answer.

Improved student response

Jews believe that Moses is important because God appointed Moses to lead the Israelites out of slavery in Egypt. God chose him to speak for the Israelite nation and through Moses God performed many miracles that led to their freedom. God appeared to Moses directly to give him this task, showing the special relationship he had with Moses. Jews believe Moses is the only person to have known God face-to-face. Another reason why Moses is important in Judaism is that he received the Torah from God on Mount Sinai. This is important as the Torah forms the basis of Jewish law and morality. God gave it to Moses so he could teach it to the Israelites and so Moses is known as a great prophet. Moses also led the Israelites to the Promised Land, taking them to the home of their ancestors and uniting them as a people under God.

Over to you! Try to answer this question:

(c) Explain different Jewish beliefs about the Messiah. [8]

Helpful hints

- Include beliefs from **Judaism only**; there is no need to mention any other religion.
- For each belief, give a **source of wisdom** to support it, e.g. a quote from the Tenakh or a Jewish prayer.
- Explain **how** Jews are expected to behave as a result, e.g. doing good to bring about the Messianic Age.

Tip

Focus only on Judaism in this question as the question only mentions this religion. You will not be credited for mentioning any other religion.

Now give yourself **eight minutes** to answer this question by yourself:

(c) Explain different Jewish beliefs about life after death. [8]

Question *(d)*

*Question **(d)** tests your ability to **evaluate**. This means you need to show you have considered more than one point of view and that you have referred to religion and belief. You will need to be able to make judgements that are supported by detailed reasoning and argument.*

(d) 'All Jews should keep the 613 mitzvot (duties).'

Discuss this statement showing that you have considered more than one point of view. (You must refer to religion and belief in your answer). [8]

Student response

I disagree that all Jews should keep the mitzvot as many of them are out of date and do not fit with life in modern times. Jews should only keep the mitzvot that are helpful in modern society as this will benefit themselves and others. Also by only following the mitzvot they don't have the ability to follow their own conscience and so this could mean they make decisions they're not totally comfortable with.

Some Jews like Orthodox Jews would agree that it is important to keep the mitzvot as they were given by God, but they would say it is impossible to keep all of them as some are only for men therefore women do not need to keep them. Also, some mitzvot are impossible to keep as they relate to the Temple and so it is impossible to keep those as the Temple has been destroyed. But they would argue it's essential to try to keep as many mitzvot as possible as this means you're a better person and will have a better relationship with God.

Improved student response

Some people such as Orthodox Jews would agree that all Jews should keep the 613 mitzvot as they were given by God (Exodus 20) and so they are divine. Orthodox Jews are traditional in their approach to Judaism and believe they should follow the duties given in the Torah, as God has given them so they can live a moral life and create a fair and just society. This also helps to create a closer relationship with God as you are keeping his covenant. However, they understand that it is impossible to keep some mitzvot such as the ones which relate to the Temple; as this is outside of human control they should instead simply keep all of the ones they are able to. The only time they believe the mitzvot should not be followed is in a situation where they must consider pikuach nefesh. As God gave life and created it in his 'image and likeness' (Genesis 1:26), the only time that the mitzvot can be broken is to save a life in need because life is so sacred, for example by performing a life-saving operation on Shabbat. This is a strong argument as Jews believe that God is a Law-Giver, therefore he has given the mitzvot so that Jews will follow them and live life according to his commands. They also believe that God is a Judge who will judge their actions based on their life on earth and how well they follow the mitzvot, so it is important for Jews to follow as many mitzvot as they possibly can in order to be ethical people, obey God's laws and receive a good judgement from him.

Other people such as Reform Jews would disagree that all Jews should keep the 613 mitzvot as they believe that Judaism needs to be interpreted in a more modern way to fit in with modern society. As the mitzvot are thousands of years old they are outdated and do not deal with modern issues and therefore should not all be followed. Reform Jews might argue that it is better to focus on the Ten Commandments as these form the basis of Jewish ethics and morality and as there are only ten of them, they are much easier to follow daily than 613 duties. As Reform Jews believe the Torah can be interpreted to match modern life, they might believe they can use their conscience to help them adapt or even discard the mitzvot, as there are many different ways to live out their faith without being bound by strict rules. This is a weak argument as God gave Jews the 613 mitzvot for a reason: to know how to act and live well, therefore if

What went well

The candidate has offered two different viewpoints. Both have limited supporting evidence, although the second does briefly refer to the problem of keeping mitzvot connected to the Temple. The candidate has used some basic evaluative language to show the two different views and has mentioned that trying to follow all of the mitzvot is impossible in modern society.

How to improve

You must back up all statements, including personal statements, with evidence to support your arguments.

You should evaluate the arguments given in your essay. This will help you to come to a judgement later and to avoid simply giving different views.

You could quote sources of wisdom and authority to support your arguments.

The candidate has used the wording in the question statement to focus their answer on the right material.

Specialist language is used consistently and accurately.

Evidence of how beliefs can influence individuals today.

The candidate has given diverse Jewish beliefs and teachings to meet the demands of the question.

The candidate refers to appropriate sources of wisdom and authority.

Jews are disregarding the mitzvot they are rejecting Gods laws. Also, God is omniscient (all-knowing) and so he understands what Jews need to do to live well. Humans are imperfect and make mistakes, so by changing or ignoring the mitzvot they could be making a bad error. They may also be misled by their conscience too as humans can be ruled by their emotions leading them to make mistakes. By keeping all the mitzvot Jews ensure they are being ethical and living as God wants.

I ultimately believe that the Orthodox Jewish approach is the best approach because it recognises God's nature as a Law-Giver and Judge meaning that Jews clearly understand their obligation to God, which is to keep the mitzvot. Also, by keeping the mitzvot they remain his people as the mitzvot are the condition of the covenant with Moses. If Jews reject the mitzvot then they are rejecting this covenant and undermining their relationship with God. The mitzvot cover all aspects of Jewish life, ethics and practice, so Jews know how to act and respond in all situations. This means that in everything they do they are following what God wants. This will lead them to have a strong relationship not only with God but with other Jews as they are united in belief and practice.

The candidate has offered their judgement on the question.

Over to you! Try to answer this question:

(d) 'Belief in the afterlife is not important in Judaism.'

Discuss this statement showing that you have considered more than one point of view. (You must refer to religion and belief in your answer). [15]

Tip

Remember to show a diversity of beliefs within Judaism to ensure that you are meeting the requirements of the question. For example, you could refer to Orthodox and/or Reform Jewish beliefs.

Helpful hints

If you find it difficult to answer this question effectively, you could try using this structure to help you set out your paragraphs:

- **Argument** – Clearly state a religious view about the question.
- **Back it up** – Give some evidence or an example of teaching or behaviour that shows this view.
- **Challenge** – Offer a counterargument that directly opposes the view you have previously stated.
- **Back it up** – Support this response with evidence or examples.
- **Decide** – Weigh up which views are the best and why.

This could be one paragraph. Repeat the formula again for a second paragraph and at the end conclude with a final decision. Make sure you only talk about Jewish perspectives in your answer!

Now give yourself **fifteen minutes** to answer this question by yourself:

(d) 'Keeping the Ten Commandments is the most important part of Judaism.' Discuss this statement showing that you have considered more than one point of view. (You must refer to religion and belief in your answer.) [15]

Chapter 6: Practices

Introduction

Judaism is a diverse religion that has many significant religious practices which connect Jews to their community and to God. The practices are based on the core beliefs that you studied in the previous chapter. In this chapter, you will consider important Jewish practices such as worship in the synagogue and at home, initiation rituals, rites of maturity, marriage, mourning, rituals in daily life and key festivals.

As Judaism is diverse in practice, this chapter will reflect the different ways in which Orthodox and Reform Jews live out their faith and the reasons behind this. For both Orthodox and Reform Jews, the Torah is a key text which contains the foundational texts of Judaism and stories which help to inform Jewish self-understanding and identity. The Torah is used to inform Jewish rituals and ceremonies and therefore is a key component in how different Jews practice their faith.

Another key component of Judaism is that of the community. Many Jews believe very strongly that the community is important as it provides support when people need it. It also shares in the joy of individuals and is a means by which people can connect with their Jewish history, culture and traditions. The practices that are covered in this chapter reflect how many Jews engage with their faith and demonstrate their identity as Jews.

Things to remember

- Jewish practices are the ways in which Jews act, worship and live out their faith due to the beliefs they hold and the religious teachings they follow.
- Orthodox and Reform Jews practise their faith in different ways due to their relationship with the mitzvot, where they live and their proximity to places of worship. There is diversity within these groups too, meaning that there is no one way that all Jews live out their faith.
- For the exam, you will need to explain different Jewish views on the practices described in this chapter and show why you think some of these practices are relevant and essential, or why you think they are morally wrong or out of date.

Concepts

Covenant – a promise or agreement between two parties. Covenants were made between God with Noah, Abraham and Moses

Kosher – ('fit' or 'proper') foods that are permitted to be eaten according to Leviticus Chapter 11. It is also used to refer to the purity of ritual objects such as Torah scrolls

Messiah – the anointed one who Jews believe will bring in a new era or age for humankind. This will include rebuilding the Temple and bringing in an age of universal peace

Mitzvot – the term has a mix of meanings. It is often used to refer to duties (such as the 613 in the Torah) and good deeds

Shabbat – day of spiritual renewal and rest. Beginning at sunset on Friday and closing at nightfall on Saturday

Shekhinah – the place where God's presence rests and can be felt

Synagogue – house of assembly; building for Jewish public prayer, study and assembly

Torah – the five books of Moses (Genesis, Exodus, Leviticus, Numbers and Deuteronomy). Regarded as the holiest books of the Tenakh

Orthodox and Reform synagogue services

The nature and importance of synagogue services

Prayer in the **synagogue** is important in Judaism as it is a public acknowledgement of a Jew's relationship with God. Jews can pray anywhere at any time, but it is considered more beneficial and meaningful to pray with the community as it enhances the connection that the community has to each other and to God.

Prayer in the synagogue allows Jews to take time out to be with God. It also connects Jews with the Temple, as the daily prayers that take place in the synagogue have become substitutes for the sacrifices that used to take place in the original Temple.

There are official times for daily prayers in the synagogue that happen during the morning, afternoon and evening, but there are also services on **Shabbat** and festivals. Morning prayers are the longest and contain numerous blessings, readings from the books of Psalms, and prayers including the Shema and **Amidah**.

In Orthodox synagogues, a **minyan** of men only is required for all services where the **Torah** is read and certain prayers, including those for mourners. This demonstrates that there is much community support within regular worship. In Orthodox and Reform services both men and women can attend the synagogue, but in Orthodox services they are seated separately. In Orthodox synagogues, the service is led by a male **rabbi** and will usually take place in Hebrew, while the rabbi can be male or female in Reform synagogues. In Reform synagogues the service is conducted in both Hebrew and English, and the Torah portions are usually read in both languages. In both Orthodox and Reform services, the sermon is delivered in English. The main time for communal worship is Shabbat.

The Shabbat service

Shabbat is the holiest day of the week in Judaism, with the Shabbat service being when most Jews come together to worship. One of the Ten Commandments is to 'remember the Sabbath and keep it holy' (Exodus 20:8). Many Jews feel the best way to do this is to come together as a community, to develop their communal identity and their relationship with God.

Shabbat begins on Friday at nightfall, when three medium size stars can be seen and ends on Saturday at sunset. During this period, three prayer services take place: the Friday night service, the Saturday morning service and Saturday afternoon service. In Orthodox synagogues there is an additional service following the morning services which focuses on the Temple service of the past. Reform communities have shortened or more frequently dropped the additional service because its contents are not felt to be relevant today.

- Friday night service – this service is fairly short and welcomes Shabbat with songs, psalms and prayers.
- Saturday morning service – this service is the longest and, in some Orthodox synagogues, can last up to three hours. The service often starts with songs and psalms before the **Shema** and Amidah are said. There are always readings from

Specification focus

Worship: The nature and importance of Orthodox and Reform synagogue services; Shabbat service, the significance of prayer including the standing prayer (Amidah).

Prayer is very important in Judaism and helps individuals to build a strong relationship with the Jewish community and God

Useful terms

prayer – a way of communicating with God through words and actions

Amidah – means 'standing'; a prayer of central importance in synagogue services said when standing

minyan – traditionally a group of ten men over the age of thirteen; the minimum number of Jews needed for communal worship to take place

rabbi – a Jewish religious leader, also considered to be a teacher

Shema – a prayer found in the Torah which proclaims belief in one God

the Torah and Haftarah. The Haftarah portions are taken from the Prophets (Nevi'im) or the Writings (Ketuvim). The rabbi usually gives a talk to explain their meaning and relevance. Worship typically ends with a blessing over wine and food, where the community can socialise and enjoy Shabbat together.

- Saturday afternoon service – this is a short service involving a Torah reading and prayers including the Shema and Amidah.

Orthodox ceremonies include singing but no instrumental music; this has been the case since the destruction of the Temple to show mourning for its loss. Reform communities also have singing, including mixed choirs and this might also be accompanied by instrumental music. Other differences are seen in Reform services. For example, these are often shorter and include more communal readings and some variations in prayers, poems and readings. Liturgies in Reform synagogues sometimes introduce references to the Matriarchs as well as the Patriarchs and tries to minimise the use of gendered language.

The Amidah is the most important prayer in Judaism; when Jews pray it they believe they are in the presence of God

The importance of prayer

Prayer is very important in Judaism and forms the core of Jewish life. Prayers can take place in the synagogue but Jews are not restricted to this formal way of prayer, and many Jews pray informally and regularly throughout the day. For many Jews, prayer is a way of living out their faith, connecting with God and keeping the **mitzvot**. The siddur (Jewish prayer book) provides the daily prayers that a Jewish person can use, to help them focus their mind on God but also to pray in the same way as the Jewish community without having to go to the synagogue.

Jewish prayers might involve:

- Thanks – thanking God for the good things he has bestowed onto individuals and the community.
- Praise – this type of prayer recognises the power and glory of God and gives honour to him.
- Petition – this involves asking God for something for the individual or the community. Requests should not be selfish or materialistic and should focus on helping other people.
- Inspiration – these involve asking for help or guidance to act, think and do the right things.
- Hymns – these are meant to by joyful and uplifting.

The Amidah

Aside from the Shema, the Amidah is the most important prayer in Judaism and forms the core of the three daily prayer services and Shabbat services. It translates as 'standing' – Jews will stand when reciting it and face Israel. The Amidah can be prayed at home or during synagogue services. When at home, a Jew will pray the Amidah silently; during synagogue services it is prayed silently and then repeated aloud by the prayer leader. It is made up of nineteen blessings, starting with prayers of praise, followed by petitions and concluding with thanksgiving.

Many Jews believe that when they pray the Amidah they are in the presence of God, and so see it as a time to have an intimate conversation with God. It is an opportunity for a Jewish person to develop their own personal relationship with God without distractions and so it is very important for a Jewish person not to be interrupted when praying the Amidah.

Knowledge recall

1 Define the following concepts: synagogue, Shabbat, mitzvot. (You can find these definitions on page 153.)
2 List three reasons why prayer is important to Jews.
3 State one prayer that is said in a synagogue service on Shabbat.

Evaluation practice

4 'Prayer should not just happen in the synagogue.' Give one Jewish response to this statement.
5 Do you think that the synagogue is important for Jews? Give two reasons for your view.

Worship in the home

Worship at home

The home is often considered to be holy in Judaism as it allows Jews a safe space to pray, celebrate, feel the presence of God on **Shabbat**, and foster core Jewish values. It is the centre of Jewish life. **Worship** in the Jewish home usually involves the following elements:

- **Siddur** – this is the Jewish prayer book which contains the set daily prayers. It is used in the **synagogue** and at home; when used at home it allows a Jewish person to pray in the same way that they would in the synagogue, meaning they can still feel connected to other Jewish people.
- **Shema** – this is an important prayer in Judaism that reminds Jews they are monotheists. The Shema is said in the morning and evening services as well as before a Jew goes to sleep. This helps to keep its teachings in the forefront of their minds. The prayer also reminds them of their **covenant** obligation to keep the **mitzvot**. The Shema is found in Deuteronomy 6:4–9 of the Torah. The opening line states 'Hear, O Israel! The Lord is our God, the Lord alone.'
- **Modeh Ani** – many observant Jews pray the Modeh Ani as soon as they wake to thank God for returning their soul, so they can enjoy another day. They believe that during sleep the soul returns to God for renewal, therefore the Modeh Ani recognises that life is a gift from God.

> 'I thank you, living and enduring king, for you have graciously returned my soul within me. Great is your faithfulness.'
> *Modeh Ani prayer*

- **Mezuzah** – the use of the mezuzah is a mitzvah as Deuteronomy 6:9 states 'inscribe them on the doorposts of your house and on your gates'. This refers to the practice of placing a scroll with the Shema written on it in the mezuzah and attaching it to doorposts. Many Jews will touch the mezuzah as they pass it and be reminded of their faith in one God and how this should influence their actions.

Preparing for Shabbat

Shabbat is the holiest day in the week in Judaism, with many seeing it as a taste of olam ha-ba (the world to come). Jews are not supposed to engage in creative activities during this time to remember that God rested after creating the world. Therefore Jews must thoroughly prepare for Shabbat. Many Orthodox Jews take the command not to work literally and will clean the home and prepare food in advance and even set timers to turn lights on and off to ensure they do not break the mitzvot. One of the things to do to prepare for Shabbat is to ensure that the table is set with two candles and two **challah** loaves, so that when Shabbat is welcomed into the home everything is ready.

Celebrating Shabbat

Jews celebrate Shabbat to keep the mitzvah 'remember the sabbath day and keep it holy' (Exodus 20:8). They remember God creating the world and freeing the Israelites, and keep the day holy by worshipping God.

Specification focus

Worship: Worship in the home; siddur, recitation of Shema and Modeh Ani, display of mezuzah. The importance of preparing for and celebrating Shabbat: Exodus 20:8–10; Items worn for worship; tallith, tefillin and kippah.

The mezuzah is a small decorative case containing a scroll with the Shema written on it

Useful terms

worship – showing respect and reverence for God
siddur – a Jewish prayer book
Shema – a prayer found in the Torah which proclaims belief in one God
Modeh Ani – a prayer recited by many observant Jews when they first wake up
mezuzah – a small scroll of parchment in a decorative case with the Shema written on it. Mezuzahs are attached to doorposts in Jewish homes
challah – a plaited loaf made of white leavened bread. It is usually baked to celebrate the Shabbat

On Friday evening, Shabbat is welcomed into the home with a woman in the house lighting two candles around eighteen minutes before sunset. These candles represent the two commandments zakhor (to remember) and shamor (to observe). Following this, the family may attend the synagogue before returning home to say blessings, including the Kiddush over wine. Wine is included in the Shabbat meal to indicate that it is a time to celebrate. After this there are blessings over the two challah loaves. These loaves represent the belief that God always provides, and each person takes a piece of bread. The family then enjoys each other's company with a meal together.

On Saturday morning many Jews will attend a synagogue service, followed by a meal at home, and then spending time with family. The requirement to do no work remains.

On Saturday evening the family prepares for the end of Shabbat. At nightfall they will carry out the Havdalah ceremony. Havdalah means 'separation', so this ceremony marks that they have separated from Shabbat and are back to ordinary life. The family light the plaited Havdalah candle, share blessed wine and smell sweet spices in the hope of a sweet week.

Items worn in worship

Tallith – this is a prayer shawl traditionally worn by Jewish men during prayer. There are two types: the Talith Gadol which is a large blue and white shawl worn over clothes, and the Talith Katan which is smaller and worn under clothes. Both have tzitzit.

Tzitzit – these are knotted fringes attached to the tallith and they represent the wearer's commitment to keep the 613 mitzvot. They come from the command 'the Lord said to Moses as follows: Speak to the Israelite people and instruct them to make for themselves fringes on the corners of their garments... look at it and recall all the commandments of the Lord and observe them' (Numbers 15:37–39).

Kippah – these are skull caps traditionally worn by Jewish men. Although it is not a mitzvah to wear these, many men do to show that they are Jewish. It is also a sign of respect for God as the wearer acknowledges that God is above them and is transcendent.

Tefillin – these are leather boxes that contain parts of the Shema and are traditionally worn by men during prayer. Tefillin are not worn on Shabbat or during other festivals. One box is tied to the head and the other to the arm. It is a mitzvah to wear tefillin: 'Bind them as a sign on your hand and let them serve as a symbol on your forehead' (Deuteronomy 6:8). They remind Jews to love God in thought and action.

Reform Judaism is egalitarian and both men and women are entitled to wear tallith, tefillin and kippah. It is less common for Reform Jewish men and women to wear tefillin because they do not participate in the daily services where these are worn, but they still have the option to do so.

Knowledge recall

1 Define the following concepts: Shabbat, covenant, Torah. (You can find these definitions on page 153.)
2 List three things that happen on Shabbat.
3 State one source of wisdom which shows why Shabbat is important.

Evaluation practice

4 'Prayer is not important for Jews.' Give one Jewish response to this statement.
5 Do you think Shabbat is the most important time of the week for Jews? Give two reasons for your view.

The synagogue

Specification focus

The synagogue: Features of different synagogues in Britain: significance of bimah, aron hakodesh, Torah scrolls, ner tamid, seating, minyan; Exodus 20:4–5; Worship, social and community functions of synagogues serving Jewish communities in Britain.

Features of the synagogue

Synagogues are very diverse and vary based on where they are in the world, the age of the synagogue and the type of Jewish group they represent. Typical features of a synagogue include the following:

① The **bimah** – this is a raised platform which is the centre of focus in the synagogue. It has a podium on which the **Torah** scrolls are placed and read. In Orthodox synagogues it is usually in the centre of the congregation while in Reform synagogues it is usually at the front, close to the aron hakodesh.

② The **aron hakodesh** – this is also known as 'the holy ark' or just 'the ark'. It is the holiest place in the synagogue as it is where the Torah scrolls are kept. It is on the wall that faces Jerusalem so the congregation faces this way during prayer. The ark symbolises the Ark of the Covenant that housed the Ten Commandments after they were given to Moses. There is usually a curtain in front of the ark, and on certain occasions the curtain is pulled back and the doors of the ark are opened to intensify the holiness of the prayers taking place. The ner tamid hangs above the ark.

The **Torah scrolls** – these are large scrolls that contain the complete text of the Torah and are handwritten by a scribe. They are read using a pointer known as a yad. This is used for practical reasons so that people do not touch the scrolls or smudge or damage the letters. The outside is covered in a mantle (a decorated cloth covering) and they are stored in the ark to keep them safe.

③ The **ner tamid** – this translates as 'eternal light' and is considered to represent God's everlasting presence. It is a light placed above the ark and is never put out as the Israelites were told to keep a lamp burning 'from evening to morning before the LORD' (Exodus 27:21).

The seating – this is arranged differently in Orthodox and Reform synagogues. In Orthodox synagogues the seating for men and women is separate; sometimes women sit upstairs in a gallery. This is to ensure that each can concentrate fully on prayer. In Reform synagogues men and women sit together.

The **minyan** – Orthodox synagogues require a minyan of men to facilitate prayer. Certain prayers such as the Amidah require a minyan in the synagogue. Reform synagogues allow the minyan to be made up of men and women.

Images – synagogues contain no statues or images of God, humans or animals to ensure the statues or images do not become a focus of worship. Worshipping idols is banned in the Ten Commandments.

> ❛You shall not make for yourself a sculptured image, or any likeness of what is in the heavens above, or on the earth below, or in the waters under the earth. You shall not bow down to them or serve them.❜
> *Exodus 20:4–5*

The role of the synagogue

The synagogue serves the Jewish community and has many functions. It is:

A place of assembly – the word synagogue means 'house of assembly' or 'meeting place' in Greek. Jews sometimes refer to the synagogue as 'beth knesset', which in Hebrew also means 'house of assembly'. This shows that the synagogue is a safe space for Jewish people to gather together as a community for worship, learning, social activities and support. The synagogue is also a place for children to assemble and therefore there are many activities for children to take part in so they can socialise with friends.

A place of prayer – synagogues can also be called 'beth ha-tefilla', meaning 'house of prayer'. This reflects one of their main functions as a place of worship, where people can gather for daily prayers and **Shabbat** services. The synagogue facilitates communal worship and so reinforces Jewish communal identity. It allows Jews to connect with God and each other through prayer. Within synagogues there are services for children too, to allow them to participate in prayer and worship and to pray at their own pace.

Reform synagogues can look a little different but serve the same purposes in the community

'I will pay my vows to the LORD in the presence of all of His people.'
Psalms 116:14

A place of study – synagogues can also be called 'beth ha-midrash', meaning 'house of study', or sometimes 'shul' meaning 'school'. Synagogues help Jewish people to develop their understanding of the faith by offering study of the Tenakh. They also often offer Hebrew classes for children, so they can learn about the Torah and prepare for Bar/Bat Mitzvahs.

A place of community – synagogues also play a big role in bringing Jews together through social activities and are often the hub of Jewish communities. Synagogues will organise charity events and fundraisers, put on entertainment for the elderly and isolated, and host events for families. They offer a place for the Jewish community to come together outside of worship so they can socialise while still maintaining their faith. For example, events will provide **kosher** food and accommodate religious requirements that may be difficult for other community settings to follow. There are often many activities for children and young people within the synagogue so that they can participate in and enjoy being part of the synagogue community.

Useful terms

bimah – a raised platform in a synagogue where the Torah scrolls are read
aron hakodesh – the Holy Ark; where the Torah Scrolls are kept and the most important area of the synagogue
Torah scrolls – a handwritten copy of the Torah; the most sacred object in the synagogue
ner tamid – the 'eternal light'; a light that is never put out in the synagogue
minyan – traditionally a group of ten men over the age of thirteen; the minimum number of Jews needed for communal worship to take place

Knowledge recall

1 Define the following concepts: synagogue, Torah, Shekhinah. (You can find these definitions on page 153.)
2 List three roles of the synagogue for Jews.
3 State one source of wisdom that shows the importance of the synagogue.

Evaluation practice

4 'The most important function of a synagogue is as a place of prayer.' Give one Jewish response to this statement.
5 Do you think that men and women should sit separately in synagogue services? Give two reasons for your view.

Brit Milah and Bar and Bat Mitzvah

Brit Milah

Brit Milah is a ceremony that takes place in Judaism when a baby boy is eight days old. It can take place in a hospital, the home or the **synagogue**. This is a ritual that welcomes the boy into the Jewish community and is a joyful celebration. It is the sign that the boy is entering into the Abrahamic **covenant**, as the boy is circumcised in accordance with the command God gave:

> 'You shall circumcise the flesh of your foreskin, and that shall be the sign of the covenant between Me and you. And throughout the generations, every male among you shall be circumcised at the age of eight days.'
> *Genesis 17:11–12*

Brit Milah is a sign of the covenant with God and a time when the child is formally welcomed into the Jewish community and given a name. Any male wishing to convert to Judaism must have a Brit Milah to show they have entered into God's covenant.

During Brit Milah, the following happens:

- The baby is presented for Brit Milah at eight days old unless he is ill and then it will be delayed. Only men will be present in Ultra Orthodox ceremonies. Whereas men and women can be present in Orthodox and Reform ceremonies.
- A specially chosen person will place the baby on an empty chair. This is called Elijah's chair as the prophet Elijah is believed to be present during every circumcision.
- The mohel (circumciser) will then place the baby on the knee of the sandek (the child's companion). Mohels are traditionally male in Orthodox ceremonies, but in Reform ceremonies they can be male or female.
- The mohel will circumcise the child, before blessing the child or handing him to the rabbi or distinguished person to bless him.
- A celebration will follow the ceremony.

Blessings are given to the child which reflect the hope that the child will achieve personal fulfillment and happiness, spiritual, ethical and moral fulfillment. In Hebrew, the blessings are 'toknow torah, chuppah and ma'asim tovim' (education, relationships and good deeds), which shows the importance of these things within Judaism.

Progressive Jews believe that it is important to welcome a baby girl into the Jewish community with the same importance as a boy. Therefore, there is usually a naming ceremony and a celebration which can take place either in the home or the synagogue. This would include a set ceremony and creative readings.

Bar Mitzvah

A **Bar Mitzvah** is a rite of passage into adulthood. It is a ceremony that takes place in the synagogue on the **Shabbat** after the boy has turned thirteen. Bar Mitzvah means 'Son of the Commandment' and indicates that the boy has become an adult and is now personally responsible for keeping the **mitzvot**.

Specification focus

Rituals: The role and importance of Brit Milah: covenant, identity, features of the ceremony; Bar Mitzvah: Law and personal responsibility, features of the ceremony; Orthodox and Reform views regarding Bat Mitzvah and Bat Chayil and features of the ceremonies.

Read more about the Abrahamic covenant on page 138.

Brit Milah happens when a Jewish boy is eight days old and marks his entry into the Jewish faith

Useful terms

Brit Milah – a ceremony where an eight-day-old baby boy is circumcised
Bar Mitzvah – a ceremony where a thirteen-year-old boy becomes an adult in Jewish law and is now responsible for keeping the mitzvot
Bat Mitzvah – a Reform Jewish ceremony where a twelve- or thirteen-year-old girl becomes an adult in Jewish law and is now responsible for keeping the mitzvot
Bat Chayil – an Orthodox Jewish ceremony where a twelve-year-old girl takes on an adult role in the Jewish community

During the ceremony, the boy must recognise and accept his obligation to keep Jewish law, try to be a righteous person and accept that he is responsible for his wrongdoings. After the ceremony, the boy can be counted as part of the minyan, fully take part in synagogue services, and wear tefillin.

The Bar Mitzvah is a sign that the boy has accepted the conditions of the covenant God made with Moses (the mitzvot). Consequently, a boy's Bar Mitzvah is a very important time in his life and it can take months to prepare for. A rabbi will help the boy with this by teaching him Hebrew, how to keep the mitzvot and the significance of prayer.

During Bar Mitzvah, the following happens:

- The boy goes to the synagogue on the Shabbat after his thirteenth birthday. He will have learned a **Torah** portion in preparation for this.
- The boy will be called to read his Torah portion from the bimah in front of the congregation.
- After this, the rabbi may give a talk that will include talking to the boy about his new responsibilities.
- The boy then gives a speech to the congregation.
- The boy's father recites a blessing thanking God for bringing his son to maturity.
- The boy wears tefillin for the first time.
- Finally, there will be a celebration where the boy will receive presents to congratulate him.

After his Bar Mitzvah, the boy is fully recognised as a responsible adult in Jewish law. Boys in both Orthodox and Reform Judaism will have a Bar Mitzvah when they turn thirteen.

A Bar/Bat Mitzvah confirms a thirteen-year-old boy/girl's place in God's covenant and marks them as an adult in Jewish law

Bat Mitzvah and Bat Chayil

In Reform Judaism in the UK, girls will celebrate their **Bat Mitzvah** at the age of twelve or thirteen. Bat Mitzvah means 'Daughter of the Commandment.' In Reform synagogues, the girls will have a ceremony that is identical to that celebrated by boys. This is due to egalitarian principles. After her Bat Mitzvah, the girl is classed as an adult in Jewish law, meaning she is responsible for keeping the mitzvot, can form part of a minyan and can fully participate in synagogue services. The Bat Mitzvah will take place in the synagogue on Shabbat. A celebration takes place after the ceremony.

Orthodox Jewish girls aged twelve usually have a **Bat Chayil**, rather than a Bat Mitzvah, as in Orthodox Judaism girls do not have the same responsibilities as boys and so are not required to keep the mitzvot in the same way. Bat Chayil means 'Daughter of Valour' and is a ceremony that takes place as near to the girl's twelfth birthday as possible. Although it takes place in the synagogue, it does not take place on Shabbat. The girl will give a speech about a specific topic in Judaism but will not read from the Torah. Bat Chayil marks the girl as taking up an adult role in the Jewish community.

Knowledge recall

1. Define the following concepts: covenant, Messiah, kosher. (You can find these definitions on page 153.)
2. List three things that happen in a Bar Mitzvah.
3. State one source of wisdom which shows why Jews carry out Brit Milah.

Evaluation practice

4. 'Bar/Bat Mitzvah is the most important Jewish ceremony.' Give one Jewish response to this statement.
5. Do you think it is essential for a Jewish boy to have a Brit Milah? Give two reasons for your view.

Marriage and mourning

The importance of marriage

Marriage is very important in Judaism and is seen as a time for celebration by the couple but also by the wider Jewish community, as it is the joining of two people in loving union.

By marrying, a Jewish person fulfils this mitzvah to enter into a life of love and joy. God also commands that Jews 'be fertile and increase' (Genesis 1:28). Many Jews believe that sex should only take place within marriage and should be for the purpose of procreation. Marriage therefore allows Jews to obey this mitzvah too.

Most Orthodox Jews believe it is important to marry someone who is Jewish. This is to ensure that both people fully understand the religious significance of marriage, and that their children are brought up Jewish to strengthen the continuation of Judaism. Many Reform Jews accept interfaith marriage, though will often prefer their children to marry a Jew and lead a full Jewish life. However, most Reform communities are very accepting of families of interfaith couples. The children of one Jewish parent can be brought up as Jewish and are recognised as such by Reform Judaism, if this is what the parents want.

The marriage ceremony

In Judaism marriage is a contract between two people, with the couple marrying each other under the supervision of a rabbi. Marriage ceremonies may vary but tend to have the same core practices:

- Kiddushin (the betrothal) – this is the first part of the marriage ritual. It is a ceremony which marks that a couple have agreed to marry. The couple then does not live together or have sex until the marriage takes place, but more often, it takes place a few hours before the marriage itself. The ketubah (marriage contract) is created, which sets out the roles and responsibilities of the bride and groom.
- Mikvah – some Jewish brides will attend the mikvah (a bath used for purification) to ensure they are purified before the marriage.
- Fasting – some Jews choose to fast on the day of their wedding to symbolise that they are being cleansed and entering the marriage in a fresh state.
- Ketubah – the groom signs the ketubah in front of witnesses, which marks the beginning of the marriage ceremony. This sets out the husband's obligations to his wife. This shows that they understand and accept their individual roles and responsibilities. The ketubah is a legal document that will be important if the couple decide to divorce in the future. In Reform ceremonies, the ketubah has been rewritten to acknowledge the equal status of husband and wife. It shows the roles and responsibilities and the aspiration for a good marriage.
- Bedeken – this takes place after the signing of the ketubah. The groom puts a veil over the bride's face to symbolise that he will clothe and protect her.
- Chuppah – the groom waits for the bride under the chuppah, which is a canopy that has two open sides. It symbolises the home the couple will make and that it is open to the community. The bride circles the groom seven times, showing she encircles him with love. In Reform ceremonies, the bride will often not circle the groom to show that they are equal in marriage. The bride will remain veiled until the ceremony is completed.

Specification focus

Rituals: Marriage: Genesis 2:24, features of the ceremony; mourning rituals: onan, kaddish, sheva, yarzheit. Role of chevra kaddisha.

> 'Hence a man leaves his father and mother and clings to his wife, so that they become one flesh.'
> *Genesis 2:24*

Jews marry under a chuppah to symbolise the home that they will build together

Useful terms

marriage – in Judaism, a legal and spiritual bonding of a man and woman
onan – the lead mourner
chevra kaddisha – a group of Jews that prepares the body for burial. Each synagogue has its own group
Kaddish – a prayer praising God
shiva – the seven-day period of mourning that happens straight after a funeral
yahrzeit – the anniversary of the death of a loved one

- Rings – two blessings are said, then the groom gives the bride a plain gold ring which is placed on her index finger. As he does this, he says 'With this ring, you are consecrated to me according to the Law of Moses and of Israel.' In Reform ceremonies, there is a mutual exchange of rings to show that the couple are equals in marriage.
- Nisuin – this is the second part of the ceremony where seven blessings are said. The blessings are said to convey a sense of joyfulness and hope for the successful future of the couple. They also show the connection that the couple share with the wider Jewish community.
- Stamping on the glass – the groom smashes a glass by stamping on it as a reminder of the destruction of the Temple.
- Time alone – after the ceremony, the couple spend a few minutes alone to mark their status as a married couple.

In Reform synagogues, many rabbis will carry out ceremonies for LGBTQ couples.

Read about Jewish beliefs on resurrection on pages 131.

Jews place stones on the headstone of a loved one to show their respect for the deceased

Mourning rituals

When a Jewish person dies, it is important that various rituals are observed to ensure that person is treated properly and with respect. The **onan** is someone appointed to assume responsibility over the funeral. They are a relative of the deceased who is obliged to mourn, for example, a son for a father. Their sole concern is to ensure that the deceased is treated properly and with dignity at all times. They help to arrange the funeral and during this time they do not have to keep the **mitzvot**. All this is a sign of utmost respect for the dignity of the person.

The onan will be assisted by the **chevra kaddisha**, which is a voluntary group of people who care for the body after death. They wash the body and clothe it in white, ensuring that all is ready for the burial. The chevra kaddisha must stay with the deceased until the burial takes place. The burial should take place as soon as possible, ideally within 24 hours of death. Orthodox Jews only permit burial, whereas Reform Jews also allow cremation due to different beliefs about resurrection. The deceased is placed in a plain wooden coffin and the funeral takes place in a cemetery. The funeral is simple, with psalms and the **Kaddish** being said to help the mourners feel closer to God. Once the burial is over the onans will move into the next phase of mourning, which is **Shiva**.

Shiva is the first and most intense stage of mourning after the burial. Shiva means 'seven' and this is a seven-day period when mourners will not leave the home, sit on low chairs, cover mirrors, and receive visitors who offer condolences. The kaddish will be recited daily and a candle will be kept lit as a symbol of the person's soul. The community will ensure that the material needs of those in mourning are cared for so that they can focus on mourning the deceased.

The next stage of mourning is shloshim, which is 30 days of less intense mourning. During this time, mourners are not permitted to attend celebrations. For most Jews mourning ends after shloshim. But if a Jew has lost a parent then mourning will continue for one year, and this period is called avelut. During this time, the mourner says the kaddish daily and does not attend any celebrations.

The **yahrzeit** is the anniversary of a death and is marked yearly. Before the first yahrzeit, a headstone is put on the grave to allow people to visit and remember the dead. Visitors place stones on the headstone to show their respect for the deceased. On the anniversary itself a yahrzeit candle is lit for 24 hours and the Kaddish is said. The yahrzeit and stone setting allows the family and community to respect, celebrate and honour the life of the deceased.

Knowledge recall

1. Define the following concepts: mitzvot, Shekhinah, Torah. (You can find these definitions on page 153.)
2. List three things that happen when someone dies in Judaism.
3. State one source of wisdom which shows why marriage is important for Jews.

Evaluation practice

4. 'Marriage is the best state for a Jew to be in.' Give one Jewish response to this statement.
5. Do you think that shiva is important? Give two reasons for your view.

The Tenakh and the Talmud: keeping kosher

Specification focus

Daily life: Significance of use of the Tenakh and the Talmud in daily life; Dietary laws: kosher/treyfah, parev, the prohibition of milk with meat, requirements of a kosher kitchen: Leviticus 11:1–23; keeping kosher in Britain: benefits and challenges.

The Tenakh and the Talmud

The **Tenakh** is the main sacred text in Judaism. The **Torah** is the most important part of the Tenakh as it contains the **mitzvot** (the duties of Judaism given by God). The Torah teaches Jews how to act, live, worship and be good people, and forms the basis of daily life.

The Tenakh also contains the Nevi'im and Ketuvim. The Nevi'im are the books of the prophets, which many Jews read to understand Jewish history (including their covenantal relationship with God). The Ketuvim are sacred writings and include the psalms, which are used in daily worship by many Jews. Many Jews believe that by using the Tenakh in daily life they can create a stronger personal relationship with God, as it helps them to understand what God wants of them.

The **Talmud** is a collection of writings that clarify areas of the Torah. It has two parts: the Mishnah and the Gemara. The Mishnah is the first written version of Jewish oral law. It includes teachings that were originally passed down orally (by word of mouth) on how to interpret the Torah and apply its rules to daily life. The Gemara is a commentary on the Mishnah by early Jewish rabbis. It discusses the Mishnah further and gives additional explanations to help understand difficult areas of the Torah.

Many Jews will study the Torah and the Talmud to better understand how to follow the mitzvot in their daily life

The Talmud is used in daily life to help understand and apply the teachings of the Torah. Many Orthodox Jews study the Talmud and Torah at yeshivas (Jewish academies); study of the Torah is emphasised in the Talmud. For Orthodox Jews the Torah is the most important revelation that God has given and as it was revealed in its final form at Sinai, they try to follow it as closely as possible as it remains eternally relevant. Most Reform Jews view the Tanakh as very important, however they believe that the Torah was written by humans with divine inspiration and so should be interpreted in light of modern society. Some Reform Jews place great emphasis on the ethical teachings of the Prophets and other parts of the Torah and Tanakh which they use to inform their daily lives. Today, Reform Jews give more consideration of the Talmud than they did in the past, as they see this as showing an evolution of many Jewish ideas and debates.

‘If you have learned much of the Torah, do not claim credit for yourself, because for such a purpose were you created.’
Pirkei Avot 2:4

Useful terms

Tenakh – the Jewish Bible, consisting of the Torah (the five books of Moses), Nevi'im (prophets) and Ketuvim (writings)
Talmud – a collection of writings on Jewish law and tradition, made up of the Mishnah and Gemara
treyfah – meaning 'torn'; food that is not permitted to be eaten in Judaism
parev – neutral foods that do not contain milk or meat and so can be eaten with either

Jewish dietary laws

Kashrut are laws in Judaism which deal mainly with food. They outline foods that can and cannot be eaten, and how to prepare, cook and store food. These laws are found in the Torah, mainly in the book of Leviticus.

There are two divisions of food in Judaism: **kosher** and **treyfah**.

- Kosher food is food that Leviticus lists as acceptable. These foods include animals which have split hooves and eat grass, fish with scales and fins, poultry, and produce from kosher animals. Any meat that is to be consumed must be killed in a certain way: the animal's throat must be cut with a sharp knife and the blood must be drained.

- Treyfah food is food that Leviticus lists as unacceptable. This includes animals without split hooves, those that do not eat grass, shellfish, meat with blood in it, animals that have died of natural causes, birds of prey and animals that have not been killed properly.
- **Parev** food is 'neutral' food that is not meat or dairy (and so can be eaten with either), such as vegetables, fruits, rice and pasta. It must be checked and washed before being eaten to ensure it has not been contaminated.

> 'Any animal that has true hoofs, with clefts through the hoofs, and that chews the cud – such you may eat.'
> *Leviticus 11:3*

> 'Everything in water that has no fins and scales shall be an abomination for you.'
> *Leviticus 11:12*

Keeping kosher means being mindful not just of what is being eaten, but also how it was prepared

Many Orthodox Jews try to keep all the rules of kashrut. This has a big impact on their daily lives as they must prepare food carefully and ensure they are mindful of what they eat, particularly if they are eating out. Reform Jews may only keep kosher at home or may choose which rules they wish to follow to fit their lifestyle.

Meat, milk and the kosher kitchen

A major law of kashrut is that meat and dairy cannot be eaten together, as Exodus 23:19 states 'you shall not boil a kid in its mother's milk'. Many Orthodox Jews would never eat a cheeseburger, for example, and some would even wait three to six hours after eating meat to then consume dairy. Reform Jews may choose not to keep this law due to the difficulties it poses in modern life.

All Orthodox Jewish kitchens will have separate areas for preparing dairy and meat, including separate sinks, plates, cutlery and utensils. Meat and dairy will be prepared in separate areas of the kitchen but can be stored in the same fridge. Reform Jewish homes may not do this due to the expense and difficulties involved.

Benefits and challenges of keeping kosher in Britain

In Britain today there are many benefits for a Jewish person keeping kosher, but modern life can also make it challenging.

Benefits	Challenges
Keeping kosher follows the mitzvot, which were given by God.	It can be very expensive to get kosher food.
It connects the person with their Jewish history.	Those who live in small Jewish communities may not have easy access to kosher food or supermarkets.
It ensures traditions are followed and will more likely be carried on by the next generation.	It is difficult to eat out if there are no kosher restaurants nearby.
It is a physical manifestation of faith and connects the whole Jewish community, including their ancestors	Preparation of food must be thorough and planned well in advance.

Knowledge recall

1 Define the following concepts: kosher, Messiah, covenant. (You can find these definitions on page 153.)
2 List three challenges of keeping kosher in Britain.
3 State one source of wisdom to show why milk and meat cannot be eaten together.

Evaluation practice

4 'There are more challenges than benefits to keeping kosher.' Give one Jewish response to this statement.
5 Do you think that a person is only truly Jewish if they keep kosher? Give two reasons for your view.

Rosh Hashanah and Yom Kippur

The origins and meaning of Rosh Hashanah

Rosh Hashanah is the festival which celebrates the Jewish New Year and commemorates God creating the world. It takes place over two days in September, on the 1st and 2nd of the Jewish month of Tishrei. During this festival, Jews look forward to the year to come and reflect on the special relationship they have with God, remembering all that he has done for them.

Rosh Hashanah is mentioned in the Bible as a day of rest, and in the Mishnah as a time when God judges everyone. Today, Rosh Hashanah is still known as the Day of Judgement. Jews believe that at this time, God will judge every person on the actions of the previous year and then decide what the coming year will bring for them. Rosh Hashanah marks the start of a ten-day period when Jews ask and work for forgiveness before Yom Kippur, the Day of **Atonement**. During these ten days, often referred to as the Ten Days of **Repentance**, Jews consider their wrongdoings of the previous year and try to make up for them. It is a time for self-reflection and improvement, with the aim of entering the new year with a clean slate. This means that even though Rosh Hashanah is a time for celebration, it is also a time for serious contemplation.

> ‘In the seventh month, on the first day of the month, you shall observe complete rest, a sacred occasion commemorated with loud blasts.’
> *Leviticus 23:24*

Celebrating Rosh Hashanah

The month leading up to Rosh Hashanah prepares Jews for the Day of Judgement. During this time, many Jews will start considering their faults and the **shofar** is blown daily. The day before Rosh Hashanah is a day of preparation. Many Jews clean their homes, buy the special foods that are eaten during the festival and attend the **synagogue** to pray. Some Orthodox Jews also have a mikvah (a bath of ritual purification) to be in a pure state for the festival. Families will gather both on the eve of Rosh Hashanah and also at lunchtime. Many people will travel to be back at home with the wider family during this festival to celebrate in this joyous time.

All Jewish festivals start in the evening, and the night before Rosh Hashanah (Erev Rosh Hashanah) Jews will have the first taste of apples and honey. On the morning of Rosh Hashanah, many Jews attend the synagogue. During this service, various prayers and blessings are said. The shofar is also blown 100 times as a call to repentance, and this marks the start of the period of repentance.

When the service ends many Jews return home for a meal, with food that has special significance. A Kiddush (blessing) is said and then apples dipped in honey are eaten in the hope of a sweet new year. There will also be a round challah loaf to symbolise the circle of life and the kingship of God. Many Jews also eat pomegranates which contain a lot of seeds – symbolic of the number of **mitzvot** a Jew will aim to uphold in the coming year.

Specification focus

Festivals: The origin, meaning and celebration of the following festivals among different Jewish communities in Britain: Rosh Hashanah, Yom Kippur; diversity of practice between different Jewish traditions.

The shofar is blown during Rosh Hashanah to call Jews to begin repenting for the sins of the previous year

Useful terms

Rosh Hashanah – 'head of the year'; the Jewish New Year
atonement – making amends for one's wrongdoings
repentance – being sorry for one's wrongdoings and making up for them
shofar – a ram's horn
Yom Kippur – 'Day of Atonement'; the holiest day of the year for Jews

Some Jews also perform the Tashlich ritual, where they throw pieces of bread into a stream to show they are symbolically throwing away their sins.

Within Judaism there is diversity in how Rosh Hashanah is celebrated. For example, Orthodox Jews will celebrate the two days of Rosh Hashanah and attend the synagogue on both days. Reform Jews might only celebrate and attend the synagogue on the first day.

The origins and meaning of Yom Kippur

After Rosh Hashanah and the Ten Days of Repentance, Jews celebrate **Yom Kippur**. This is described in the Tenakh as a day of atonement and abstinence. One original custom mentioned in Leviticus involved symbolically putting people's sins on a goat and driving it out into the desert. Today it is the most solemn day of the year and a time when forgiveness should take place. It is a day that many Jews will spend in the synagogue in prayer and worship. It is important to note that whilst the focus of Yom Kippur is repentance, this is not restricted to only this time of year. Jews are able to repent for wrongdoings at any time during the year.

Yom Kippur is the holiest day of the year in Judaism; many Jews believe that God's Final Judgement in the future will happen on Yom Kippur

> 'Mark, the tenth day of this seventh month is the Day of Atonement. It shall be a sacred occasion for you: you shall practice self-denial.'
> *Leviticus 23:26*

Celebrating Yom Kippur

Many Jews perform acts of charity and clean their homes in preparation for Yom Kippur. They eat before sunset on the day before Yom Kippur and this will be the last meal which marks the start of a twenty-five-hour fast. Some Orthodox Jews will visit the mikvah to cleanse themselves before the festival.

On the day of Yom Kippur, Jews who are over the age for Bat or Bar Mitzvah and are healthy and fit enough to do so will not eat or drink as a sign that they are atoning for their sins. Many Orthodox Jews and some Reform Jews wear white to symbolise purity and sinlessness and spend the day in continuous prayer. Many synagogues have five prayer services instead of the usual three to mark that it is the holiest day of the year. During this time, Jews ask for forgiveness from God and will also remember the dead and light yahrzeit candles in their memory.

During Yom Kippur the doors of the aron hakodesh are opened to show the close connection Jews have with God and that the gates of heaven are open. The prayer services cover various themes such as justice, redemption and God's willingness to forgive the truly sorry. The last service is Neillah ('closing') and is the most sacred. It symbolises the closing of the gates of heaven, which Jews believe will happen after the Final Judgement. At the end of Yom Kippur, the shofar is blown once to show this holy time has ended, and Jews believe they enter the year with a fresh start, reconciled with God and other people. Jews believe that before facing God, people should ensure that they have asked for forgiveness and said sorry to those who they have wronged in the past to ensure they have made up for their misdeeds. In Hebrew, the words for 'sin' are varied and include the concept of 'missing the mark'. Therefore, Yom Kippur is a time to make up for when Jews have missed the mark.

Knowledge recall

1 Define the following concepts: synagogue, Shekhinah, Shabbat. (You can find these definitions on page 153.)
2 List three things that Jews do to celebrate Rosh Hashanah.
3 State one reason why Jews fast during Yom Kippur.

Evaluation practice

4 'Yom Kippur is the most important day of the year.' Give one Jewish response to this statement.
5 Do you think that it is important for Jews to try to atone during Yom Kippur? Give two reasons for your view.

Pesach and Sukkot

The origins and meaning of Pesach

Pesach or Passover is the Festival of Freedom for Jews as well as a spring harvest festival. It is a very important festival as it celebrates the Israelites' escape from slavery in Egypt and their subsequent freedom. Its name comes from the fact that the Israelites were 'passed over' by the final and worst plague that God sent to free them (the deaths of the firstborn sons). The Israelites had painted lambs' blood onto the lintels and doorposts of their homes and so were spared. Pesach takes place during the Jewish month of Nisan (March to April), and it remembers the history of the Jews and the reasons why they are free.

> 'This day shall be to you one of remembrance: you shall celebrate it as a festival to the LORD throughout the ages; you shall celebrate it as an institution for all time.'
> *Exodus 12:14*

Celebrating Pesach

Pesach is celebrated for seven days in Israel and by Reform Jews around the world, and eight days by Orthodox Jews in countries other than Israel. During this time no **chametz** is eaten, therefore before Pesach begins many Jews prepare by extensively cleaning and removing all chametz from the home. Children are involved in helping search out the last crumbs before the start of the festival, therefore this is a time of great fun and joy. Some Jewish families may have separate kitchenware, cutlery and plates to avoid any contamination. The reason for the prohibition of chametz is that when the Israelites fled from Egypt there was no time for their bread to rise. Therefore during Pesach, **matzah** is eaten instead.

At the beginning of Pesach, candles are lit to mark the start of the festival. Many families then go to an evening synagogue service before returning home to the Pesach or Seder meal. For many families, Seder night is the the ultimate intergenerational family gathering of the Jewish calendar year as family members of all ages gather to celebrate. For Orthodox Jews this meal is eaten twice, on the first and second nights of Pesach; for many Reform Jews it is just eaten on the first night. Seder means 'order', indicating that there is a special order and significance to what is in the meal. The Haggadah is a book used during the meal to tell the story of the Israelites' escape from Egypt. Many Jews take this time to think about how they can actively help those who are oppressed and in contemporary forms of slavery as they remember the history of the Jewish people.

The meal begins with the youngest person in the family asking questions about the origins and significance of Pesach. After these are explained the family enjoy the meal, which contains the following symbolic foods and wine. Pesach is a time for lots of family cooking and recipes to be included in meals, which represents the closeness of the family.

- Z'roa: usually a lamb's bone; Reform Jews will use a sweet potato instead if they are a vegetarian. Represents the lambs' blood the Israelites painted on their doorposts to spare them from God's tenth plague.

Specification focus

Festivals: The origin, meaning and celebration of the following festivals among different Jewish communities in Britain: Pesach: Exodus 12:14, Sukkot; diversity of practice between different Jewish traditions.

Seder means order. The Seder plate is an ordered plate which contains symbolic foods connected with Pesach

Useful terms

Pesach – a festival celebrating the Israelites' freedom from slavery in Egypt
chametz – leavened foods: food that contains grain and water and has been left to rise
matzah – flatbread or unleavened bread
Elijah – an important prophet in Judaism; it is believed he will declare the coming of the Messiah
Sukkot – also known as the Festival of Shelters; a festival that thanks God for protecting and providing for the Jews
sukkah – a temporary shelter built during Sukkot

- Karpas: green leaves or vegetables that are dipped into salt water to represent the pain felt by the slaves.
- Maror and chazaret: bitter herbs to represent the bitterness of slavery.
- Charoset: represents the mortar (cement) that was used to make the pyramids in Egypt. Apples and walnuts are chopped and mixed with wine to make a paste.
- Beitzah: a roasted egg that symbolises the life cycle. This links to the new life the Israelites received after their freedom.
- Wine: this symbolises that Pesach is a joyous occasion. Four glasses are poured to symbolise the four times God promised to free the Israelites. An extra glass is also poured for **Elijah**.
- Matzah: flatbread eaten to remember the haste the Israelites were in to leave Egypt.

The origins and meaning of Sukkot

Sukkot is one of three harvest festivals in Judaism and traditionally marked the final harvest in early autumn. Leviticus commands Jews to celebrate Sukkot to commemorate the Israelites' journey to the Promised Land. During the forty years spent wandering in the desert, the Israelites had to build and live in temporary homes; by celebrating Sukkot, Jews remember the difficult conditions that the Israelites had to endure. It is a joyful and festive time, during which many Jews feel more connected to God and nature.

> 'You shall live in booths seven days; all citizens in Israel shall live in booths, in order that future generations may know that I made the Israelite people live in booths when I brought them out of the land of Egypt.'
> *Leviticus 23:42–43*

The sukkah represents the Jews' dependence on God for provision and security

Celebrating Sukkot

Sukkot begins five days after Yom Kippur. It lasts for seven days, with the first two being days of rest. Before Sukkot, many Jewish families will build a **sukkah** outside, which must have three walls and a simple roof (such as branches or reeds) through which the stars can be seen. This is to emulate the way the Israelites lived in the desert. The open nature of the sukkah represents that Jews are open to the presence of God and that God is their one source of protection and security. During Sukkot, many Jews will eat and spend time in the sukkah, and some Jews may sleep in the sukkah too. Families often decorate their sukkah to reflect the joyous nature of the festival.

Jews are required to place a lulav and etrog in the sukkah. A lulav is made up of a palm, a myrtle branch and a willow branch bound together. An etrog is a large citrus fruit. These together with Hadissim and Aravot are known as the Four Species. Jews are required to wave these in all four directions to show that God is everywhere. The Four Species also represent the blessings in the lives of Jews. Many Jews wave the lulav in the four directions of the compass every morning of Sukkot (excluding **Shabbat**) to represent the omnipresence of God. The waving of the lulav replicates some of the worship that used to happen in the original Temple.

Orthodox Jews are more likely to build their own sukkah if they can and throughout the festival only eat meals in the sukkah. Reform Jews may choose to build a sukkah or celebrate in a communal sukkah, such as one built by their local **synagogue**. They may also choose not to eat all of their meals in the sukkah. Many Jewish communities use the open nature of their sukkah to extend hospitality to their friends and neighbours. Many Reform synagogues will organise interfaith events in the communal sukkah to encourage community cohesion.

Knowledge recall

1. Define the following concepts: covenant, Messiah, mitzvot. (You can find these definitions on page 153.)
2. List three things that Jews do when celebrating Sukkot.
3. State one source of wisdom which shows why Jews celebrate Pesach.

Evaluation practice

4. 'Pesach is the most important Jewish festival.' Give one Jewish response to this statement.
5. Do you think Jews have a duty to observe Sukkot? Give two reasons for your view.

Skills practice

On these exam practice pages you will see example answers for each of the exam question types: **a**, **b**, **c** and **d**. You can find out more about these on pages 8–9.

Question *(a)*

*Question **(a)** tests your knowledge and understanding. You will always be asked to **define a key concept** in this question. You can find a list of the concepts at the beginning of the chapter.*

(a) What do Jews mean by 'mitzvot'? [2]

Student response

The mitzvot are found in the Torah and there are 613 of them, they are rules that Jews have to follow.

Improved student response

The term mitzvot has different meanings, it is often used to refer to duties (such as the 613 in the Torah) and good deeds. An example is 'do not kill'.

Over to you! Try to answer this question:

(a) What do Jews mean by 'kosher'? [2]

Helpful hints

To help you answer this question effectively, you could use the check list below to make sure you include the most important things:

- Mention that the concept comes from the Torah.
- Give an example of something that is kosher.

Now give yourself **two minutes** to try to answer this question by yourself:

(a) What do Jews mean by the 'Torah'? [2]

Question *(b)*

*Question **(b)** tests your knowledge and understanding. It will always ask you to **describe** a belief, a teaching, a practice, or an event that is included on the specification.*

(b) Describe how Pesach (Passover) is celebrated. [5]

What went well

The candidate has given a general definition of what mitzvot means and mentioned where they are found and how many there are.

How to improve

You must show that the word means more than just rules.

You should learn the exam board's definition of the word at the start of this chapter.

You could give an example to support your definition.

Tip

The easiest way to make sure you get full marks for this question is to learn the definitions found on page 131.

Student response

Pesach is celebrated each year by Jews. One thing Jews do to prepare for Pesach is to remove all chametz from the house, this is anything that can rise, as this remembers when the Israelites fled Egypt. Jews will have a special symbolic meal with their family when they will tell stories about Pesach.

What went well

The candidate briefly mentions two different ways Jews celebrate Pesach.

How to improve

You must make sure that you fully develop each way Pesach is celebrated to show what happens.

You should describe the symbolism behind each practice.

You could make reference to or even quote sources of wisdom or authority to support your answer.

Improved student response

Pesach is often referred to as the Festival of Freedom in Judaism and it commemorates when the Israelites escaped slavery in Egypt. Jews celebrate Pesach by first removing all chametz from the home, this is any products which contain grain and can rise. This remembers that when the Israelites were fleeing Egypt, they did not have time to let their bread rise, therefore Pesach is celebrated with the eating of matzah.
Jews celebrate Pesach as it is commanded in the Torah, which states 'this day must be one that you will remember. You must keep it as a festival to God for all generations. It is a law for all time that you must celebrate it'. Jews will welcome Pesach into the home by lighting candles and going to the synagogue. They will then have a special meal called the Seder meal, Seder means 'order' and so it is an ordered plate with specific foods on it which symbolise the plight of the Israelites, for example there is charoset to represent the mortar the Israelites used when building the pyramids. During the meal the origins and meaning of Pesach are explained.

Tip

The best answers reference all aspects of the question. Here, the candidate talks about:

- some of the main ways that Pesach is celebrated
- why Pesach is celebrated like this
- scripture which supports one of the points made.

Over to you! Try to answer this question:

(b) Describe the origin and meaning of Sukkot.	[5]

Helpful hints

Use the check list below to make sure you include the most important things:

- **Describe** the origins or a meaning of Sukkot.
- Give an **example** from the Torah to support your point.
- Then **repeat** the above process to make sure you describe both how Sukkot originated **and** what it means for Jews.

Now give yourself **five minutes** to try to answer this question by yourself:

(b) Describe how Jewish women might worship differently to men.	[5]

Question *(c)*

*Question **(c)** tests your knowledge and understanding. You need to give detailed evidence and reasoning to support your explanation of the topic.*

(c) Explain why the synagogue is important in Judaism.	[8]

Student response

The synagogue is important in Judaism as it a place of prayer and worship. Jews come here to pray, feel part of a community and feel God's presence. Jews believe they have been given the synagogue by God. The synagogue is important as many Jews go to synagogue on Shabbat, the Jewish day of rest, so it forms the heart of Jewish worship.

What went well

The response gives a number of brief reasons why the synagogue is important, focusing on its role as a place of worship.

Improved student response

Synagogue means place of assembly. The synagogue is important in Judaism as a place where Jews can come together, pray, learn and socialise. Jews can attend the synagogue during the week to participate in daily prayers so they can connect with God and pray. Many Jews attend the synagogue on Shabbat to pray, feel the presence of God and also be part of the wider Jewish community. It is the heart of Jewish worship.

The synagogue is also important in Judaism as a house of study. This means that in the synagogue Jews can access sacred texts to learn about their faith and speak to a rabbi who can give guidance on religious issues. Many rites of passage also take place in the synagogue such as Bar and Bat Mitzvahs and marriages. Jews are required to prepare for these and learn about their importance and they do so in the synagogue with the help of a rabbi.

How to improve

You must define the word 'synagogue'.

You should make links to the features and roles of the synagogue to show why it is important.

You could include some quotes or examples to support the reasons you are giving.

Over to you! Try to answer this question:

(c) Explain why the home is important in Judaism. [8]

Helpful hints

- Include Jewish beliefs only. Responses from other religions will not be credited.
- For each belief give a source of wisdom to support it (e.g. the Tenakh, the mitzvot).
- Explain why Jews believe this (e.g. how the home becomes holy during Shabbat and their beliefs about the importance of the family).
- Explain how Jews behave as a result (e.g. prayers within the home, Shabbat preparations).

Tip

Focus only on Judaism in this question – you will not be credited for mentioning any other religion.

Now give yourself **eight minutes** to try to answer this question by yourself:

(c) Explain why Shabbat is important in Judaism. [8]

Question *(d)*

Question ***(d)*** *tests your ability to* ***evaluate****. This means you need to show you have considered more than one point of view and that you have referred to religion and belief. You will need to be able to make judgements that are supported by detailed reasoning and argument.*

(d) 'Shabbat is the most important celebration for Jews.'

Discuss this statement showing that you have considered more than one point of view. (You must refer to religion and belief in your answer). [15]

Student response

Some Jews agree that Shabbat is the most important Jewish celebration as it takes place on a weekly basis, this means it's the celebration that is done the most for Jews. Observing Shabbat is a mitzvah and so many Jews believe it's more important than other celebrations as God has commanded the Jews to celebrate Shabbat and by doing so they are building a closer relationship with God. It's a time when Jews can rest and refresh themselves and spend time with their family ready for the coming week.
I disagree, I believe that a Bar or Bat Mitzvah is the most important celebration for Jews because it marks them as an adult in the Jewish faith and means they are responsible for themselves, keeping the mitzvot and their personal relationship with God. After this celebration, others like Shabbat become more meaningful as the person can take a more active role in the worship that takes place on Shabbat. Also a Bar or Bat Mitzvah marks the covenant relationship that the person has with God and so has more personal significance than Shabbat as the person is reminded of their own responsibility to follow the mitzvot in their daily life.

What went well

The candidate has offered two different viewpoints. They have offered some explanation but have limited evidence to support the points they have made. Basic evaluative language has been used to show two opposing arguments.

How to improve

You must back up all statements, including personal statements, with evidence to support your arguments.

You should evaluate the arguments given in your essay. This will help you to come to a judgement later and to avoid simply giving different views.

You could quote sources of wisdom and authority to support your arguments.

Improved student response

Many Orthodox Jews would agree that Shabbat is the most important Jewish celebration because it happens each week and therefore is the celebration that happens most often in Judaism. Shabbat is a time for rest and renewal each week so that Jews can get ready for the week to come. It is also a time to remember God as the creator of the world and to give thanks for creation as it is considered to be the anniversary of the seventh day of creation: 'on the seventh day God finished the work that he had been doing, and he ceased on the seventh day from all work' (Genesis 2:2). To observe Shabbat is also a mitzvah, in the Ten Commandments God stated that Jews should 'Remember the Sabbath to keep it holy' (Exodus 20:8). Therefore, as Orthodox Jews try to keep all the mitzvot, they observe Shabbat each week and keep it holy through prayer and worship. This helps them to reinforce their relationship with God and ensure they start the new week with God in mind. For Orthodox Jews, Shabbat is a taste of Olam Ha-Ba. It is a time outside of the ordinary, set aside for God and family. This is a strong argument because it shows that Shabbat is the central event of each week, which many Jews look forward to as a time of peace and reflection. It is also a reminder of the covenant that God made with Moses and therefore reinforces the special connection that Jews have with God. It also reminds them of their covenantal responsibility to keep the mitzvot, which for Orthodox Jews is the foundation of their religion.

Other Jews would argue that Bar and Bat Mitzvahs are the most important celebrations for Jews. These are celebrations of maturity in Judaism and mark that a Jewish boy or girl is personally responsible for keeping the mitzvot and for upholding their own covenantal relationship with God. For both boys and girls, they happen at age thirteen, with Bar/Bat Mitzvah meaning Son/Daughter of the Commandment. It also means that boys can be counted as part of a minyan and wear tefillin in prayer – in Reform Judaism girls will also be able to do this. This means that the individual can have a more active role in worship and develop their personal relationship with God. This is a fairly strong argument as it recognises the status of the individual as having their own responsibility to keep the mitzvot. It is a celebration that happens only once, so it is an important standalone event in a person's life and requires a lot of preparation. However this argument is weakened as Orthodox Jewish girls cannot usually have a Bat Mitzvah and instead have a Bat Chayil, which does not have the same depth of meaning.

The candidate has used the wording in the question statement to focus their answer on the right material.

Appropriate sources of wisdom and authority have been used.

Specialist language is used consistently and accurately.

The candidate has used diverse Jewish beliefs and teachings to meet the demands of the question.

The candidate has included evidence of how beliefs can influence individuals.

In contrast, some Jews would argue that Yom Kippur is the most important celebration. Although it only happens once a year, it is the most solemn day of the year and it is a time to atone for sin. Yom Kippur means the Day of Atonement, it is a day for a new start with God and others, so Jews can go into the new year clean, without sin and with good relationships with others. During this festival Jews will fast for twenty-five hours to show their repentance, they will confess their sins to God and reflect on the fact that it is important to be truly sorry. This is a weak argument as Jews should work on atoning for their sins throughout the year as they do them rather than waiting for this one time a year. Also it is not as joyous as other Jewish celebrations such as Rosh Hashanah and Sukkot so some Jews may be less inclined to participate in it.

I ultimately think that Shabbat is the most important celebration for Jews as it happens weekly and therefore is a time to focus on God and be with family. Also, it develops the relationship with God and helps Jews to remember their obligation to God. Although Yom Kippur is important, I believe that Jews should work on atoning for sins and wrongdoings as they do them rather than waiting until the end of the year as it means they are constantly improving themselves throughout the year and are mindful of how they treat people. Also as Shabbat is a time for family it remembers the first thing God said after creating humans: 'be fertile and become many' (Genesis 1:28). Therefore, by spending time with their family Jews are showing that they have fulfilled this command and their love for both God and their family.

The candidate has offered a judgement supported by evidence.

Over to you! Try to answer this question:

(d) 'You have to keep kosher to be Jewish.'

Discuss this statement showing that you have considered more than one point of view. (You must refer to religion and belief in your answer). [15]

Helpful hints

If you find it difficult to answer this question effectively, you could try using the structure below to help you set out your paragraphs:

- **Argument** – Clearly state a religious view about the question.
- **Back it up** – Give some evidence or an example of teaching or behaviour that shows this view.
- **Challenge** – Offer a counterargument that directly opposes the view you have previously stated.
- **Back it up** – Support this response with evidence or examples.
- **Decide** – Weigh up which views are the best and why.

This could be one paragraph. Repeat the formula again for a second paragraph and at the end conclude with a final decision. Make sure you only talk about Jewish perspectives in your answer!

Tip

Remember to evaluate the arguments that you give by saying if you think they are strong or weak arguments and why.

Now give yourself **fifteen minutes** to try to answer this question by yourself:

(d) 'You have to go to the synagogue to be a Jew.'

Discuss this statement showing that you have considered more than one point of view. (You must refer to religion and belief in your answer). [15]

Glossary

Terms with a **yellow background** are key concepts which you will need to make sure you remember.

abortion – the removal of a foetus from the womb to terminate a pregnancy

Abraham – 'Father of many'; the founder of Judaism

absolute – the idea that truth and principles are final and universal

absolution – the assurance that God has forgiven the person's sins after their confession

absolutism – the belief that there are certain actions that are always right or always wrong. The belief that moral laws exist eternally and are not just human inventions.

acclamation – a prayer said or sung together to express shared belief

agape – love or selfless charity

Amidah – means 'standing', a prayer of central importance in synagogue services said when standing

apostolic succession – the authority given from Jesus to his apostles, passed on to their successors, the Pope and bishops

apse – a large, usually domed roof at the eastern end of a church

aron hakodesh – the Holy Ark; where the Torah Scrolls are kept and the most important area of the synagogue

assisted suicide – providing an ill person with the means to end their own life

Atheist – a person who does not believe in God

atonement – making amends for one's wrongdoings

Bar Mitzvah – a ceremony where a thirteen-year-old boy becomes an adult in Jewish law and is now responsible for keeping the mitzvot

Bat Chayil – an Orthodox Jewish ceremony where a twelve-year-old girl takes on an adult role in the Jewish community

Bat Mitzvah – a Reform Jewish ceremony where a twelve- or thirteen-year-old girl becomes an adult in Jewish law and is now responsible for keeping the mitzvot

Beatitudes – a list of people, given by Jesus, who God will look on favourably because of their actions

Bible – the Christian scriptures, which contain the Old Testament and the New Testament

bimah – a raised platform in a synagogue where the Torah scrolls are read

bishop – the leader of a local area in the Catholic Church (called a diocese), who continues the work of the apostles

blasphemy – using God's name in a disrespectful way

Blessed Sacrament – the consecrated host, which Catholics believe is Jesus' body. It can also refer to the consecrated wine, which Catholics believe is Jesus' blood

Brit Milah – a ceremony where an eight-day-old baby boy is circumcised

CAFOD – the Catholic Agency for Overseas Development, a Catholic charity which works to bring about social justice

Catholic social teaching – the official teachings of the Catholic Church on matters of social justice

causation – the idea that everything has a cause and God is the cause of the universe

challah – a plaited loaf made of white leavened bread. It is usually baked to celebrate the Shabbat

chametz – leavened foods: food that contains grain and water and has been left to rise

charity – an organisation set up to help those who are less fortunate

chevra kaddisha – a group of Jews that prepares the body for burial. Each synagogue has its own group

Chi Rho – a symbol formed from the first two letters of the Greek word 'Christ'

circumcision – the removal of the foreskin from the penis

Communion – another term for the Eucharist; the body and blood of Jesus

conception – when sperm meets an egg and fertilisation occurs

conscience – human reason making moral decisions. The knowledge we have of what is right and wrong and the God-given compulsion within all human beings to do what is right and to avoid what is evil

Council of Nicaea – the first full 'meeting' of the Church that took place in the fourth century to clarify particular beliefs

covenant – a promise or agreement between two parties. Covenants were made between God with Noah, Abraham and Moses

Creation *ex nihilo* – creation out of nothing. Before God created the universe, nothing existed. Only God can create out of nothing

crucifix – a cross which displays the dying Christ

death – the end of physical life. When the physical body ceases completely to function

denomination – a branch of Christianity, such as Catholicism

descendant – a person who is related to you and lives on after you, such as a child or grandchild

doctrine – a Church teaching

dominion – having power or control over nature and the environment

dwelling – a place of living or a home

Elijah – an important prophet in Judaism; it is believed he will declare the coming of the Messiah

eternal – without beginning or end

eternal life – the term used to refer to life in heaven after death. Also, the phrase Jesus uses to describe a state of living as God intends which leads to this life in heaven

Eucharist – meaning 'thanksgiving'. The name Catholics use to describe the rite where the bread and wine become the body and blood of Jesus and is received by the people. Also the name for the real presence of Jesus in the Sacrament of Holy Communion

Eucharistic prayer – the part of the Mass where Jesus' sacrifice is remembered and the bread and wine are consecrated, becoming Jesus' body and blood

euthanasia – the painless killing of someone who is suffering

evangelisation – literally means spreading the 'good news' which we translate as Gospel. The sharing of the Gospel and life of Jesus with others

evangelist – one of the four Gospel writers: Matthew, Mark, Luke and John

Evangelium Vitae – an encyclical (letter) written by Pope St John Paul II in 1995 about the sanctity of life. The title means 'the gospel of life'

evil – the absence of good and the impulse to seek our own desires at the expense of the good of others which often results in suffering

Evolution – the process of mutation and natural selection which leads to changes in species over time to suit particular environments

extempore prayer – prayer that is improvised by individuals to express a particular intention

Final Judgement – the judgement of the whole human race at the end of time

forgiveness – the act of pardoning someone for the offences they have caused you. Overlooking a person's faults

formulaic prayer – traditional prayer with set words

free will – the decision making part of a person's mind is called the will. A will is free if a person is able to choose right from wrong without being controlled by other forces

God's Kingdom – when all people live as God calls them to, according to his will

Golden Rule – one of Jesus' main teachings which summarises all of his others: treat others as you would want to be treated

Good News – the Christian teaching about salvation brought about by Jesus

goodness – the quality of being like God: seeking the well-being of others selflessly

grace – the freely given love of God

Hades – another name for hell

Heaven – those who have accepted God's grace and forgiveness in this life will enjoy an eternal existence in God's presence in the next life. This face-to-face encounter with God is what we call 'Heaven'

Hell – those who through the exercise of their own free will ultimately reject God's grace and forgiveness, will have chosen to live eternally outside of God's presence. This total lack of God for all eternity is what we call 'Hell'

hospice – a place that provides care for people with life-limiting or terminal illness

host – a disc of unleavened bread used in Holy Communion

Humanist – a non-religious person who follows the principles of Humanism

human rights – the basic rights and freedoms that all people have, no matter who they are

hymn – a religious song offered in praise to God, usually sung communally

idolatry – worshipping something that is not God as if it was God

imago Dei – in the image of God. The belief that human beings are uniquely a reflection of God's personhood. Unlike the other animals, human beings are rational, free and moral

immanent – God is close to his creation and involved with the world so that he can make himself known

immortality of the soul – the idea that the soul lives on after the death of the body

Incarnation – 'made flesh'. The Christian belief that God became man in the person of Jesus, fully human and fully divine

inconsistent triad – an argument that questions how an omnibenevolent, omnipotent God can exist while there is evil and suffering in the world

interfaith dialogue – engagement between those of different faiths and no faith to bring about positive outcomes such as respect, tolerance and social harmony

inspiration – 'God breathed'. The belief that the Spirit of God guides an individual to act or write what is good and true

Judgement – the belief that each individual will be held to account by God for the things they do, or fail to do, during their lives

Kaddish – a prayer praising God

Kosher – ('fit' or 'proper') foods that are permitted to be eaten according to Leviticus Chapter 11. It is also used to refer to the purity of ritual objects such as Torah scrolls

laity – the members of the Church community who are not ordained

literal – to read the words of the Bible as factually true

Magisterium – the teaching authority of the Church, exercised by the bishops in communion with the Pope. The Magisterium is given grace by the Holy Spirit to faithfully interpret the Scriptures and Tradition

marriage – in Judaism, a legal and spiritual bonding of a man and woman

matzah – flatbread or unleavened bread

meditative – a form of prayer that is often very focused and reflective

mercy – compassion shown by someone who has the power to punish

Messiah – the anointed one who Jews believe will bring in a new era or age for humankind. This will include rebuilding the Temple and bringing in an age of universal peace

Messianic Age – a new era or age for humankind; a time of peace

metaphorical – to read the words of the Bible as stories or myths that contain truths

mezuzah – a small scroll of parchment in a decorative case with the Shema written on it. Mezuzahs are attached to doorposts in Jewish homes

minyan – traditionally a group of ten men over the age of thirteen; the minimum number of Jews needed for communal worship to take place

miracle – an event that cannot be explained by the laws of science

Mitzvot – the term has a mix of meanings. It is often used to refer to duties (such as the 613 in the Torah) and good deeds

Modeh Ani – a prayer recited by many observant Jews when they first wake up

monotheism – belief there is only one God

monotheistic – believing in one God

Moses – a prophet who led the Israelites out of slavery in Egypt

moral authority – having the capacity to teach others right from wrong

moral evil – evil caused by the actions of humans

mortal sin – a grave sin which means a person will be separated from God unless they repent for it

multi-faith society – a society in which there are people of many different religions and people of no religion

natural evil – evil caused by natural occurrences, such as an earthquake

Natural Law – the moral laws of right and wrong which are universal and not dependent on human laws. The belief in natural law is the belief that the moral law is discoverable by every human being and is the same for all human beings in all places at all times

natural selection – a process in which animals that are better adapted to their environment are more likely to survive

near-death experience – an experience a person has as they are dying, which they are then able to recount to others

ner tamid – the 'eternal light'; a light that is never put out in the synagogue

non-voluntary euthanasia – ending a person's life when they are unable to request this for themselves

numinous – a sense of awe and wonder at God's creation

offertory – when the gifts of bread and wine are given to the priest in preparation for the Eucharistic prayer

olam ha-ba – 'the world to come'; the afterlife

olam ha-ze – 'this world'; life on earth

omnibenevolent – all loving

Omnipotence – the belief that God is all powerful

omnipotent – all powerful

omniscient – all knowing

onan – the lead mourner

Oral Torah – a commentary on the written Torah, giving explanation and descriptions

Original Sin – the belief that all humans have inherited sin from the first human beings

palliative care – symptom and pain management given to a person who is seriously unwell

parev – neutral foods that do not contain milk or meat and so can be eaten with either

particular judgement – the judgement of an individual following their death

Paschal candle – a candle first lit at the Easter Vigil each year, which represents Jesus' resurrection

patron saint – a saint to which a parish, country, school or cause is dedicated

penal system – the justice system; the way in which crime is punished

Pesach – a festival celebrating the Israelites' freedom from slavery in Egypt

pieta - a painting or sculpture of Mary holding Jesus after his death

pikuach nefesh – the obligation to save a life in need

plague – a widespread disease or disaster sent by God

polytheism – believing in many gods

Pope – the head of the Catholic Church, who continues the role of St Peter and has pastoral responsibility for the universal Church

popular piety – a commonly practised type of worship or devotion that is not part of the official liturgy of the Church

prayer – a way of communicating with God through words and actions

primary precepts – five purposes that humans naturally strive towards

privation – the loss or absence of a quality or something that is normally present. Evil is a privation of good

pro-choice – the belief that the mother has the right to choose what happens to her body and so can have an abortion if she wants one

pro-life – the belief that abortion is wrong in every circumstance and all humans have the right to life

Promised Land – the land God promised to Abraham and his descendants

prophesising – making a prediction about something that will happen in the future

punishment – the consequences of a wrong decision and a penalty imposed by a person in authority on the person who has committed wrongdoing

quality of life – the idea that life must have benefits for it to be worth living

rabbi – a Jewish religious leader, also considered to be a teacher

reason – the ability to think logically

reconciliation – the act of bringing individuals or groups together in peace after conflict

redemption – the belief that Jesus paid the 'ransom' to free humans from sin by dying on the cross

reincarnation – a cycle where a soul is born into a new body

relative – the idea that truth and moral values are not fixed but depend on the situation

relativism – the belief that there is no moral law and that rules that govern what is right and wrong are human inventions and change from place to place and from age to age

repent – to feel sorry for wrongdoing

repentance – being sorry for one's wrongdoings and making up for them

resurrection – the raising of the body to life again after death. Christians believe that Jesus has already experienced resurrection and that all people will experience it at the end of time

Revelation – the word used to describe all of the ways in which God makes himself known to human beings. Christians believe that God does this finally and fully in the person of Jesus Christ

rite – a religious ceremonial act with prescribed words and actions

rosary beads – a string of beads used as an aid to prayer

Rosh Hashanah – 'head of the year'; the Jewish New Year

Sacred Heart – a statue of Jesus where his heart is clearly visible

sacrifice – to give up something valuable for the sake of someone or something else

salvation – the belief that through Jesus' death and resurrection humanity has achieved the possibility of life forever with God

sanctity of life – the belief that human life is sacred because it is a gift from God

sanctuary – the area surrounding the altar, which is considered to be especially holy because it is where the Eucharist is consecrated

sarcophagus – a stone coffin, usually adorned with symbolic markings, words or images

Second Vatican Council – a gathering called by Pope St John XXIII where leaders of the Catholic Church and other representatives addressed the relationship between the modern world and the Catholic Church. It ran from 1962 to 1965

Shabbat – day of spiritual renewal and rest. Beginning at sunset on Friday and closing at nightfall on Saturday

Shekhinah – the place where God's presence rests and can be felt

Shema – a prayer found in the Torah which proclaims belief in one God

shiva – the seven-day period of mourning that happens straight after a funeral

shofar – a ram's horn

siddur – a Jewish prayer book

sin – acting against the will or laws of God

social cohesion – when members of society are bound together through respect and tolerance, and share common values

social justice – the aim to have a society that is fair, where all people have access to and an equal share in wealth, opportunities and basic necessities

soul – the eternal part of a human being given at conception which lives on after the death of the body. Also a name for a human being's rational nature – their mind

speciesism – the idea that human life is more important than any other life

spiritual renewal – reinforcing or restoring a person's religious faith

Stewardship – the duty to care for creation responsibly, as stewards rather than consumers, and to protect it for future generations

suffering – pain or loss which harms human beings. Some suffering is caused by other human beings (often called moral evil); some is not (often called natural evil)

sukkah – a temporary shelter built during Sukkot

Sukkot – also known as the Festival of Shelters; a festival that thanks God for protecting and providing for the Jews

survival of the soul – the belief that the soul does not die

sustainable – using natural resources responsibly to ensure they do not run out

SVP – the St Vincent de Paul Society, a Catholic charity which aims to alleviate poverty by helping those who are in need in local communities

symbolism – images used to show or represent religious beliefs

Synagogue – house of assembly; building for Jewish public prayer, study and assembly

Talmud – a collection of writings on Jewish law and tradition, made up of the Mishnah and Gemara

Tenakh – the Jewish Bible, consisting of the Torah (the five books of Moses), Nevi'im (prophets) and Ketuvim (writings)

Ten Commandments – ten laws handed directly from God to Moses

the Law – the rules given by God to Moses teaching people how to behave and worship

The Lord's Prayer – the prayer that Jesus taught, which is used by all Christians

the Word – another name for Jesus to describe the idea that he is God's word made flesh

Torah – the five books of Moses (Genesis, Exodus, Leviticus, Numbers and Deuteronomy). Regarded as the holiest books of the Tenakh

Torah scrolls – a handwritten copy of the Torah; the most sacred object in the synagogue

Transcendence – existing outside of space and time; God exists in a way that makes him nothing like anything else that exists, above and beyond creation

transcendent – existing outside of space and time

transgression – an act against a rule or law

transubstantiation – the belief that through the power of the Holy Spirit, bread and wine become the body and blood of Jesus

treyfah – meaning 'torn'; food that is not permitted to be eaten in Judaism

venerate – show honour and respect

venial sin – a minor sin which need not separate a person from God in heaven

vestments – the garments worn by the priest when he leads worship

viaticum – the holy communion received during the sacrament of the sick if the person is physically able to receive it. It means 'food for the journey'

virtues – morally good characteristics

vision – seeing a religious figure when in a dream or trance

voluntary euthanasia – ending a person's life at their request

worship – showing respect and reverence for God

yarzeit – the anniversary of the death of a loved one

yetzer ha ra – the tendency to do bad actions

yetzer ha tov – the tendency to do good actions

Yom Kippur – 'Day of Atonement'; the holiest day of the year for Jews

Index

Headings in **bold** indicate key concepts.

Acknowledgements

We are grateful to the authors and publishers for use of extracts from their titles and in particular for the following:

Scripture quotations are from **New Revised Standard Version Bible: Catholic Edition**, copyright © 1989, 1993 National Council of the Churches of Christ in the United States of America. Used by permission. All rights reserved worldwide.

Excerpts from **Catechism of the Catholic Church**, http://www.vatican.va/archive/ccc_css/archive/catechism/ccc_toc.htm (Strathfield, NSW: St Pauls, 2000). Reproduced with permission from The Vatican. © Libreria Editrice Vaticana

Excerpts from **The William Davidson Talmud**, English from The William Davidson digital edition of the Koren Noé Talmud, with commentary by Rabbi Adin Even-Israel Steinsaltz korenpub.com Koren Publishers Ltd., used with permission, The Noé Edition Koren Talmud Bavli.

Barukh She'amar prayer taken from the Centenary edition of the **Authorised Daily Prayer Book of the United Hebrew Congregations of the Commonwealth.** © Singer's Prayer Book Publication Committee, 1990. Reproduced with permission from Cambridge University Press through PLSclear.

Excerpt from **the English translation of The Roman Missal** © 2010, International Commission on English in the Liturgy Corporation (ICEL). All rights reserved.

Excerpt from **the English translation of Order of Christian Funerals** © 1985, 1989, International Commission on English in the Liturgy Corporation (ICEL). All rights reserved.

C. Darwin: *Darwin Correspondence Project*, Letter no. 2814 to Asa Gray, 22 May 1860, https://www.darwinproject.ac.uk/letter/DCP-LETT-2814.xml (Cambridge Univesrity Press, accessed on 28 October 2020). Reproduced with permission from Cambridge University Press through PLSclear.

Pope Francis: *Address to a Meeting at the Ponitifcal Academy of Sciences*, October 2014. (The Vatican, 2014). © Libreria Editrice Vaticana. Reproduced with permission from The Vatican.

Pope Francis: *Laudato Si*, 24 May 2015. (The Vatican, 2015). © Libreria Editrice Vaticana. Reproduced with permission from The Vatican.

Pope John XXIII: *Gaudet Mater Ecclesia*, 11 October 1962. (The Vatican, 1962). © Libreria Editrice Vaticana. Reproduced with permission from The Vatican.

Pope John Paul II: *Evangelium Vitae*, March 25th 1995 (The Vatican, 1995). © Libreria Editrice Vaticana. Reproduced with permission from The Vatican.

Pope John Paul II: *Message to the Pontifical Academy of Sciences: on Evolution*, 22 October 1996. (The Vatican, 1996). © Libreria Editrice Vaticana. Reproduced with permission from The Vatican.

Pope John Paul II: Letter of his Holiness to the Bishops Delegates to the Fifth Plenary Assembly of the Federation of Asian Bishops' Conference, 23 June 1990. (The Vatican, 1990). © Libreria Editrice Vaticana. Reproduced with permission from The Vatican.

Pope John Paul II: Address to the Professors and Students of the Pontifical Institute of Sacred Music, 19 January 2001. (The Vatican, 2001). © Libreria Editrice Vaticana. Reproduced with permission from The Vatican.

Pope Leo XIII: *Rerum Novarum,* on Capital and Labour, 15 May 1891. (The Vatican, 1891). © Libreria Editrice Vaticana. Reproduced with permission from The Vatican.

Pope Paul VI: *Nostra Aetate*, 28 October 1962. (The Vatican, 1965). © Libreria Editrice Vaticana. Reproduced with permission from The Vatican.

Pope Paul VI: *Gaudium et Spes*, Pastoral Constitution on the Church in the Modern World, 7 December 1965. (The Vatican, 1965). © Libreria Editrice Vaticana. Reproduced with permission from The Vatican.

Pope Paul VI: *populorum progression*, on the Development of Peoples, 26 March 1967. (The Vatican, 1967). © Libreria Editrice Vaticana. Reproduced with permission from The Vatican.

P. Singer: *Animal Liberation: A New Ethics for our Treatment of Animals*, (Random House, 1975). Reproduced with permission from Pr P. Singer, AC.

We have made every effort to trace and contact all copyright holders before publication, but if notified of any errors or omissions, the publisher will be happy to rectify these at the earliest opportunity.

Excerpts from *Tanakh: The Holy Scriptures* (Jewish Publication Society Inc., 1991). © 1985, The Jewish Publication Society, Philadelphia. Copyright holder not established at time of going to print.

Excerpt from **Maimonides' Thirteen Principles of Jewish Faith** https://www.chabad.org/library/article_cdo/aid/332555/jewish/Maimonides-13-Principles-of-Faith.htm Copyright holder not established at time of going to print.

Excerpts from **Pirkei Avot** https://www.sefaria.org/Pirkei_Avot Fuchsberg **Jerusalem Center, 2020.** Copyright holder not established at time of going to print.

St Augustine: *Augustine: Confessions and Enchiridion*, edited by Albert Cook Outler, St Augustine Confessions XII, 7. The Library of Christian Classics (Penguin Books Ltd., 2011). Copyright holder not established at time of going to print.

G. Fauré: quote, 1921. (G. Fauré, 1921). Copyright holder not established at time of going to print.

M. Shapiro: Maimonides' Thirteen Principles: The Last Word in Jewish Theology The Torah U-Madda Journal, Vol. 4 (Yeshiva University Press, 1993). Copyright holder not established at time of going to print.

Cover illustrations: Eleanor Grosch

Photos: p11: NASA images/Shutterstock; **p12a**: Inga Maya/Shutterstock; **p12b**: Grejak/Shutterstock; **p13**: Heritage Images/Hulton Fine Art Collection/Getty Images; **p14**: Design Projects/Shutterstock; **p15**: Ryan M. Bolton/Shutterstock; **p16**: DEA / A. DAGLI ORTI/De Agostini/Getty Images; **p17**: Henrik5000/E+/Getty Images; **p18**: Steve Pyke/Premium Archive/Getty Images; **p19**: VGstockstudio/Shutterstock; **p21**: Mimagephotography/Shutterstock; **p22**: Tanvir Aziz/Shutterstock; **p23**: Dmytro Zinkevych/Shutterstock; **p24**: ChristianChan/iStock; **p25**: ZDL/Shutterstock; **p26**: Scala/Art Resource, New York; **p28**: Catholic Talks; **p29**: Catholic Talks; **p29**: Rom, Basilika San Clemente, Apsis/Dnalor 01; **p30**: DGLimages/Shutterstock; **p31**: Lee Thomas/Alamy Stock Photo; **p32**: Monkey Business Images/Shutterstock; **p33**: Fairfax Media/The AGE Getty Images; **p34**: Caroline Penn/Alamy Stock Photo; **p35**: Washington Imaging/Alamy Stock Photo; **p41**: JOHN KELLERMAN/Alamy Stock Photo; **p44**: Gerard van Honthorst (1592-1656)/Wallraf–Richartz Museum/Codart; **p45**: Keith McIntyre/Shutterstock; **p46**: Jorisvo/Shutterstock; **p47**: Mylu/Shutterstock; **p48**: Creative Travel Projects/Shutterstock; **p50**: Victoria 1/Shutterstock; **p51**: Giulio napolitano/Shutterstock; **p52**: Geoff Caddick/PA Images/Alamy Stock Photo; **p53**: Giacomo Gori/Shutterstock; **p55**: Everett Collection/Shutterstock; **p56**: Granger Historical Picture Archive/Alamy Stock Photo; **p57**: Halfpoint/Shutterstock; **p58**: SPboy13/Shutterstock; **p59t**: Immaculate/Shutterstock; **p59m**: GrahamMoore999/Shutterstock; **p59b**: Zvonimir Atletic/Shutterstock; **p61**: Vitaly Minko/Shutterstock; **p62**: Spirit Stock/Shutterstock; **p63**: Cristian baitg reportage/Alamy Stock Photo; **p64**: Praweena style/Shutterstock; **p65**: Duncan Andison/Shutterstock; **p71**: Gabriel P. Pinheiro/Shutterstock; **p72**: Renata Sedmakova/Shutterstock; **p73**: Kaiser/Agencja Fotograficzna Caro/Alamy Stock Photo; **p75**: Chronicle/Alamy Stock Photo; **p76**: Michelangelo (1475-1564); **p77**: Brucegerencser; **p78**: Aldeca Studio/Shutterstock; **p80**: Adrian Sherratt/Alamy Stock Photo; **p81**: RealyEasyStar/Fotografia Felici/Alamy Stock Photo; **p83**: Granger Historical Picture Archive/Alamy Stock Photo; **p84**: Album/Alamy Stock photo; **p85**: Paula Solloway/Alamy Stock

Photo; **p86**: Art Images for College teaching; **p87a**: Art Images for College Teaching; **p87b**: Jastrow (2006)/Vatican Museums; **p87c**: Art Images for College Teaching; **p87d**: Art Images for College Teaching; **p88**: Fotomax/iStock; **p89t**: Alexandros Michailidis/Shutterstock; **p89b**: JOERG KOCH/DDP/Getty Images; **p90**: Jeff Morgan 16/Alamy Stock Photo; **p91**: Odile Noel/Lebrecht Music & Arts/Alamy Stock Photo; **p92**: Spencer Grant/ArkReligion.com/Art Directors & TRIP/Alamy Stock Photo; **p94**: Southern Stock/Digital Vision/Getty Images; **p95**: Lebrecht Music & Arts/Alamy Stock Photo; **p101**: Godong/Alamy Stock Photo; **p102**: Fizkes/Shutterstock; **p103**: Photofusion Picture Library/Alamy Stock Photo; **p105**: PA Images/Alamy Stock Photo; **p107**: Alessia Pierdomenico/Shutterstock; **p109t**: Boris Stroujk/Shutterstock; **p109b**: Nagel Photography/Shutterstock; **p110**: Robrt_s/Shutterstock; **p112**: Fine Art/Alamy Stock Photo; **p113**: Jose Luis Pelaez Inc/DigitalVision/Getty Images; **p114**: Chronicle/Alamy Stock Photo; **p115**: Renata Sedmakova/Shutterstock; **p116**: Florian Kopp/ImageBroker/Alamy Stock Photo; **p118t**: Kamira/Shutterstock; **p118b**: ChiccoDodiFC/Shutterstock; **p119t**: Mazur Travel/Shutterstock; **p119m**: Onfilm/iStock; **p119b**: MarioGuti/iStock; **p121**: BMD Images/Alamy Stock Photo; **p122**: Pope Francis. [@Pontifex]. (2020, September 28). Twitter.; **p123**: Missio; **p125**: David Warren/Alamy Stock Photo; **p131**: The world in HDR/Shutterstock; **p132**: GarikProst/Shutterstock; **p133t**: Stockbroker/MBI/Alamy Stock Photo; **p133b**: Dmitriy Feldman svarshik/Shutterstock; **p134**: Lu Yang/Dreamstime.com; **p135**: ChameleonsEye/Shutterstock; **p136**: Flik47/Shutterstock; **p138**: NicePng; **p139**: DES E GERSHON/Alamy Stock Photo; **p140**: Zu_09/Digital Vision/Getty Images; **p141**: Batman2000/Dreamstime.com; **p142**: Stock-Asso/Shutterstock; **p143**: Eddie Gerald/Alamy Stock Photo; **p144**: BrAT82/Shutterstock; **p145**: Photograph by Yakir Zur; **p146**: Richard B. Levine/Alamy Stock photo; **p147**: EyeJoy/iStock; **p154**: Stockbroker/MBI/Alamy Stock Photo; **p154**: dpa picture alliance archive/Alamy Stock Photo; **p155**: Assetbank /Shutterstock; **p156**: kolderal/Moment/Getty Images; **p157**: Idris Ahmed/Alamy Stock Photo; **p158t**: Maurice Savage/Alamy Stock Photo; **p158m**: GODONG-PHOTO/Shutterstock; **p158b**: Godong/Alamy Stock Photo; **p159**: Ron Zmiri/Shutterstock; **p160**: Adam Murphy/Alamy Stock Photo; **p161**: Miriam Reik/Alamy Stock Photo; **p162**: Dennis Degnan/Getty Images; **p163**: Laura Caldwell/iStock; **p164**: Syda Productions/Shutterstock; **p165**: Heisenferg/Shutterstock; **p166**: Dan Kitwood/Getty Images; **p167**: Godong/Robert Harding Picture Library; **p168**: Luvo/Getty Images; **p169**: Chameleonseye/iStock.

Artwork by Integra Software Services.